The Hershey Bears

Sweet Seasons

PROGRAM AND GUIDE

Hershey Hockey Club

POPULARLY KNOWN AS THE "HERSHEY B'ARS"

1934-'35

Championship Season

of the

Eastern Amateur Hockey League

Also a Series of

Inter-Sectional Matches

with

Outstanding Canadian

and

American Hockey Teams

1056

SKATING PERMITTED AFTER HOCKEY GAME WITHOUT ADDITIONAL CHARGE

HERSHEY ICE PALACE

HERSHEY, PENNSYLVANIA

"THE CHOCOLATE TOWN"

Here is a program from the 1934–1935 EAHL season. (Bruce C. Cooper collection.)

The Hershey Bears
Sweet Seasons

Tim Leone

ARCADIA
PUBLISHING

ISBN 978-0-7385-1333-1

Published by Arcadia Publishing
Charleston, South Carolina

Printed in the United States of America

Library of Congress Catalog Card Number: 2003109613

For all general information contact Arcadia Publishing at:
Telephone 843-853-2070
Fax 843-853-0044
E-mail sales@arcadiapublishing.com
For customer service and orders:
Toll-Free 1-888-313-2665

Visit us on the Internet at www.arcadiapublishing.com

For Amy, Tamara, and Andrew

On the cover: Seen in the front-cover color photograph is Mike McHugh with the Calder Cup in 1997. In the back-cover color photograph is the 1997 Calder Cup celebration. (Front: Michael Fernandez/*Patriot-News*; back: Bill Duh and Bruce Tyson/Just Sports.)

Contents

ACKNOWLEDGMENTS

I wish to thank Scott Newkam, chairman of the board and president and chief executive officer of Hershey Entertainment & Resorts Company, and Doug Yingst, Hershey Bears president and general manager, for championing this project and opening the club's archives. Thanks also go to David Newhouse (executive editor), Nick Horvath (sports editor), and Jim Carlson (assistant sports editor) of the *Harrisburg Patriot-News* for giving the green light and opening the newspaper's photograph archives. Thanks to Tiffany Howe (sports history editor) of Arcadia Publishing for reviving a good idea that had become dormant.

I am also grateful to Denny Ott, Don Scott, Dave Sottile, and John Walton for their work on the Bears record book. The same to Dave Mishkin, Kelly Ritz, Dan Sernoffsky, and Scott Smith for their work on the team's 1995–1996 media guide, which remains a valuable historical document. Special thanks to Bruce "Scoop" Cooper for his historical work, advice, and invaluable proofreading.

Since this is a pictorial history, major thanks must go to the photographers whose work graces these pages. Thanks to Bill Duh, Bruce Tyson, and Nancy Attrill of Just Sports. Thanks to M. Jaffe, Barry Ford, and Dorothy Scott, who have taken pictures for the Bears. Thanks to *Harrisburg Patriot-News* photographers Mike Fernandez, Joe Hermitt, Laura Mathews, Gary Dwight Miller, Chris Millette, Peter Rekus, Amiran White, and John Whitehead. Added thanks goes to *Harrisburg Patriot-News* Photo Editor Mark Pynes for navigating the newspaper's digital photograph archives. Also, thanks to the anonymous photographers whose names have been lost to time but whose work survives.

I am also indebted to former *Harrisburg Patriot-News* reporters John Travers, Steve Summers, and Bruce Whitman, who wrote much of the first rough draft of the Bears history. Finally, deep thanks to Brent Hancock, the indispensable man of this project. Hancock, the team's longtime publicity director, is the one most responsible for collecting and preserving the Bears' history.

INTRODUCTION

Gordie Howe once said that "everybody who is anybody in hockey has played in Hershey." Howe, or "Mr. Hockey," is not alone in recognizing Hershey's place of importance in the hockey world. The Hershey Bears are the oldest club in the American Hockey League (AHL) and have been in existence far longer than most National Hockey League (NHL) teams. The Bears, who played their 65th AHL season in 2002–2003, top most of the AHL's all-time statistics, including games played, playoff appearances, and victories. Hershey has won the Calder Cup in six different decades: 1946–1947, 1957–1958, 1958–1959, 1968–1969, 1973–1974, 1979–1980, 1987–1988, and 1996–1997. Its total of eight league championships ranks second only to Cleveland's nine.

Frank Mathers, Hershey's longtime head coach and general manager, is a member of the Hockey Hall of Fame. So are former Bears coaches Ralph "Cooney" Weiland and Bill Barber. Mathers and Hershey executive John B. Sollenberger both have been honored with the prestigious Lester Patrick Trophy for service to hockey in the United States.

Hundreds of players, an estimable honor roll who have donned the Hershey uniform, have come through on their way to the NHL. Many others made grand careers in the AHL and settled in the Hershey area, becoming living reminders of a legacy they helped build. More men have played for the Bears than any of the NHL's "Original Six" franchises.

Barber and fellow former Bears coaches Gary Green, Bryan Murray, John Paddock, and Bob Hartley went on to serve as NHL head coaches. Hartley led the Colorado Avalanche to the Stanley Cup in 2001.

The Bears now play in the $75 million Giant Center, where attendance topped 300,000 in the building's inaugural season of 2002–2003. The vast majority of their history was written in the hallowed Hersheypark Arena, which was to the AHL what Toronto's Maple Leaf Gardens, Montreal's Forum, the Boston Garden, and Chicago Stadium were to the NHL. The rink mecca, in full service from 1936 to 2002, was, quite simply, the greatest arena in the history of minor-league sports. It hosted a galaxy of events, ranging from Frank Sinatra to the Harlem Globetrotters to high-school graduations. But it was made for hockey, and most of its ghosts wear skates.

A vision conjured in the first half of the 20th century served proudly into the 21st century, becoming a community touchstone for generations who passed through its gates. The civic legacy the arena established made it a model for the way things should be done. Hersheypark Arena was privately financed and had brilliant architecture and cannon-proof construction. It had more than 7,000 seats and generated countless memories.

Fans and players created passion plays accompanied by the organ in their oblong theater. The buzz of arena workers preparing the facility and smoothing the ice amid the clatter of turnstiles, swinging seat bottoms, and pregame debate gave way to the roar of thousands thrilled by hockey's addictive combination of athleticism, courage, and ill will.

Big goals, big saves, checks, brawls, amazing passes, sudden death, Calder Cup celebrations, ceremonial handshakes, and retirement nights are all a part of the history. Through the years, millions viewed the puck drama on their frozen field of dreams.

Hersheypark Arena, an arched icon brought to life by dedicated craftsmen, still stands vigil on the central Pennsylvania skyline. It serves as a concrete embodiment of tradition. Hershey's heritage is unsurpassed in minor-league sports. The Bears have brewed a rich cup of entertainment and excellence, flavored by chocolate and ice. Enjoy these sweet seasons.

—Tim Leone, July 2003.

One

ICE ORIGINS

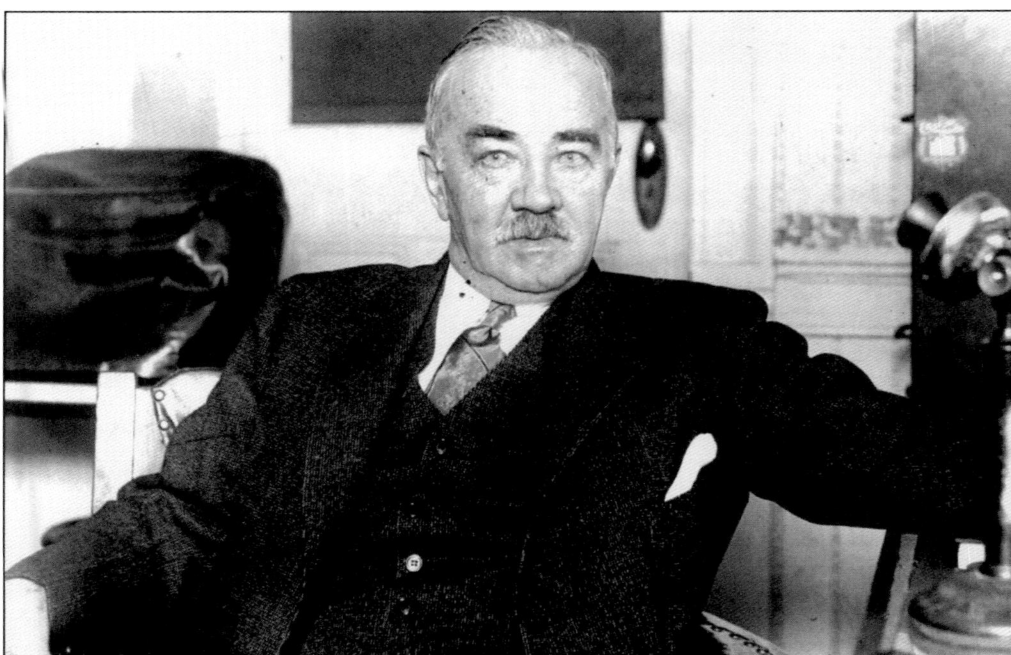

MILTON S. HERSHEY. Born a poor farm boy in Derry Township shortly before the Civil War, Milton S. Hershey (1857–1945) created a chocolate company empire in the town that would come to bear his name. The civic-minded Hershey also sought to build a model community, which included Hersheypark and a school for disadvantaged children. Among the buildings he commissioned was Convention Hall, which opened in 1915. (Hershey Bears.)

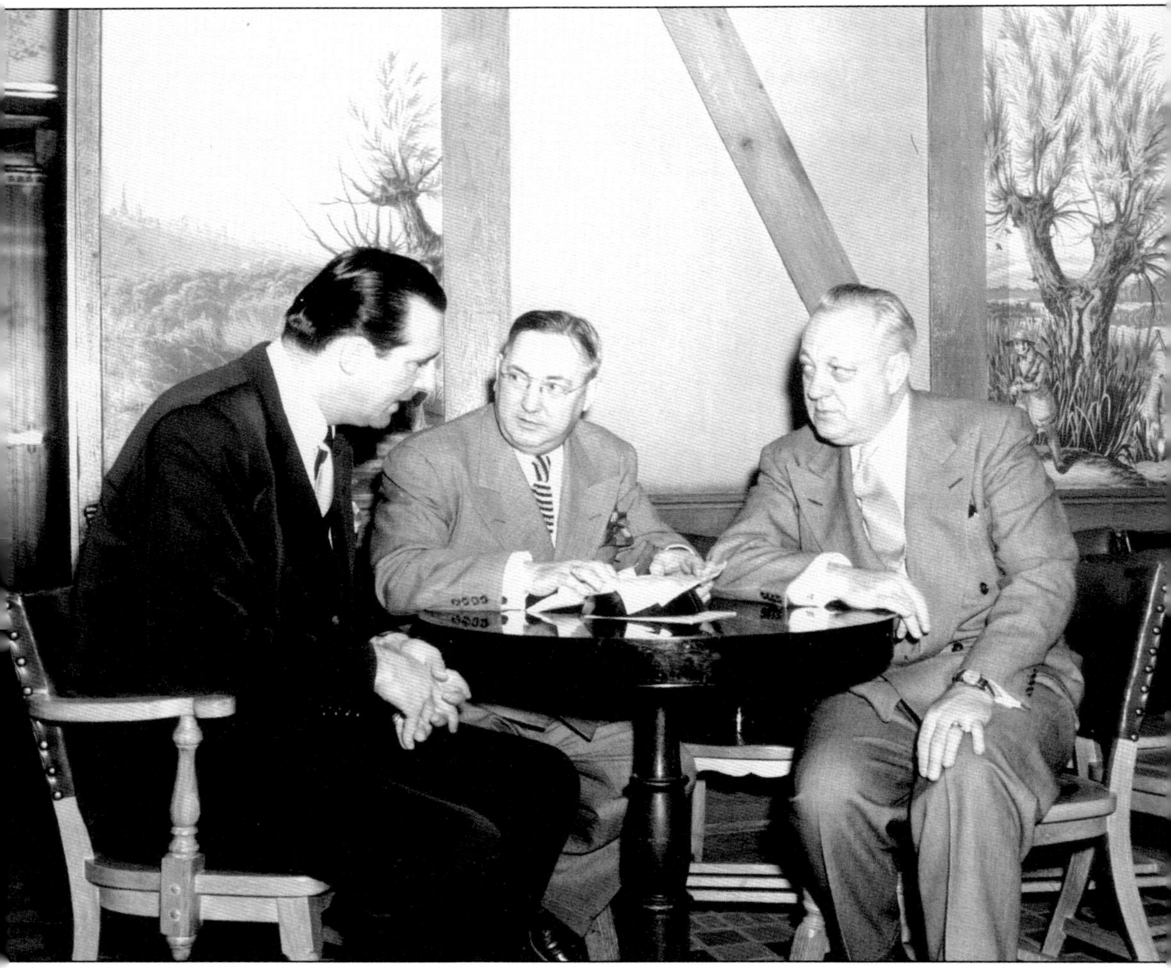

JOHN B. SOLLENBERGER. John B. Sollenberger (right) is shown in 1950 with Hank Greenberg (left) and Harvey Ensminger. Through the efforts of Milton S. Hershey, Sollenberger, and Hershey Estates President Charles F. Ziegler, hockey was introduced at Convention Hall, but Sollenberger gets most of the credit. Straight off the farm, Sollenberger went to work for Milton Hershey at age 17 reading electric meters and rose to become his right-hand executive. (Hershey Bears.)

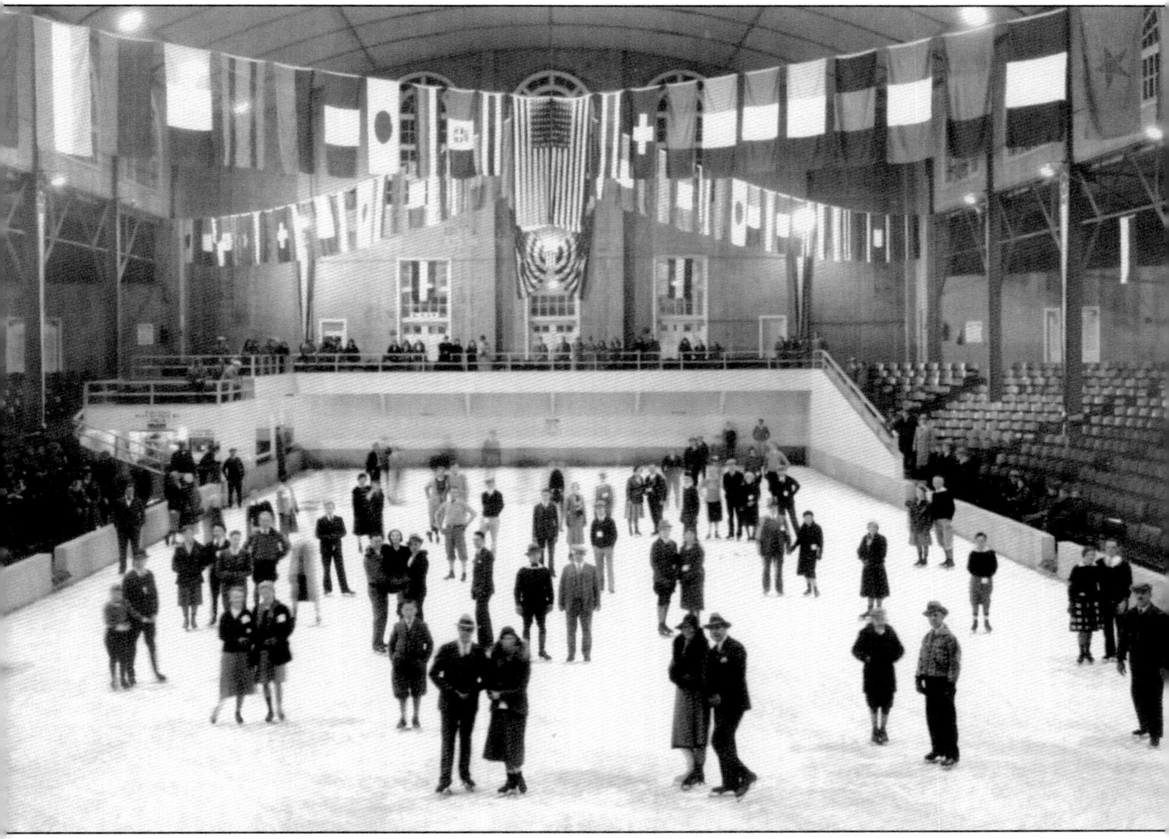

Inside the Ice Palace. An ice plant and rink were installed inside Convention Hall in 1931 to provide use for the building during the winter. Hockey quickly caught on at what would come to be known as the Ice Palace, giving birth to one of the greatest traditions in minor-league sports. The Ice Palace, which opened on January 31, 1931, also was used for public skating (shown above) and an annual ice carnival. The original ice surface was 60 by 170 feet. Indoor rinks were rare in 1931, so the Ice Palace attracted teams from Swarthmore, Villanova, and Philadelphia. The first hockey game was played there on February 18, 1931, between two amateur teams, the Pennsylvania Athletic Club (Penn A.C.) and Villanova, before a crowd of about 250. The ice surface was enlarged before the 1932–1933 season, and hockey became the building's main use. Hockey and the soon-to-be Hershey Bears outgrew the Ice Palace in less than three years. (Hershey Bears.)

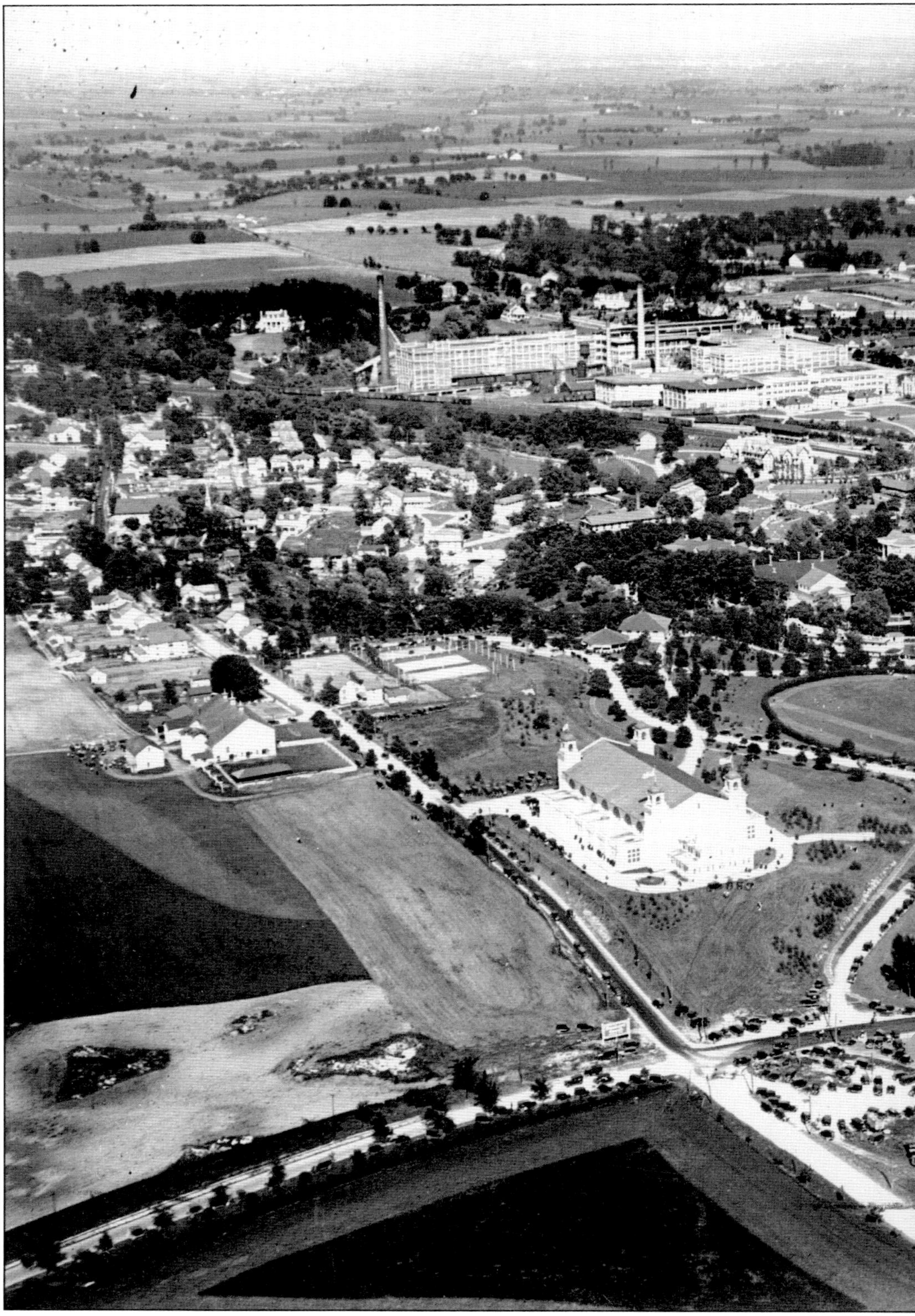

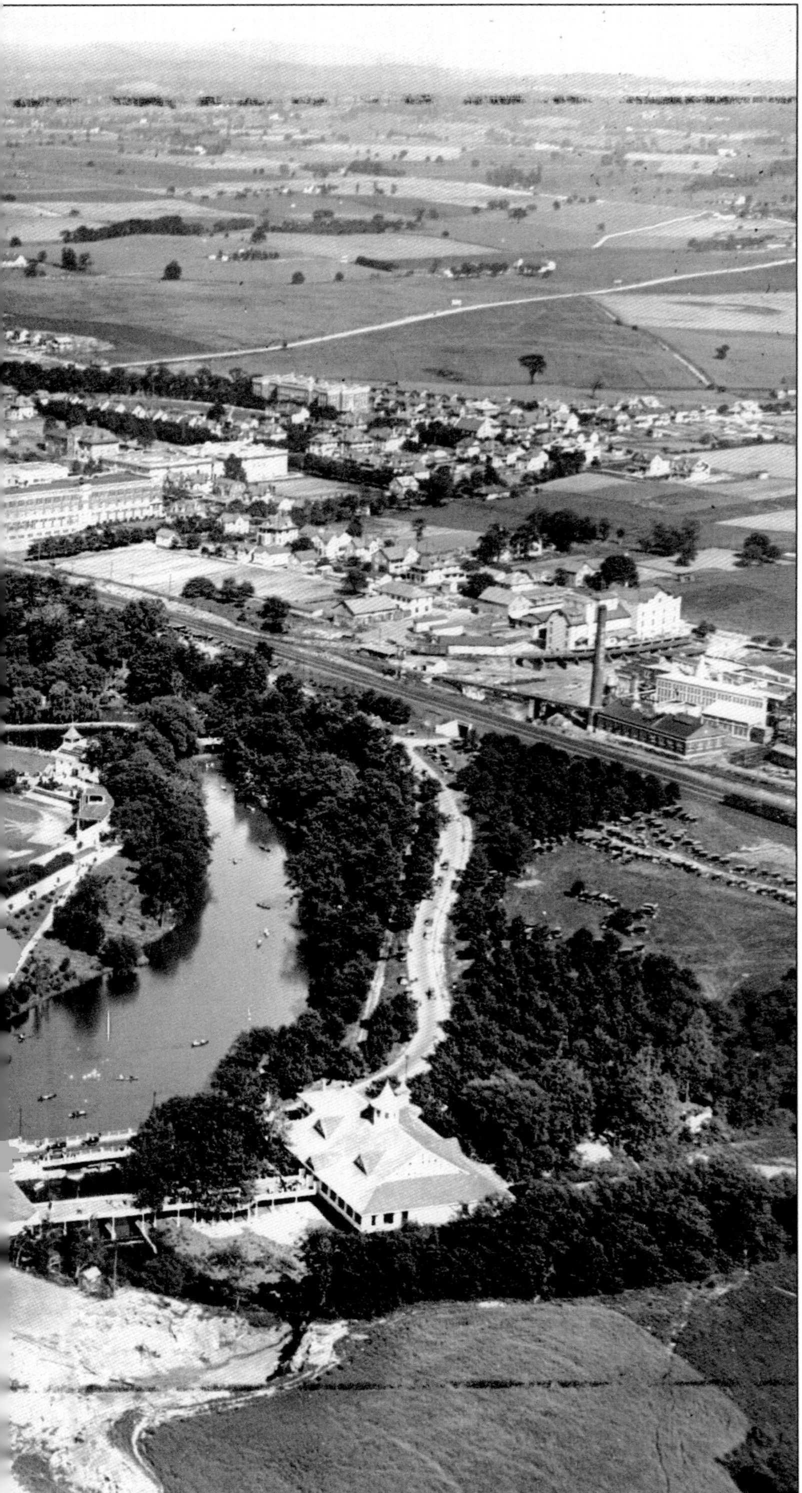

An Ice Palace Aerial. This aerial shot of the Ice Palace, with its signature four spires, was taken *c.* 1923. It seated 1,950. The Swarthmore Athletic Club (Swarthmore A.C.) was the first team to call the Ice Palace home. They played exhibitions in 1931 and regularly drew crowds of more than 900. Eventually, Hersheypark Arena was built attached to the Ice Palace on the end facing toward Milton S. Hershey's mansion, visible in the top left-hand corner. The Ice Palace now houses the Hershey Museum. (Hershey Bears.)

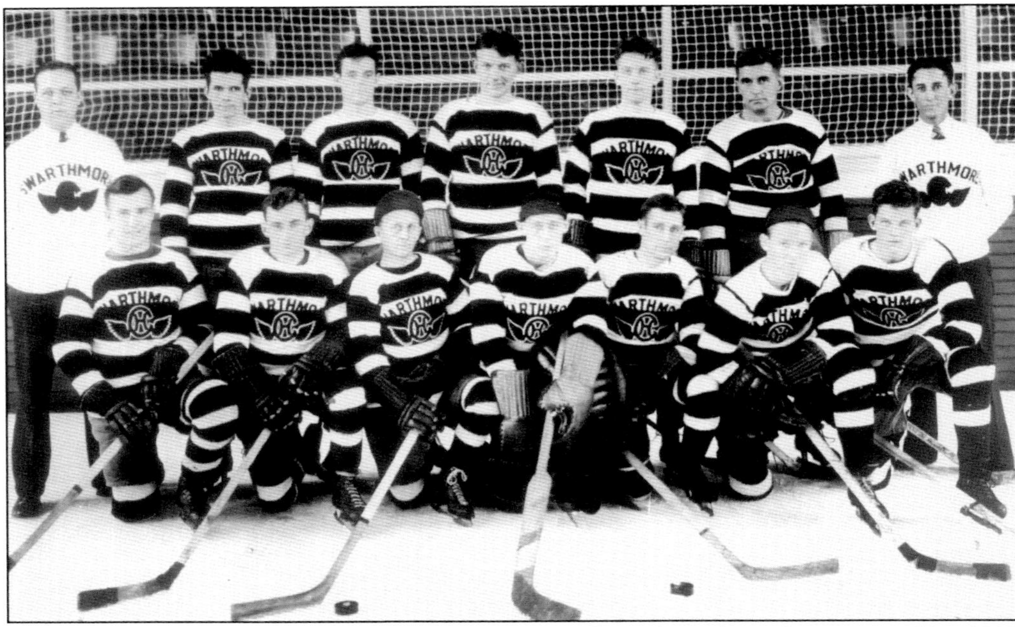

Swarthmore A.C. Hershey's first team played an independent slate of games in 1931–1932. Figure skates were standard equipment for some players, like the one kneeling in the front row, third from the left. Some players also wore caps as personal signatures. From left to right are the following: (front row) Walter Stupka, two unidentified players, goalie ? McCallen, ? Brickman, Bob Nilon, and Bob Maley; (back row) unidentified, Sam Whittingham, ? Gallagher, "Print" Manning, unidentified, coach and manager Porter Waite, and trainer and driver Chip Evans. (Hershey Bears.)

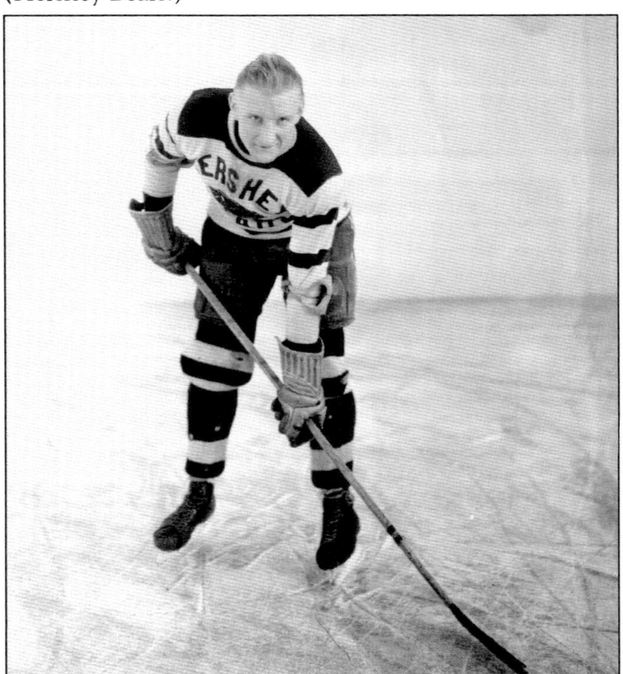

A Growing Legend. When Swarthmore A.C. played its first Ice Palace game on November 19, 1931, it encountered Lloyd S. Blinco, a center for the visiting Crescent Athletic Club (Crescent A.C.) of New York City. Grand Mere, Quebec, native Blinco had played on a Mamaroneck, New York, amateur all-star team with Lou Gehrig and was nicknamed "Bull" for his hard-nosed rushes. Blinco joined the Hershey B'ars of the Tri-State League in 1932 and played for Hershey until 1938. (Hershey Bears.)

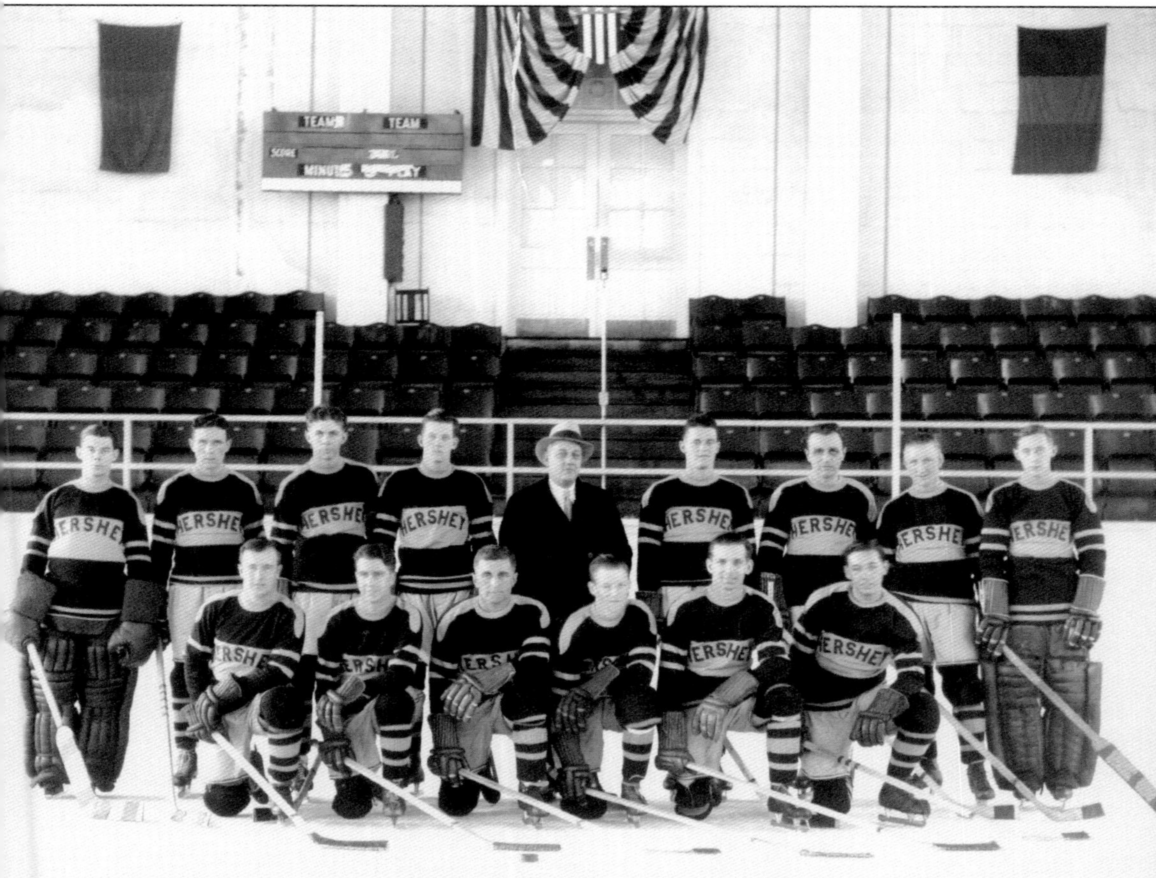

A Club Named Hershey. The 1932–1933 Hershey B'ars were the first team to carry the Hershey name. The Atlantic City Sea Gulls, Baltimore Orioles, and Philadelphia Comets were the other clubs in the newly formed Tri-State League. From left to right are the following: (front row) Walter Stupka, Porter Waite, Bob Nilon, Jerry Dupuy, Bill Dyment, and unidentified; (back row) Charlie Wicks, Sam Foxworthy, Bob "Cowboy" Gilmour, Bob Maley, manager John B. Sollenberger, ? Gallagher, ? Grant, Lloyd S. Blinco, and ? McCallen. Originally, Sollenberger was interested in signing Blinco's brother, Russ, from the Crescent Athletic Club but went after Lloyd when Russ turned professional. Russ Blinco went on to a lengthy NHL career with the Montreal Maroons and Chicago Blackhawks, but Lloyd Blinco served as a coach, general manager, and club president during a storied Hershey career that lasted until his retirement in 1973. (Hershey Bears.)

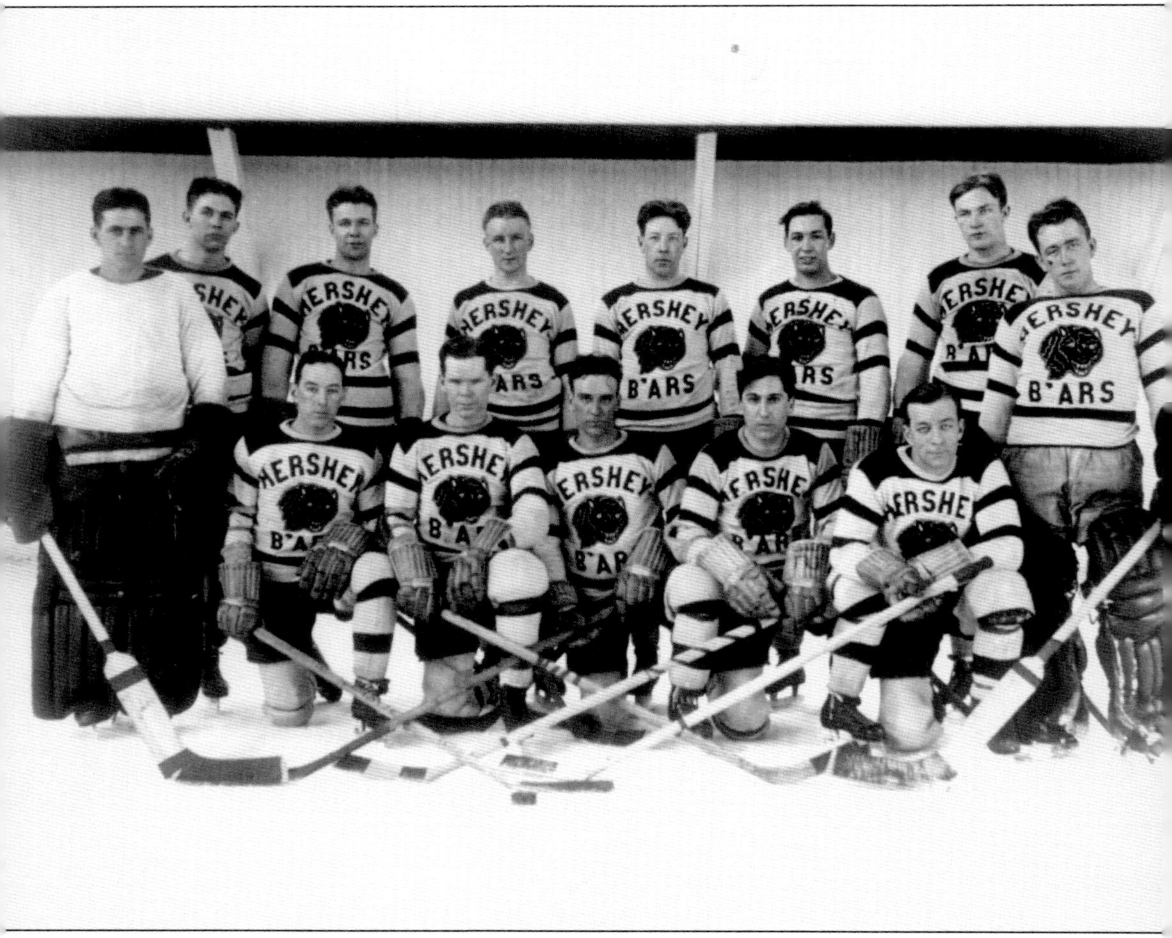

The 1933–1934 Hershey B'ars. The club was not yet known as the Bears, but a Bear logo is on the uniform. In 1933–1934, the reformed Tri-State League became the Eastern Amateur Hockey League (EAHL), a seven-team outfit that also included clubs from Atlantic City, Baltimore, and four from New York (Crescent Athletic-Hamilton, St. Nicholas Hockey Club, New York Athletic Club, and Bronx Hockey Club). Atlantic City won the championship and Hershey, under head coach "Wink" Foulis, finished third. The amateur B'ars only received travel expenses plus meal and room money. From left to right are the following: (front row) Jimmie Haldane, Red Grossman, unidentified, Mike Trimarco, and Oscar Kinghorn; (back row) Lou Murzin, Bob Gilmore, Walton Russell, Lloyd S. Blinco, unidentified, Bill Dyment, Frank Beisler, and Ted Frazier. (Hershey Bears.)

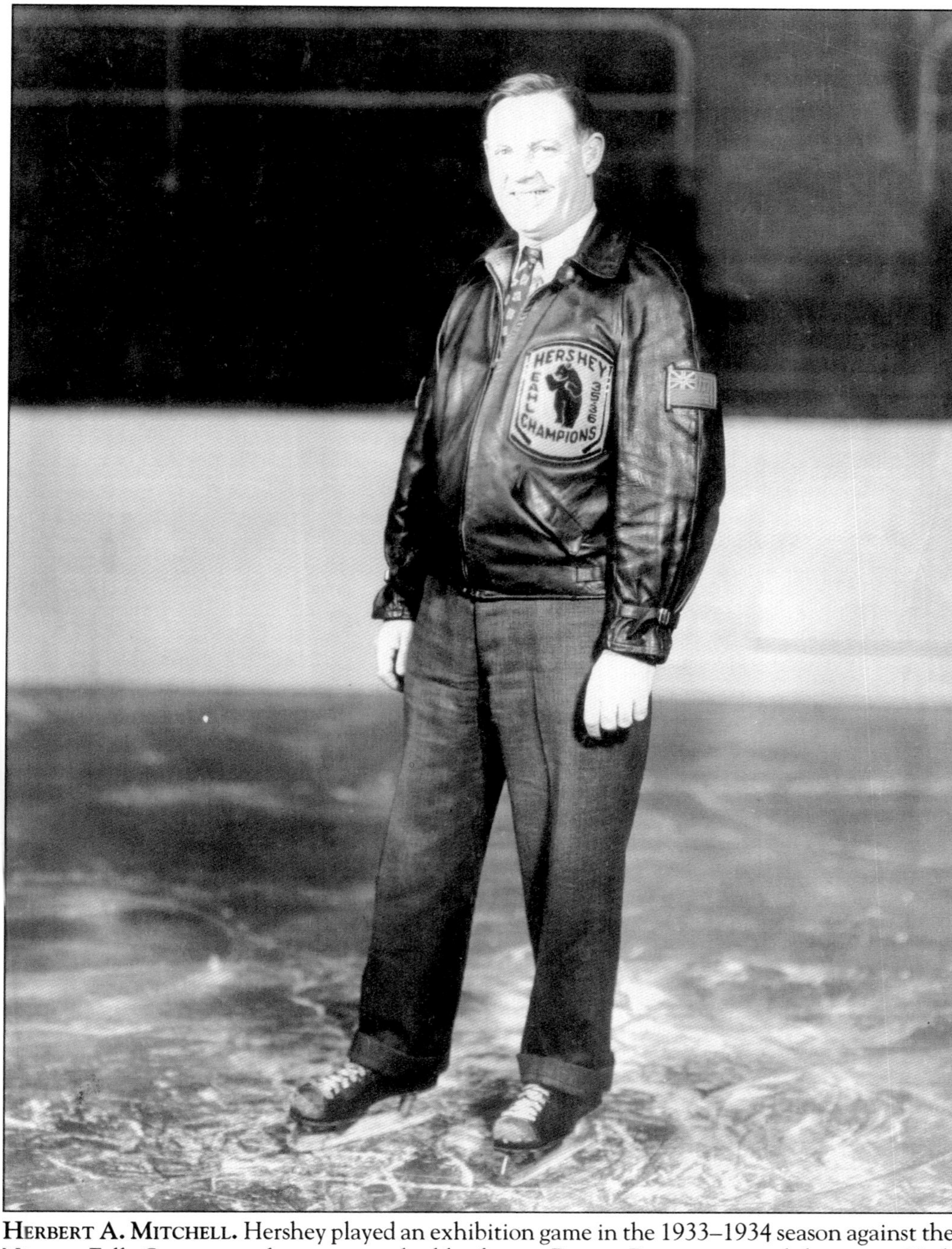

Herbert A. Mitchell. Hershey played an exhibition game in the 1933–1934 season against the Niagara Falls Cataracts, who were coached by former Boston Bruins winger-defenseman Herb Mitchell. His team's play was so impressive that Mitchell was hired as Hershey's head coach. Mitchell signed the first professional contract in Bruins history and played for the club from 1924 to 1926. He coached Hershey from 1934 to 1941, winning EAHL titles in the 1935–1936, 1936–1937, and 1937–1938 seasons. (Hershey Bears.)

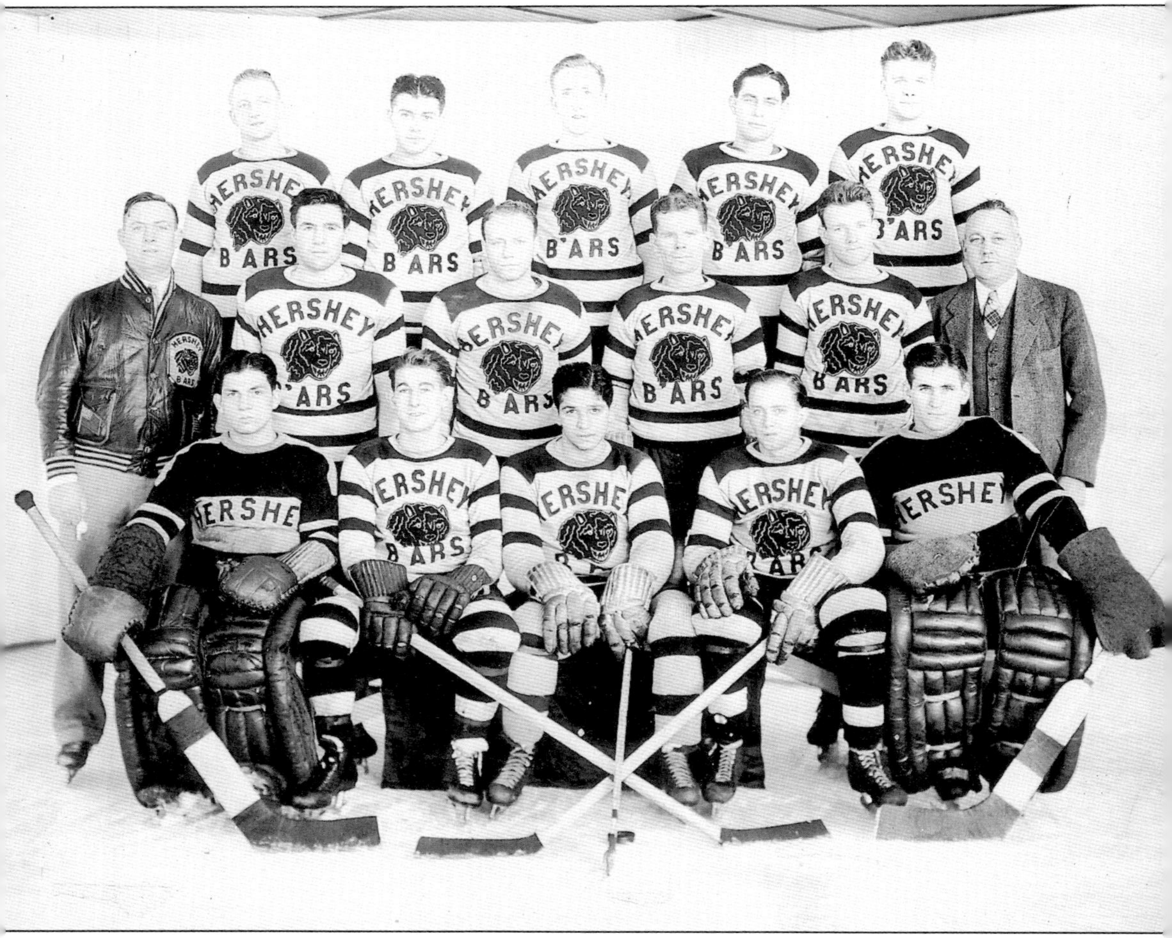

The 1934–1935 Hershey B'ars. The improving B'ars started drawing standing-room crowds to the Ice Palace. Hershey's most heated rival was the New York Crescent-Hamilton Club, which won the EAHL title. Hershey finished second, compiling a 10-9-2 record while scoring 60 goals and allowing 56. From left to right are the following team members: (front row) Nick Damore, Edgar "Chirp" Brenchley, Felix "Gus" Mancuso, Chester "Windy" Steele, and Lou Murzin; (middle row) coach Herb Mitchell, Aud Tuten, Hank Lauzon, Frank Grossman, Bob Nilon, and manager John B. Sollenberger; (back row) Lloyd S. Blinco, Roger J. Proulx, Alex Kennedy, Oscar Kaiser, and Walton Russell. Mitchell led the team during its transition from amateur to professional when Hershey joined the AHL in the 1938–1939 season. He compiled an 82-65-19 AHL record in Hershey and later served as the club's chief scout. (Hershey Bears.)

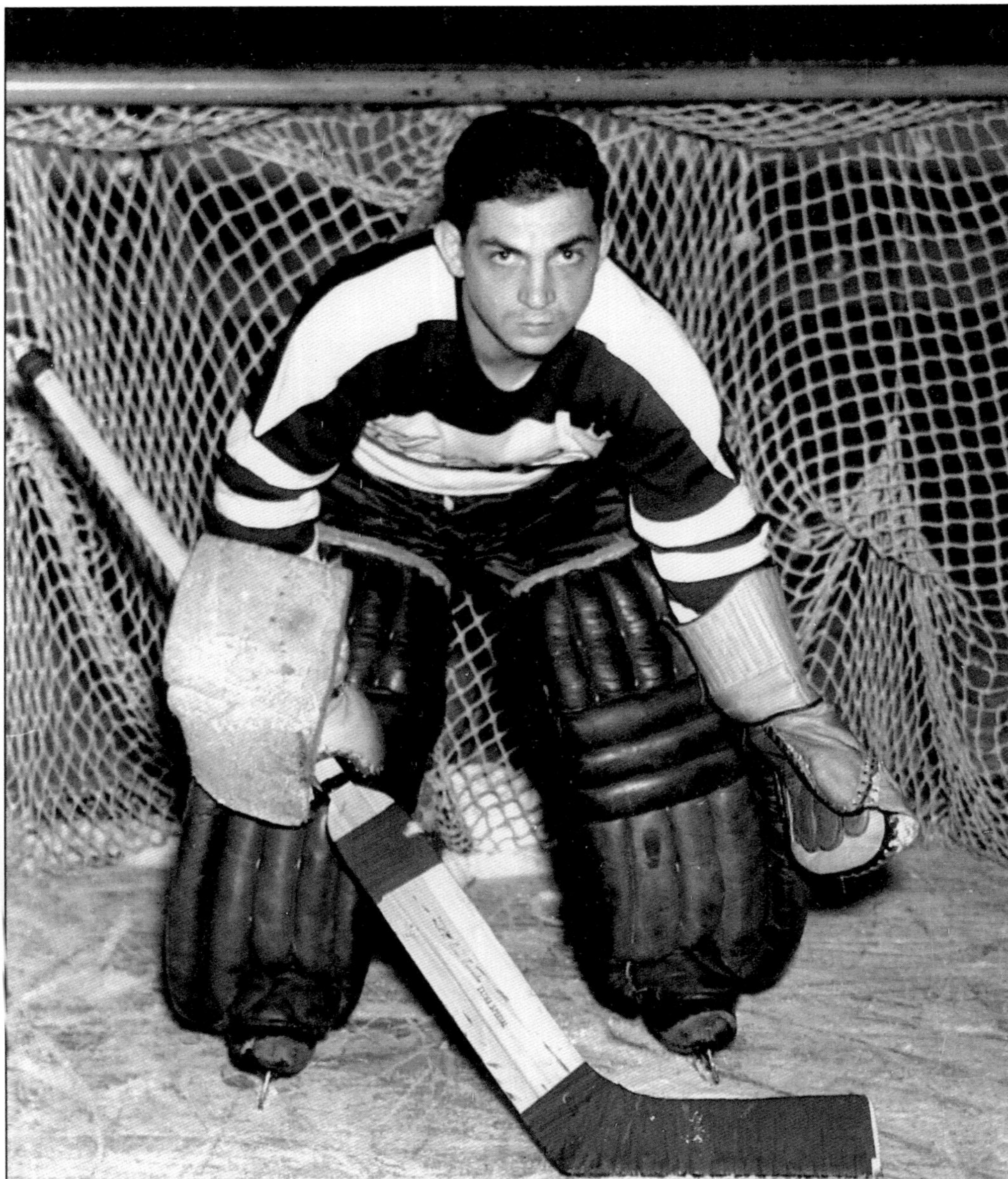

Imposing Pads. Nick Damore is one of the greatest goalies in Hershey history. He ranks No. 2 in all-time Bears games played (365) and victories (190) and No. 1 in shutouts (29)—and those are merely his AHL numbers. Damore also played for Hershey during its EAHL incarnation. After Hershey won its first EAHL title in 1935–1936, New York Mayor Jimmy Walker presented the club with the silver Jimmy Walker Cup at Madison Square Garden. (Hershey Bears.)

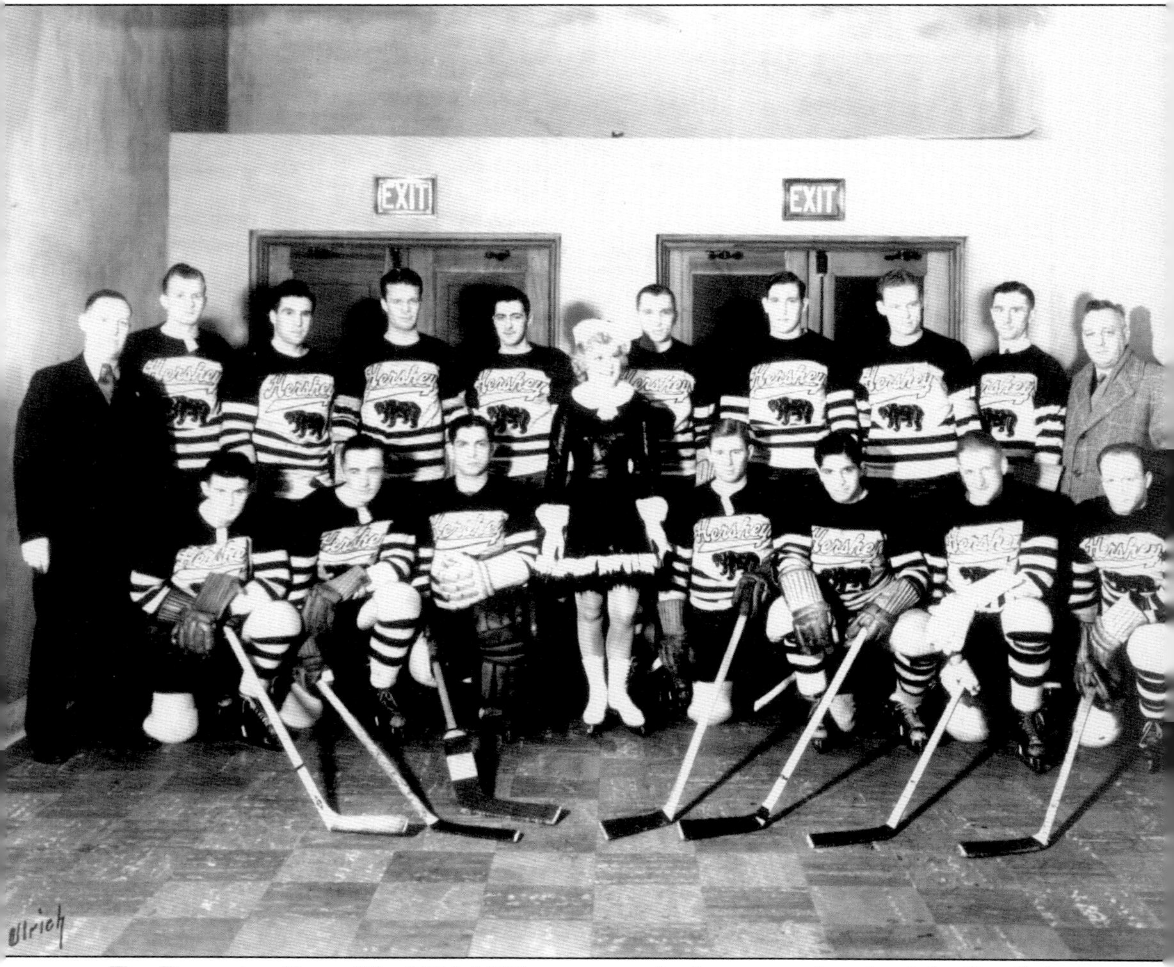

The Bears Are Born. The 1936–1937 season was the first season that the club officially became known as the Hershey Bears. New York City writers, objecting to the commerciality of the name B'ars, had taken to calling the team the "Bears from Penn's Woods." The Bears got their picture taken with three-time Olympic figure skating champion Sonja Henie on January 18, 1937, in what was originally called Hershey Sports Arena. Henie presented a 30-minute program before and between periods of an exhibition between the Bears and the Port Colborne Sailors of the Ontario Hockey Association Senior League. From left to right are the following: (front row) Matt Kelly, Bernard Blanchard, Nick Damore, Sonja Henie, Harry Currie, Felix Mancuso, Lloyd Blinco, and Hank Lauzon; (back row) coach Herb Mitchell, Harry Frost, Aud Tuten, Walton Russell, Jerry Cormier, Tony Graboski, Art Sommons, Bill Morris, Lou Gagnon, and manager J.B. Sollenberger. (Hershey Bears.)

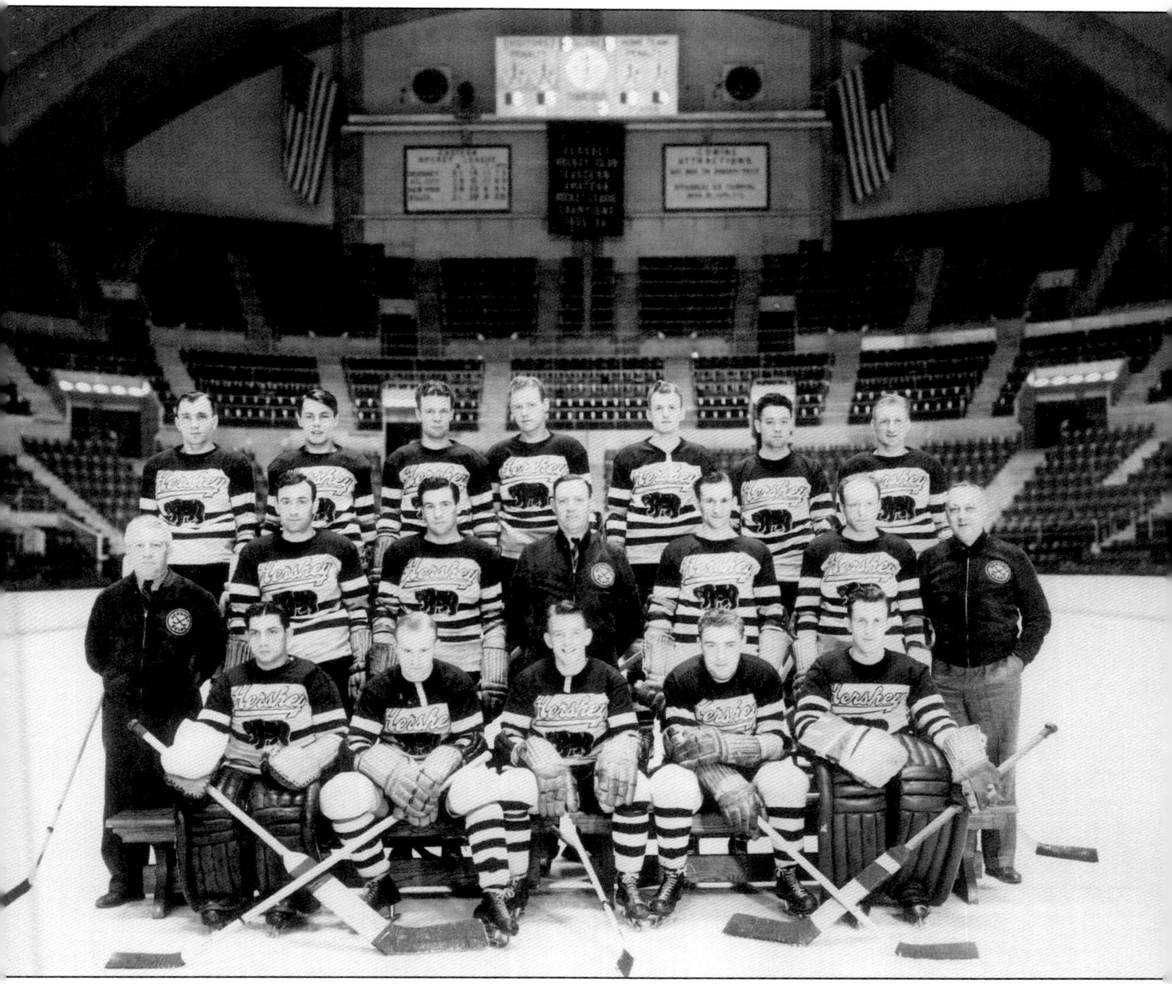

THE LAST AMATEURS. The Bears, in their final season as an amateur club, won their third straight EAHL title in the 1937–1938 season. They went 32-15-11. After winning the Walker Cup series, Hershey went on to defeat the Detroit Holzbaugh-Fords 3-2 and 5-2 at home and 2-1 in Detroit to claim the U.S. Amateur Championship. The team poses inside the new Hershey Sports Arena, which is less than a year old. Note the scoreboard, which features analog clocks for game time and penalties. From left to right are the following: (front row) Nick Damore, Stan Kawalski, Fred Hunt, Joe Catlin, and Jack Skillings; (middle row) trainer Jake Frysinger, Ab Grant, Aud Tuten, coach Herb Mitchell, Jo-Jo Graboski, Hank Lauzon, and manager John B. Sollenberger; (back row) Tony Graboski, Ray Van Daele, Russ Russell, Bill Morris, Harry Frost, Vern Buckles, and Lloyd S. Blinco. (Hershey Bears.)

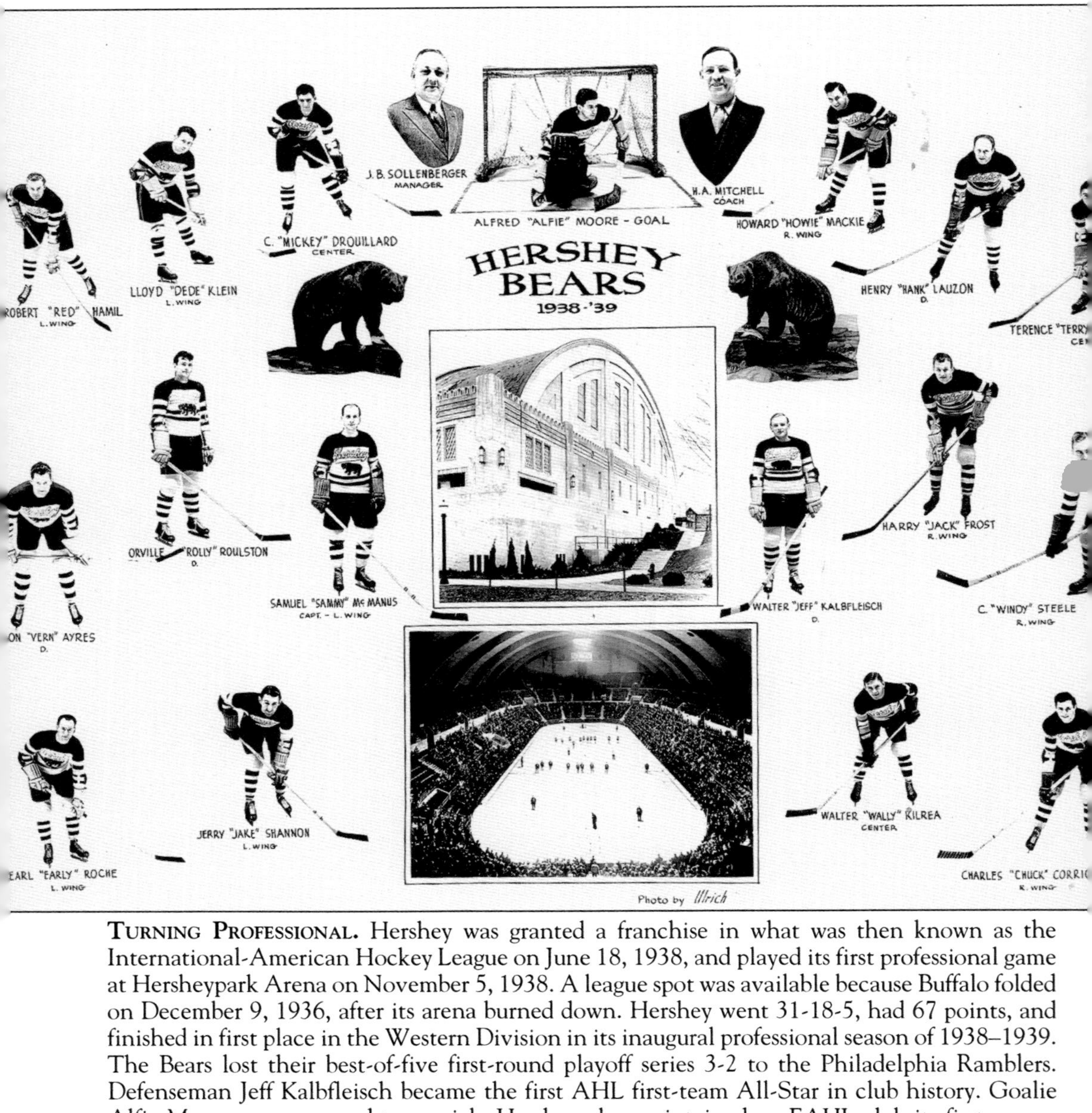

TURNING PROFESSIONAL. Hershey was granted a franchise in what was then known as the International-American Hockey League on June 18, 1938, and played its first professional game at Hersheypark Arena on November 5, 1938. A league spot was available because Buffalo folded on December 9, 1936, after its arena burned down. Hershey went 31-18-5, had 67 points, and finished in first place in the Western Division in its inaugural professional season of 1938–1939. The Bears lost their best-of-five first-round playoff series 3-2 to the Philadelphia Ramblers. Defenseman Jeff Kalbfleisch became the first AHL first-team All-Star in club history. Goalie Alfie Moore was a second-team pick. Hershey also maintained an EAHL club its first season in the AHL. The Hershey Cubs, coached by Lloyd S. Blinco, disbanded after the 1938–1939 season. (Hershey Bears.)

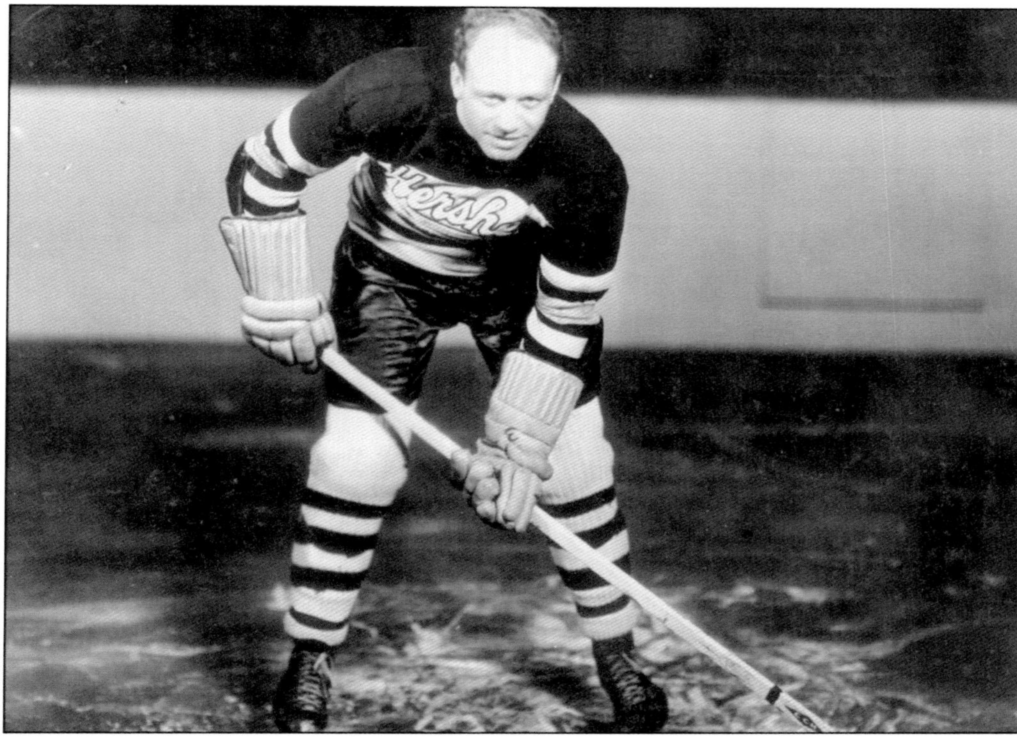

Hank Lauzon (1938–1944, 1945–1946). In February 1938, defenseman Lauzon, an EAHL All-Star, became the first player to sign a professional contract with the Bears. He came to Hershey from the Niagara Falls Cataracts, where he had played for Herb Mitchell. Lauzon still ranks 22nd in all-time scoring by Hershey defensemen (97 points in 341 games). After he retired, his Lauzon's Gulf Service Station was a successful enterprise in Hershey for many years. (Hershey Bears.)

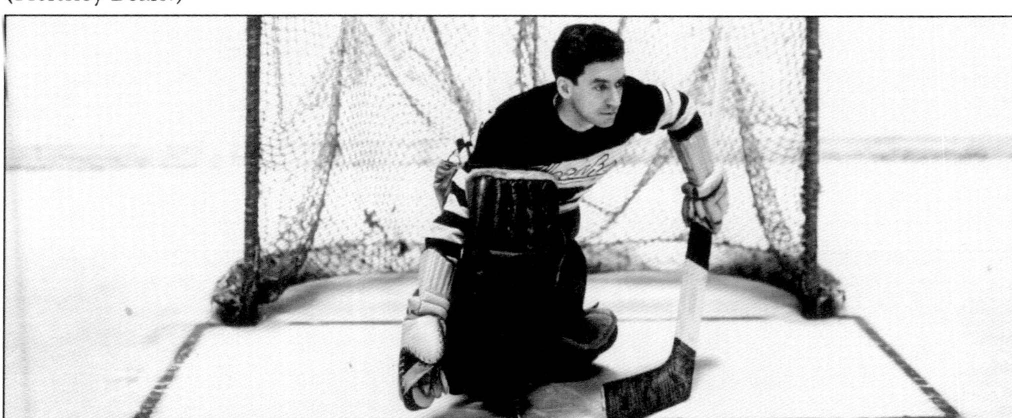

A Soap Opera. Goalie Alfie Moore was in the net when Milton S. Hershey had Hershey's cocoa-butter soap distributed to fans before a game during the 1938–1939 season. Fans pelted the ice with soap bars when referee Eddie Burke drew their ire. Moore ducked inside his net for protection, and Burke emerged unscathed. Moore (1938–1940) played just two seasons in Hershey but is tied for fifth on the club's all-time shutout list (eight) and holds the single-season goals against average (GAA) record (1.98). (Hershey Bears.)

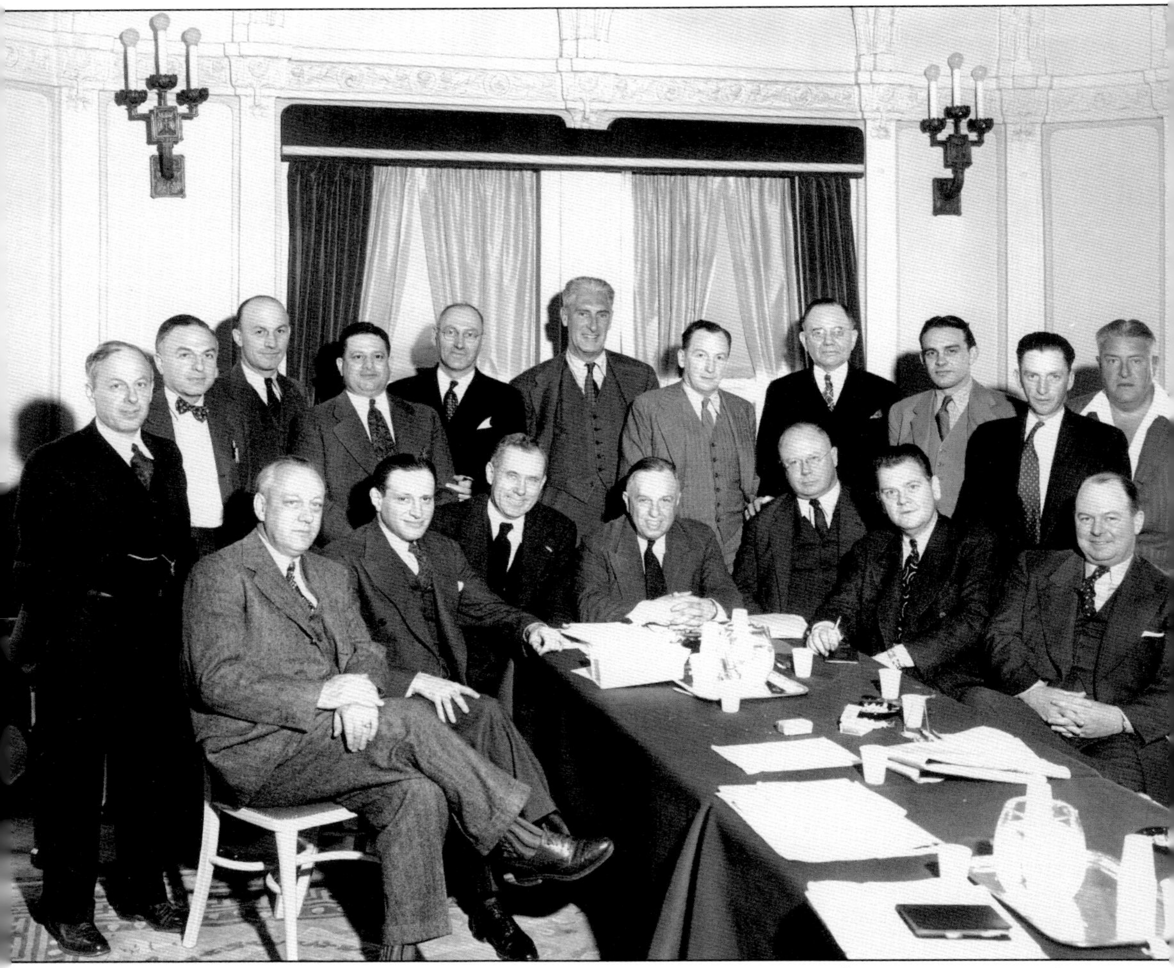

Executive Decisions. AHL leaders meet at the Hotel Traymore in Atlantic City on May 13, 1941. Though the league began in 1936, two seasons before Hershey joined, its formation actually started in 1926 when the Canadian-American and International Hockey Leagues began play. In 1936, Cleveland, Pittsburgh, Buffalo, and Syracuse of the International Hockey League (IHL) joined New Haven, Philadelphia, Providence, and Springfield of the Canadian-American Hockey League to form the International-American Hockey League. From 1936 to 1938, the two leagues played an interlocking schedule but had not yet technically become a single circuit. Those two seasons are part of the official AHL record. The formal merger came in June 1938, and the name was shortened to the American Hockey League in 1940. Hershey executive John B. Sollenberger (seated on the far left) served as AHL president during the 1953–1954 season. (Hershey Bears.)

THE LITTLE BEAR. Wally Kilrea (1938–1944) led the Bears in scoring in four of their first five seasons. A first-team AHL All-Star in the 1942–1943 season, Kilrea still ranks 16th in all-time Hershey scoring (334 points in 298 games). In the 1942–1943 season, Kilrea became Hershey's first 90-point scorer (99) and first AHL scoring champion. Before coming to Hershey, he played on Stanley Cup championship teams in Detroit in 1936 and 1937. (Hershey Bears.)

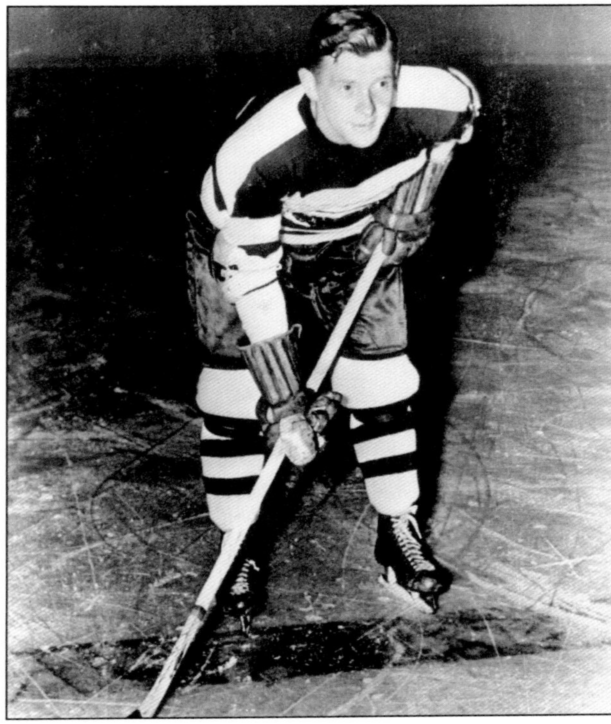

From - Jim Hendy,
American Hockey League Service Bureau
515 Madison Ave., New York 22, N. Y.

For release in morning and afternoon papers of Tuesday, Nov. 5, 1946

AMERICAN HOCKEY LEAGUE
(Standings include games of Sunday, Nov. 3)

Eastern Division

	GP	W	L	T	Pts	GF	GA
New Haven	11	7	3	1	15	45	35
Hershey	10	7	2	1	15	41	24
Providence	10	2	6	2	6	25	47
Springfield	7	3	4	0	6	24	27
Philadelphia	10	1	9	0	2	30	76

Western Division

	GP	W	L	T	Pts	GF	GA
Indianapolis	10	6	1	3	15	48	19
Cleveland	9	5	2	2	12	39	27
Pittsburg	10	4	3	3	11	49	34
Buffalo	10	3	4	3	9	24	26
St. Louis	9	1	5	3	5	30	40

Leading Scorers

	GP	G	A	TP
Norman Burns, New Haven	11	7	14	21
Wally Wilson, Pittsburg	10	9	7	16
Don Metz, Pittsburg	10	8	8	16
Jack Hamilton, Pittsburg	10	6	9	15
Gerry Couture, Indianapolis	7	10	4	14
*Tony Bukovich, Indianapolis	10	9	5	14
Lloyd Doran, Indianapolis	10	4	10	14
Les Douglas, Indianapolis	7	3	11	14
John O'Flaherty, Pittsburg	10	3	11	14
Mel Hill, Pittsburg	10	6	7	13
Gordon Bruce, Hershey	10	4	9	13
Tomy Licari, Indianapolis	10	5	7	12
Paul Ronty, Hershey	10	5	7	12
Pete Bebando, Hershey	10	4	8	12
Ab Collings, Philadelphia	10	4	8	12
Tom Burlington, Providence	10	2	10	12
Joe Bell, New Haven	7	8	3	11
Jack McGill, Hershey	10	6	5	11
Johm Holota, Cleveland	9	6	5	11
Pete Leswick, Cleveland	9	4	7	11
Mark Marquess, Hershey	10	5	6	11
Gaston Gauthier, Philadelphia	10	4	7	11
Phil Hergesheimer, Phila	10	4	7	11
Ernie Dickens, Pittsburg	10	1	10	11
John Chad, Providence	10	7	3	10
Russ Brayshaw, Providence	10	3	7	10

Schedule for week of November 4, 1946

Tues. Nov. 5...Spgfld. at St.Louis
Wed. " 6...Spgfld. at Pitt.
" " "...Cleve. at Prov.
" " "...Hershey at Phila.
Thurs. " 7...Spgfld. at Indpls.
" " "...St.Louis at New Haven
Sat. " 9...St.Louis at Hershey
" " "...Prov. at Cleve.
" " "...Buffalo at Phila.
" " "...Indianapolis at Pitt.
" " "...New Haven at Spgfld.
Sun. " 10...Hershey at Buffalo
" " "...Cleve. at Indpls.
" " "...Spgfld. at New Haven
" " "...Phila. at Prov.
" " "...Pitt. at St. Louis

* Correction: Bukovich of Indianapolis was credited with 7 assists in last week's records in error. It should have read 7 goals 4 assists for a total of 11 points. The correction is made in this week's release.

Leaders

Shutouts - Jim Henry, New Haven....2
Goals - Gerry Couture, Indpls.....10
Assists - Norman Burns, New Haven.14
Penalties - Jack McGill, Hershey..31 minutes

Goaltender

	GP	GA	SO	Avge.
Ralph Almas, Indpls.	10	19	1	1.90

HUNT AND PECK. Today's AHL statistics are available on the Internet, but there was a time when technology demanded that statistics be produced on a manual typewriter. This weekly statistics page from early in the 1946–1947 season is from the AHL office of James C. Hendy, who went on to serve as general manager of the Cleveland Barons. The James C. Hendy Memorial Award, given annually to the AHL's top executive, is named in his honor. (Hershey Bears.)

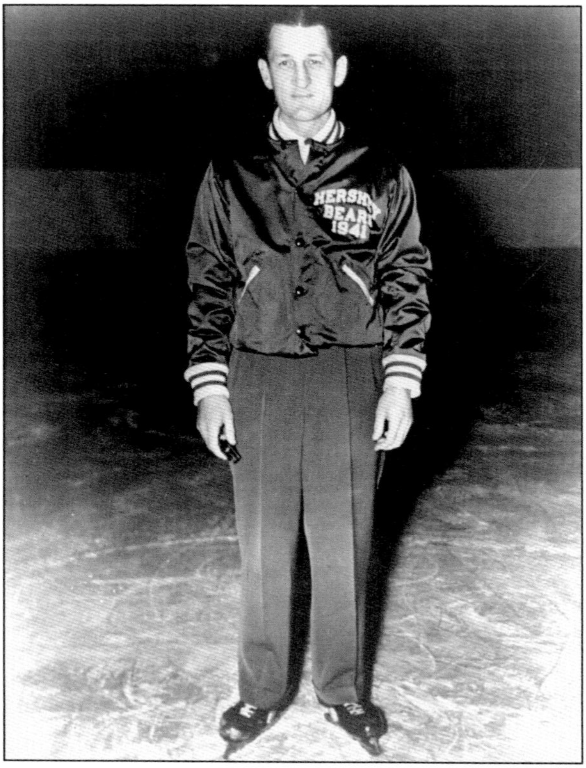

Ralph "Cooney" Weiland (1941–1945). Weiland coached Boston to the Stanley Cup in the 1940–1941 season and captained Boston's 1938–1939 Stanley Cup team. In the 1941–1942 season, he replaced Herb Mitchell as Hershey's coach and compiled a 126-70-30 record. His 1942–1943 Bears hold the club record for fewest losses (13). The Hockey Hall of Famer and Lester Patrick Trophy recipient coached New Haven in the AHL (1945–1947) before coaching at Harvard for 21 seasons. (Hershey Bears.)

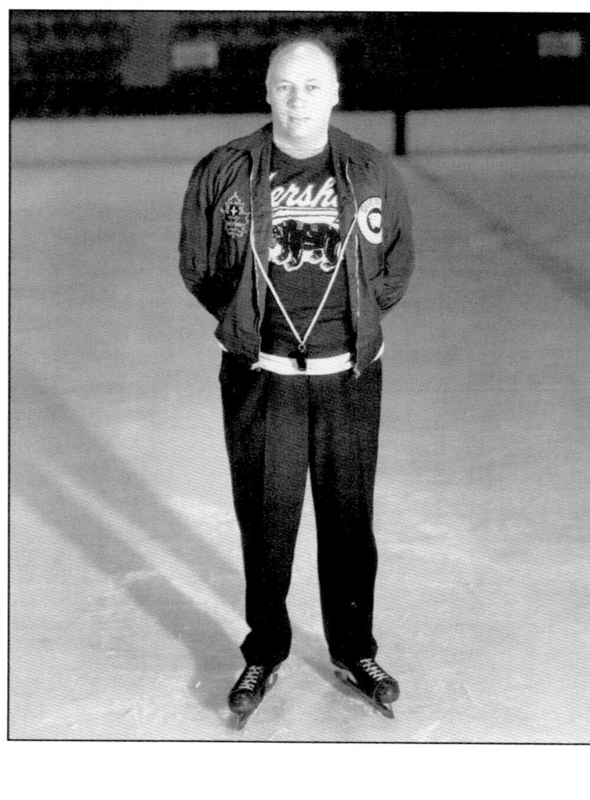

Don Penniston (1945–1950). Hershey failed to win the Calder Cup in its first eight AHL seasons. Penniston changed that after replacing Ralph "Cooney" Weiland as head coach for the 1945–1946 season. He led Hershey to the Calder Cup his second season. In five Hershey seasons, Penniston went 136-146-50 and ranks fifth in all-time Hershey coaching victories. (Hershey Bears.)

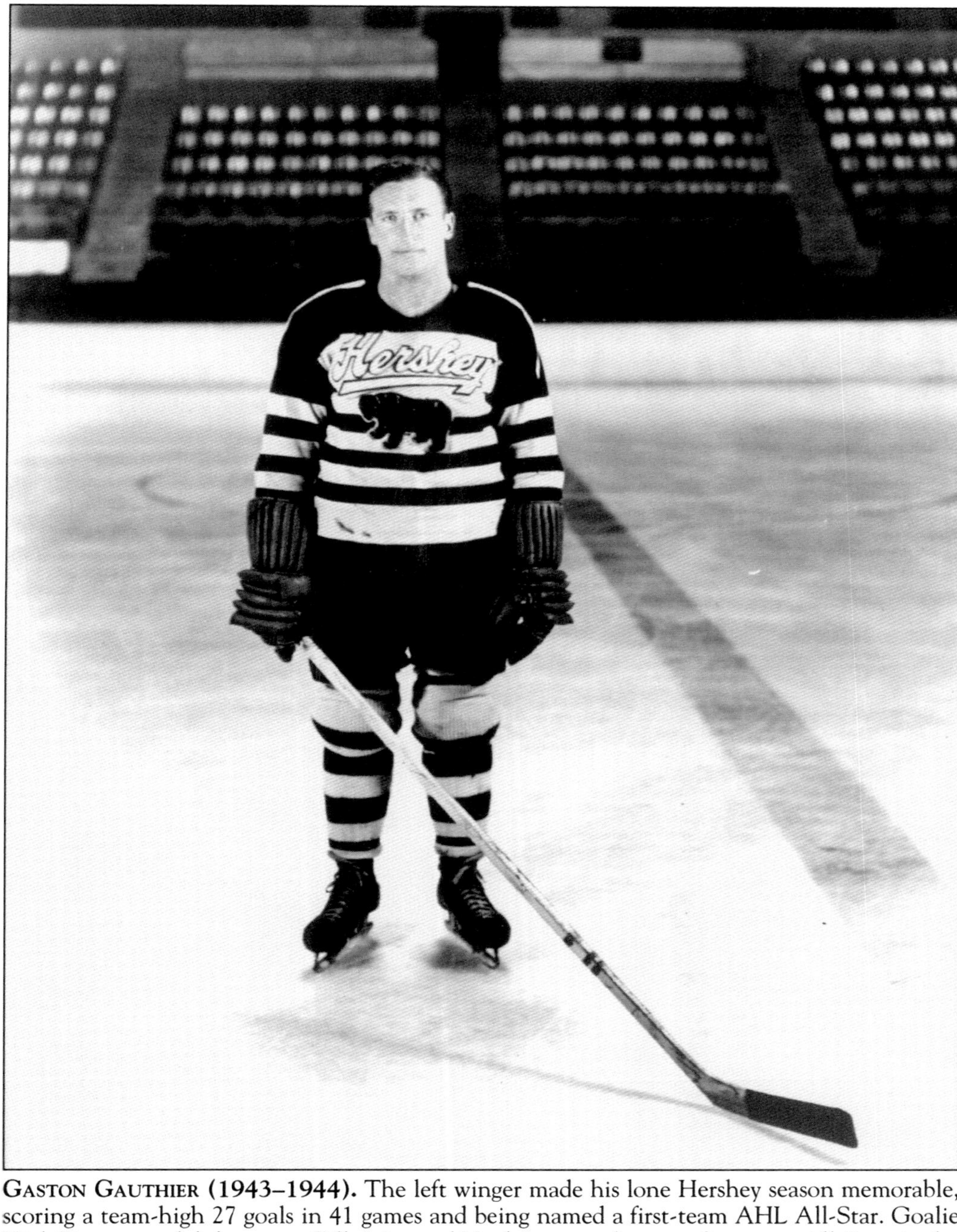

Gaston Gauthier (1943–1944). The left winger made his lone Hershey season memorable, scoring a team-high 27 goals in 41 games and being named a first-team AHL All-Star. Goalie Nick Damore and defensemen Billy Moe and Hank Lauzon also were first-team All-Stars in the 1943–1944 season. Moe went on to play five seasons with the New York Rangers. Hershey went 30-16-8, with 68 points, to win the Eastern Division but lost to Cleveland in the first round of the playoffs. (Hershey Bears.)

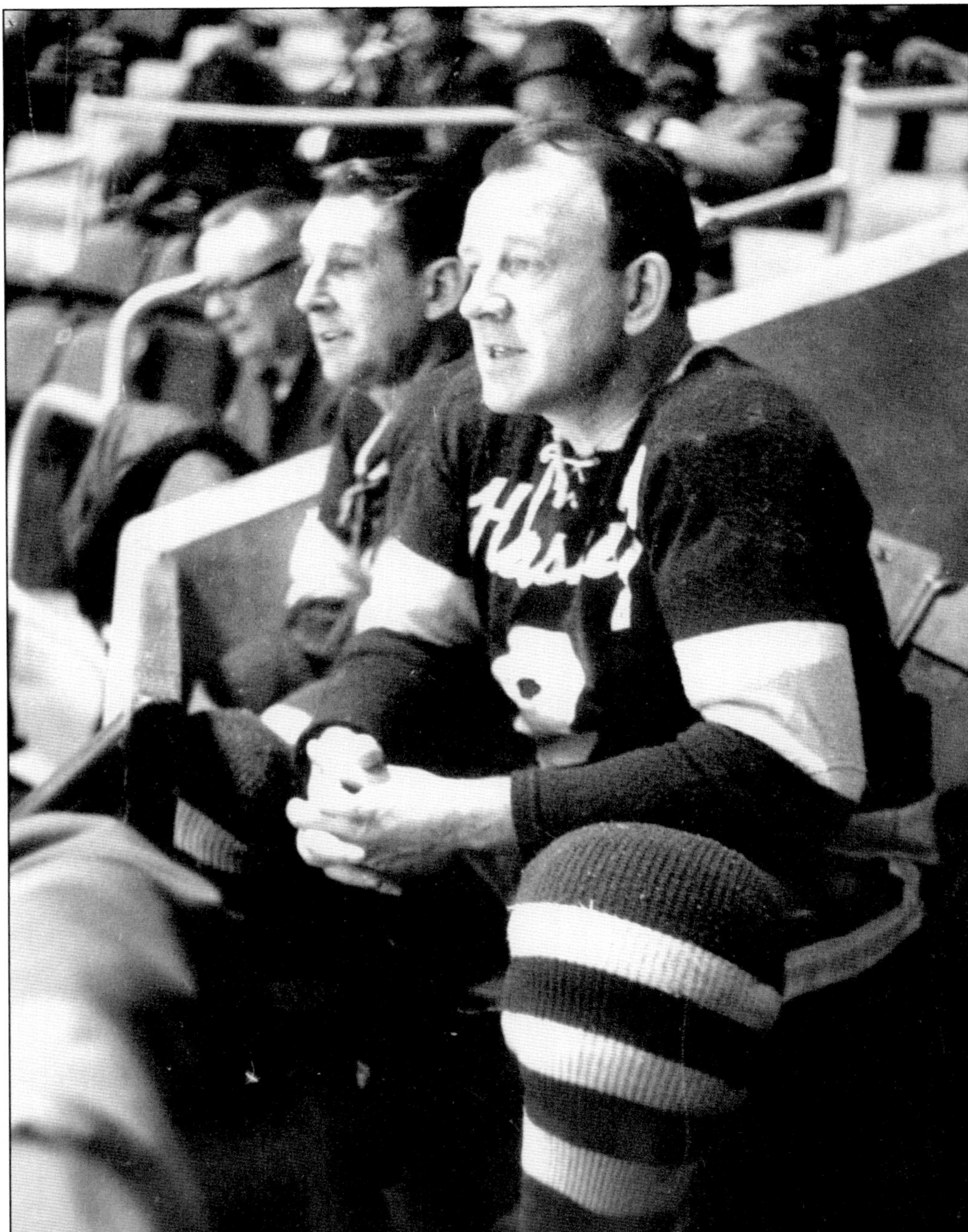

Fred T. Hunt (1948–1949). Hunt played one AHL season in Hershey and has greater renown as player, general manager, and governor for the Buffalo Bisons. He led Buffalo to six Calder Cups. Hunt scored 20 goals and added 28 assists for the Bears in the 1948–1949 season. He ranks in the top 30 in all-time AHL playoff scoring (55 points in 54 games). The AHL's Fred T. Hunt Memorial Award for sportsmanship, determination, and dedication is named in his honor. (M. Jaffe/Hershey Bears.)

Two

A Living Landmark

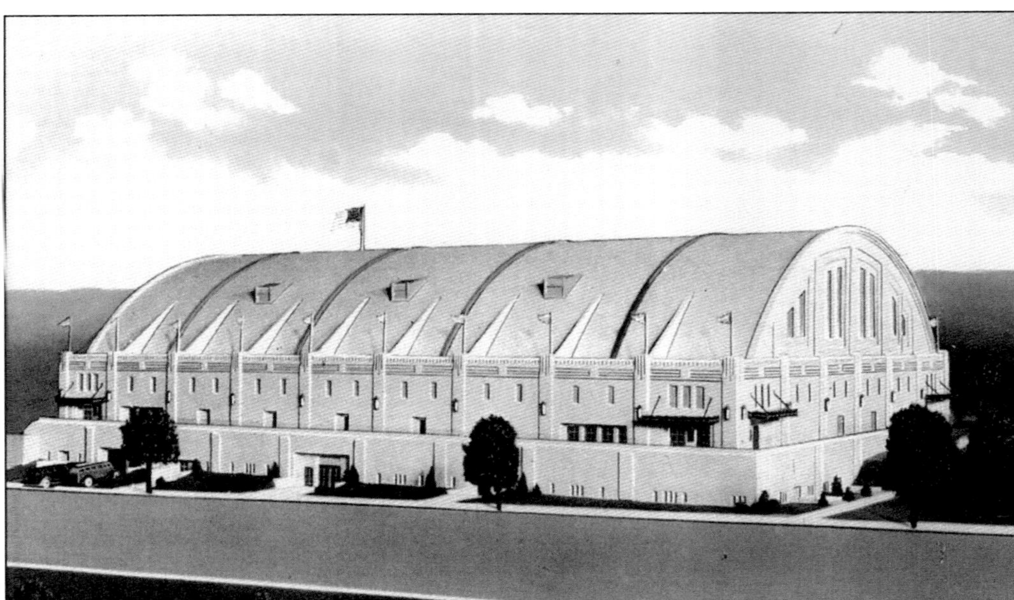

Postcard Perfect. Hershey Sports Arena is touted on the back of the above postcard: "In this gigantic building, where there are no pillars or posts to mar one's vision, professional hockey, basketball, tennis and such eye-filling spectacles as the Ice Follies and the Ice Capades take place during the Fall, Winter and Spring Months." (Hershey Bears.)

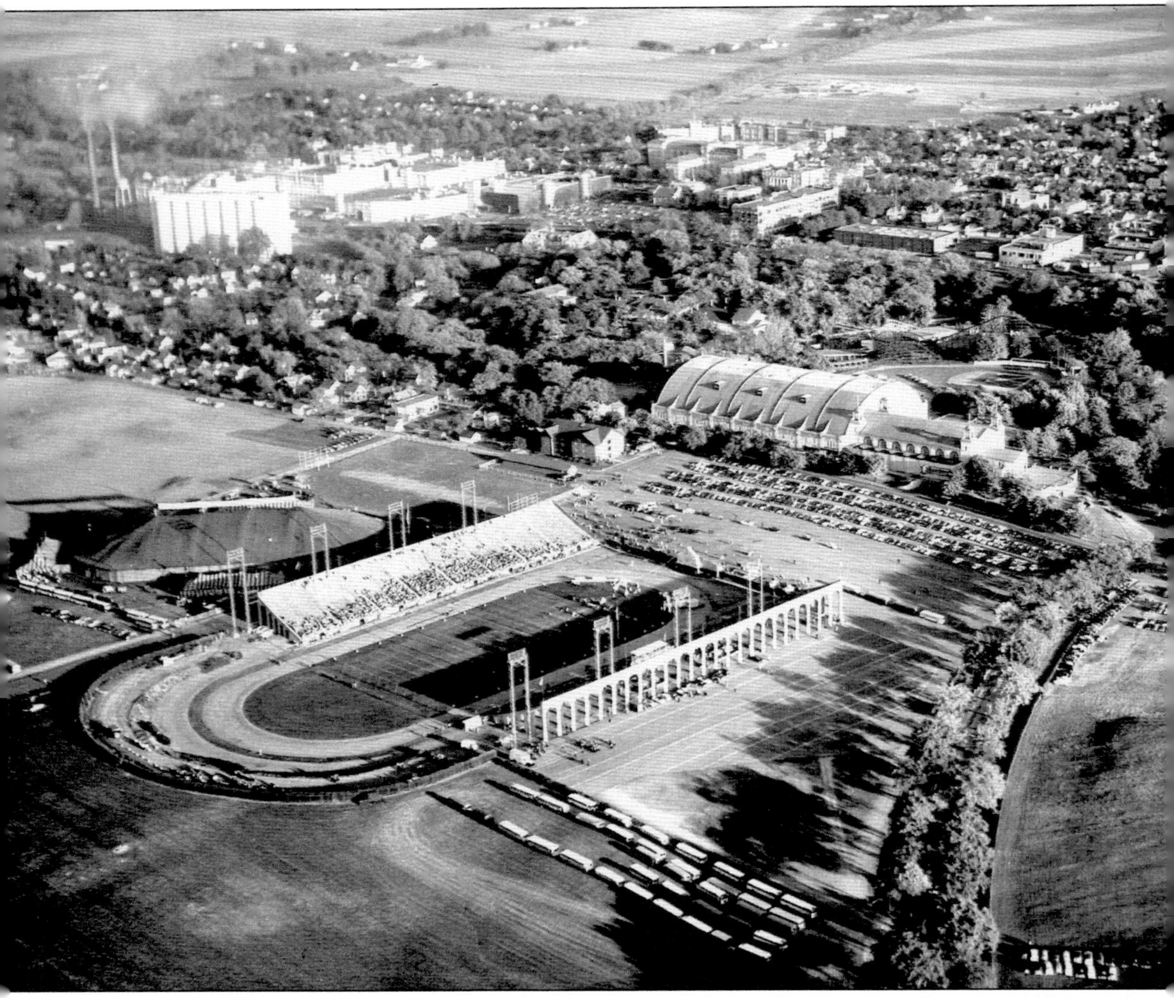

ARCHED EXCELLENCE. Ground was broken for Hersheypark Arena in January 1936, and construction began in April of the same year. The arena's signature is its arched roof, which is made of a 3.5-inch shell of concrete. The style, known as Zeiss-Dywidag roof design, had begun to be used extensively in Europe. The building was designed by architects Paul Witmer and Anton Tedesko. Witmer, manager of Hershey Lumber Products, built many of the projects Milton S. Hershey commissioned. Tedesko was the engineer of structural design for the Roberts & Schaeffer Company of Chicago. An added benefit of the arena's construction, and other buildings that Hershey commissioned at the time, was that it provided jobs during the Depression. The building just to the left of Hersheypark Arena is the Brown House, which was used to house Bears players until it was razed in the late 1980s to make room for the Hersheypark expansion. (Hershey Bears.)

"Dear Sir: For several years now I have been a regular attendant at the hockey matches, and despite the fact that I know there is a press reservation waiting forme, it is with some trepidation that I journey Hersheyward on the evening of a hockey game for the reason that the crowds are so dense that even if my reservation is waiting, I look like something the cat dragged in by the time I fight my way through the mob.

"Now, Mr. Hershey, inasmuch as the game has proved to be such a popular one around here, and they tell me that the fans journey in from points as far removed as Waynesboro and Williamsport, some even staying overnight, why can't something be done to take care of all those who haveto stand week in and week out, and whatis worse, those who drive to Hershey to watch the B'ars, only to be turnedaway at the door because there isn't even standing room"

"The effect now on turning them away is good -- they make their reservations early, and some even go supperlessto get there in time to get a seat, but it could have an op osite reaction.

"There is only one solution, Mr. Hershey, -- enlarge the Ice Palace, and while you're at it, make it such that the game can be witnessed from any seat in the house. As it is now, very few can remain seated and watch the rapid action taking place on the rink.

"I am only one, Mr. He shey, registering this complaint, but I feel that I am voicing the sentiment of hundreds when I say-- enlarge the Ice Palace seating capacity, and give all those who want to go, an op ortunity to see o e of the real games of sport."

A FINAL PUSH. Hundreds were routinely turned away from the Ice Palace, so the need for a bigger arena became obvious. A popular tale, perhaps apocryphal, holds that Milton S. Hershey decided to build a new arena when he was turned away from a game. Club records point more strongly to an open letter (typed copy above, including typos) to Hershey written by Nobe Frank in a *Harrisburg Evening Telegraph* column c. 1935 as the likely final spark. (Hershey Bears.)

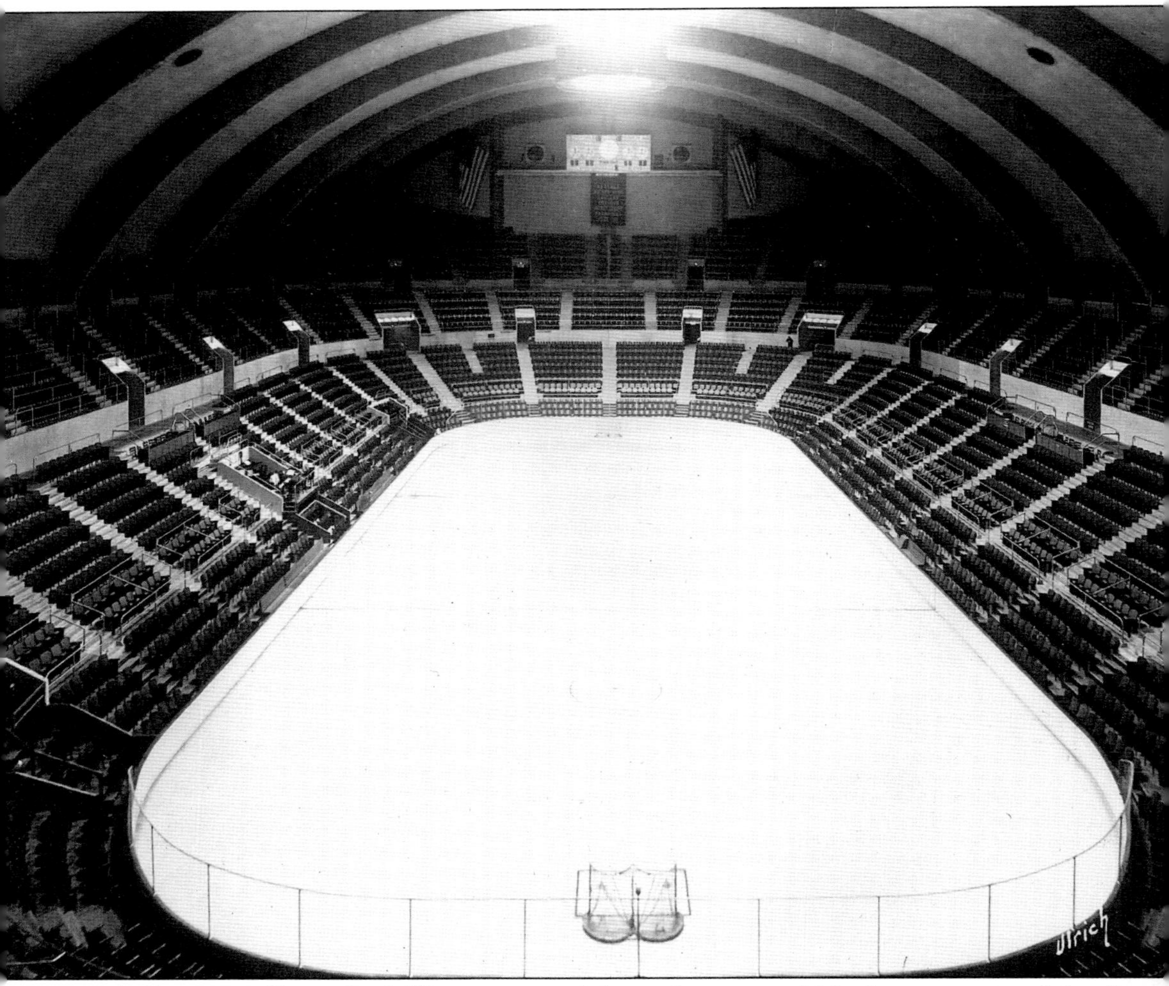

A Brilliant Plan. Paul Witmer, one of the architects, and Hershey executives John B. Sollenberger and Charles F. Ziegler visited Toronto's Maple Leaf Gardens and Montreal's Forum to use them as models for their prospective new building. Original discussions contemplated 4,800 seats, but the final decision, pushed by Sollenberger, was to go with more than 7,000 to ensure adequate growth capacity. Original capacity was 7,104 wooden folding seats, but that changed over the years. The roof, which rests on a series of hinges where the total weight is brought down to one point, was poured in five sections. There was fear that cold weather during pouring of the final section would spoil the job, but Witmer procured all the horse manure and straw he could find and used it as insulation during the 14 cure days the roof needed. A 250-man crew worked around the clock for eight months to build the arena at a cost of $1 million. (Hershey Bears.)

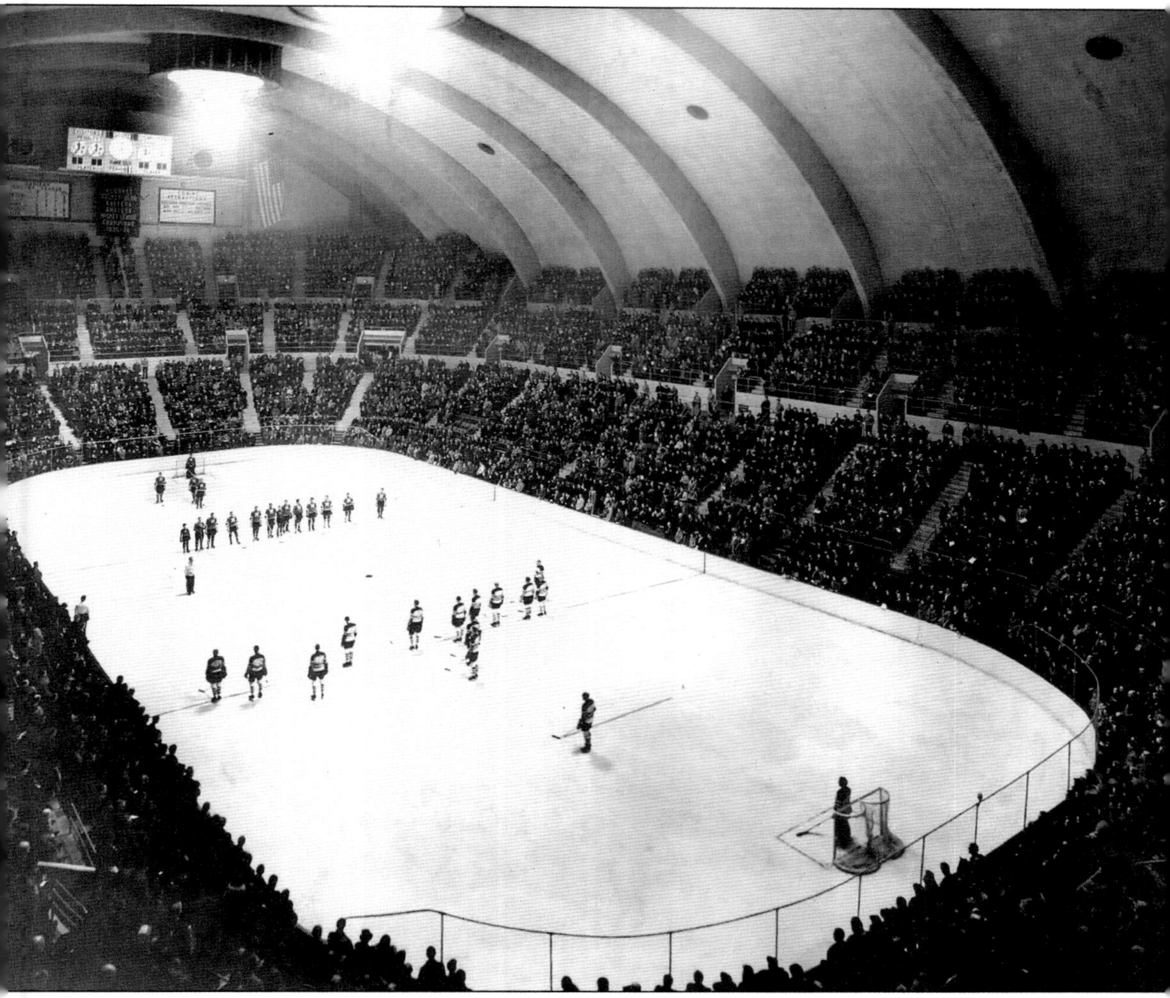

Opening Night. The above shot was taken during opening night of the 1937–1938 season. The original opening night was December 19, 1936. It was a snowy day, followed by rain that created slush. The east end of the arena, not quite finished, had a tarpaulin on it as a crowd of more than 6,000 watched the Bears beat the New York Rovers 3-2 in the inaugural game. Lloyd S. Blinco scored the first goal, assisted by Russ Russell, 1:28 into the first period. Hershey's "Tut" Tuten was the first player in the penalty box. Tuten and New York's Paul Kowel engaged in the first fight. New York fans and writers rode a special railroad train to the EAHL game. At the time of its construction, Hersheypark Arena was the only monolithic concrete structure of its kind in the United States, measuring 362 feet long by 232 feet wide, with the height of 100 feet from the roof to the floor. To the left of mid-ice, on the lower bowl, stands a pit where a five-piece orchestra performed during games. (Hershey Bears.)

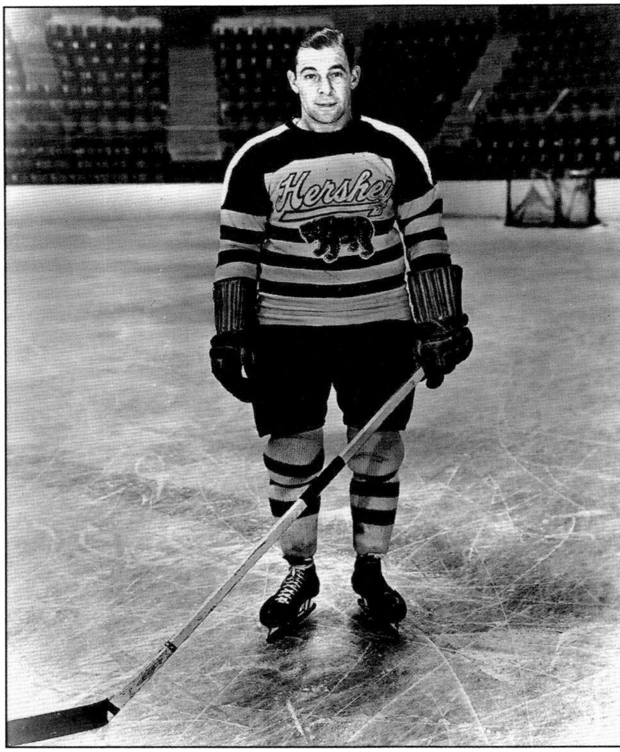

No Zamboni. Cliff Barton (1940–1941) stands on a rink originally resurfaced by a hand-drawn cart containing a drum of heated water. Underneath were 10 miles of wrought-iron pipe circulating brine. Milton Garland, a cooling expert for Frick Refrigeration, supervised the 24-hour pouring of the concrete floor. Given complimentary lifetime tickets as compensation for frequent visits to monitor the ice plant, Garland attended games until his death in 2001 at 102 years old. (Hershey Bears.)

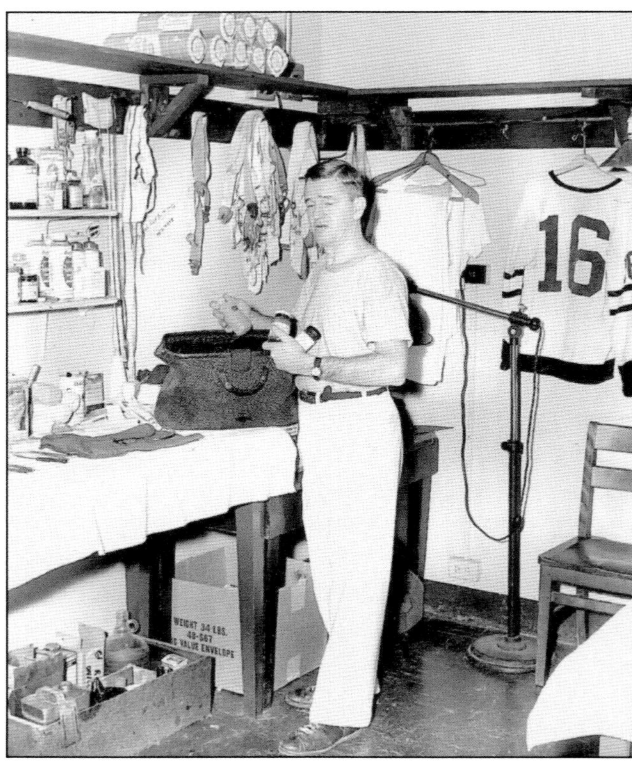

Alexander's Empire. Toronto native Scotty Alexander, who commuted to Hershey from Baltimore, Maryland, spent more than a quarter century as the Bears trainer. Here, he is in the training room at Hersheypark Arena in a shot believed to be taken in the 1950s. Alexander worked for the Buffalo Bisons before joining the Bears for the 1946–1947 season. (Hershey Bears.)

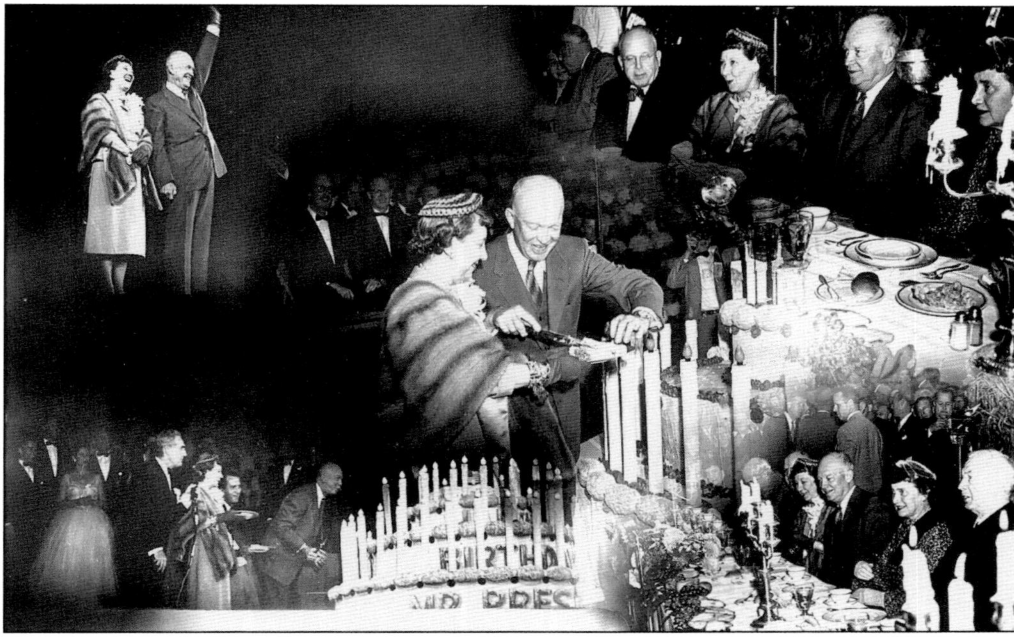

Hail to the Chief. Pres. Dwight D. Eisenhower, who owned a home in Gettysburg, celebrated his birthday on October 13, 1953, at a Hersheypark Arena gala sponsored by the National Republican Party. Milton S. Hershey celebrated his 80th birthday with an arena party on December 13, 1937. (Hershey Bears.)

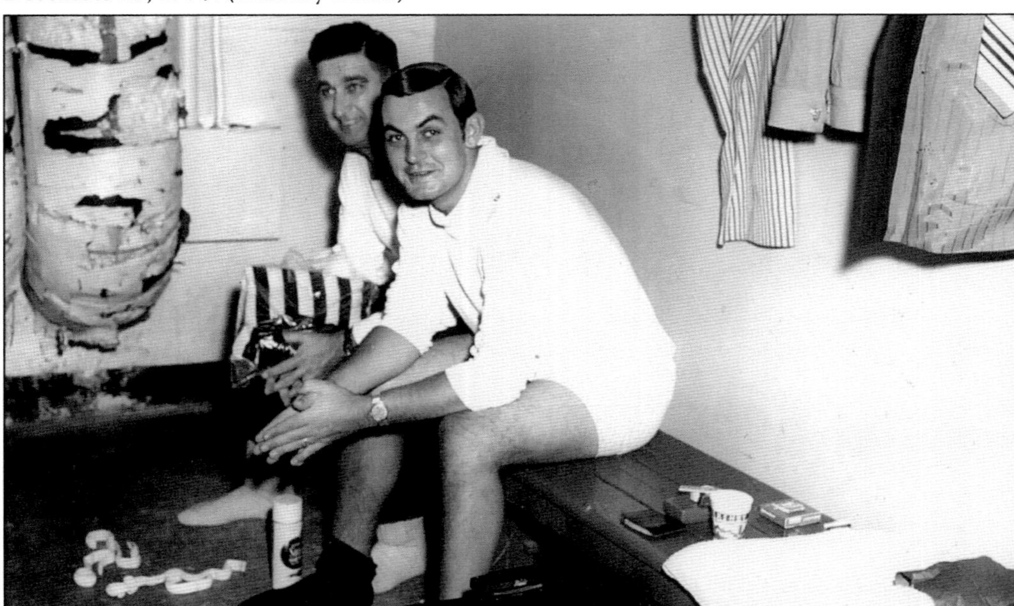

Stark Reality. Hersheypark Arena never offered plush accommodations, especially for visiting teams and officials. Longtime linesmen Art Fausnacht (left) and John McCauley get ready for a game. When Montreal's Forum, Toronto's Maple Leaf Gardens, Chicago Stadium, and the Boston Garden were replaced by new arenas in the 1990s, Hersheypark Arena became the oldest building continuously hosting hockey in North America. (Hershey Bears.)

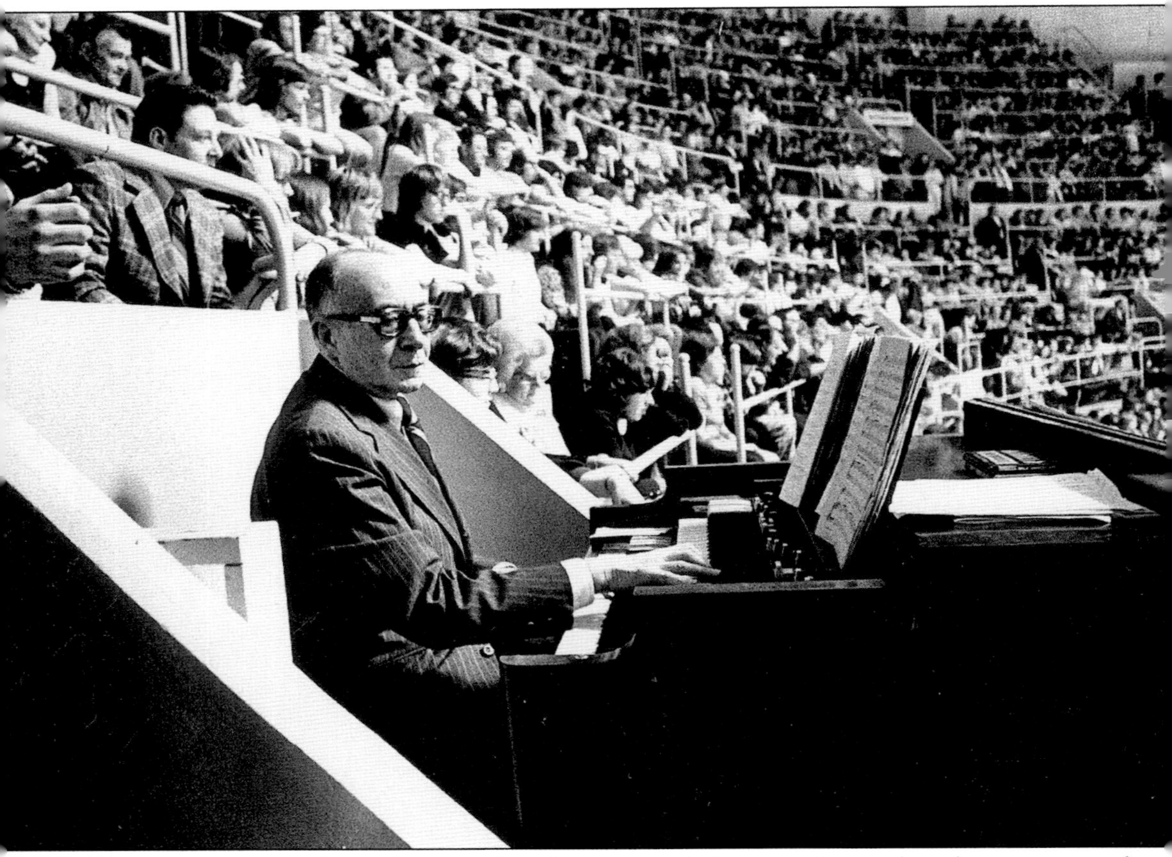

ORGANIST MITCH GRAND. He started in the orchestra led by Lou Cohan when the arena opened in 1936, but Grand ultimately became a legendary solo act when an organ replaced the orchestra after 11 years. John B. Sollenberger admonished him that "you must remember it's not Radio City Music Hall" when he got the job. He was reminded of his venue whenever kids in the upper deck bounced Hershey Kisses off his bald pate. Grand, an arena staple for more than 40 years, was known to play "Three Blind Mice" when the officials skated out. Some of his other standards were "Don't Fence Me In" for players headed to the penalty box, the "Batman Theme" after a goal, and "Mission Impossible" when the Bears were not playing well. When Mike Nykoluk scored, he would play "Hello, Dolly" in honor of the Big Bear's wife, Dolly. (Hershey Bears.)

High Gloss. This official program is from a March 9, 1946 game against the Buffalo Bisons. Future Bears trainer Scotty Alexander was on Buffalo's bench as trainer. Inside the program, it was reported that the pool for the 1946 Calder Cup playoffs, set to start on March 19, was $42,600 (to be shared by all players). Hershey was eliminated by Pittsburgh in the first round. Buffalo won the Calder Cup, beating Cleveland in the finals. (Hershey Bears.)

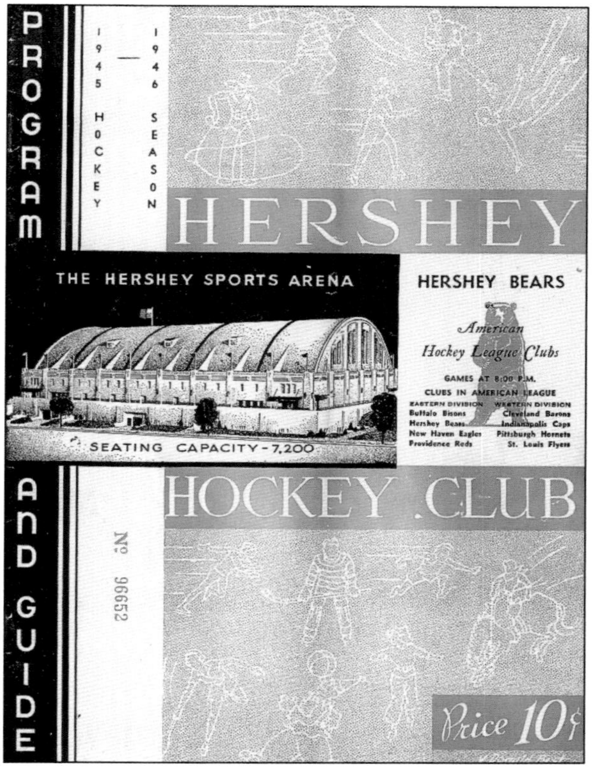

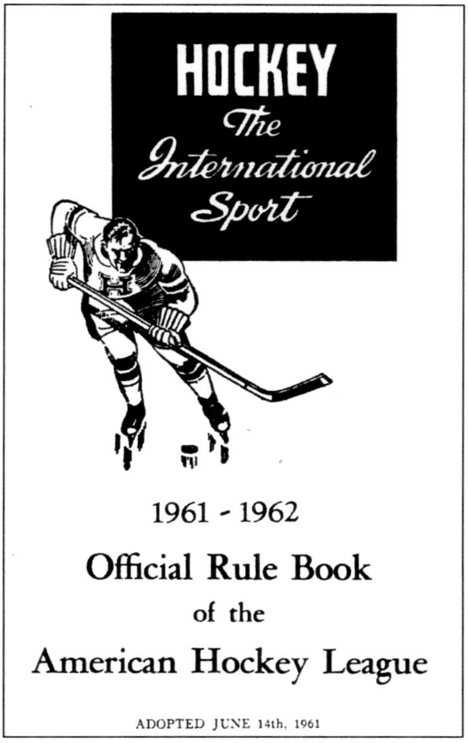

The Letter of the Law. To the left is a copy of the 1961–1962 AHL rule book. It was 64 pages long. The AHL rule book for the 2002–2003 season was 161 pages long. On October 14, 1981, at Hersheypark Arena, the Bears and Adirondack set the AHL penalty-minutes record (520) for two teams in one game. The Red Wings also set the record (264) for one team in a game. The 1986–1987 Bears hold the AHL record for most penalty minutes in a season (2,872). (Hershey Bears.)

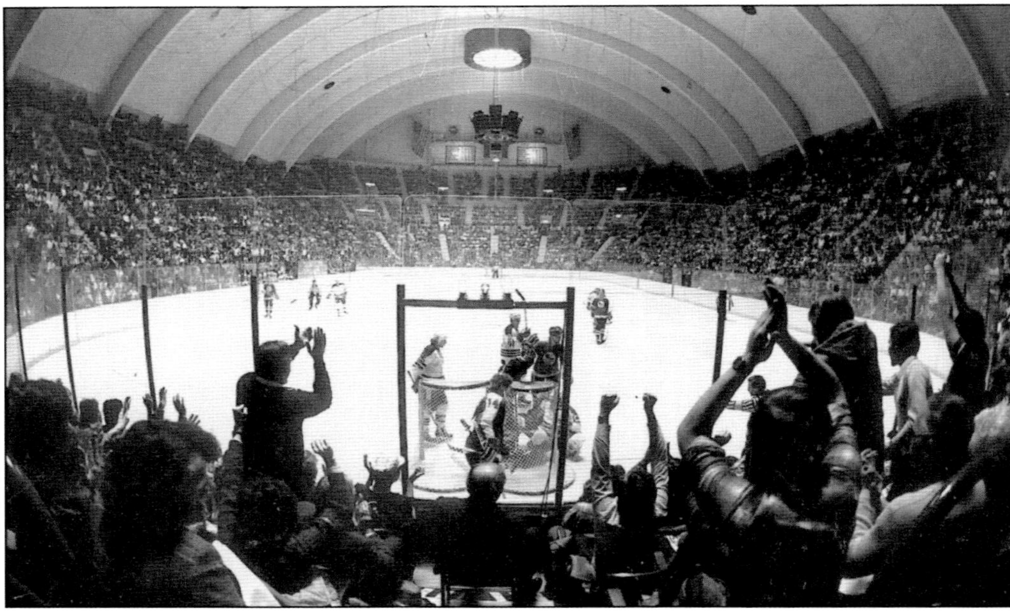

A FANATICAL FOLLOWING. Bears fans—loud, knowledgeable, and right on top of the action—provided a significant home-ice advantage at Hersheypark Arena. Renowned for the sightlines from its steeply inclined seats, the arena offered what many deem the best hockey viewing experience of any building. Alcohol was never served at the concession stands. Countless opposition players hated the idea of having to come into the "Old Barn," as they called it. (Hershey Bears.)

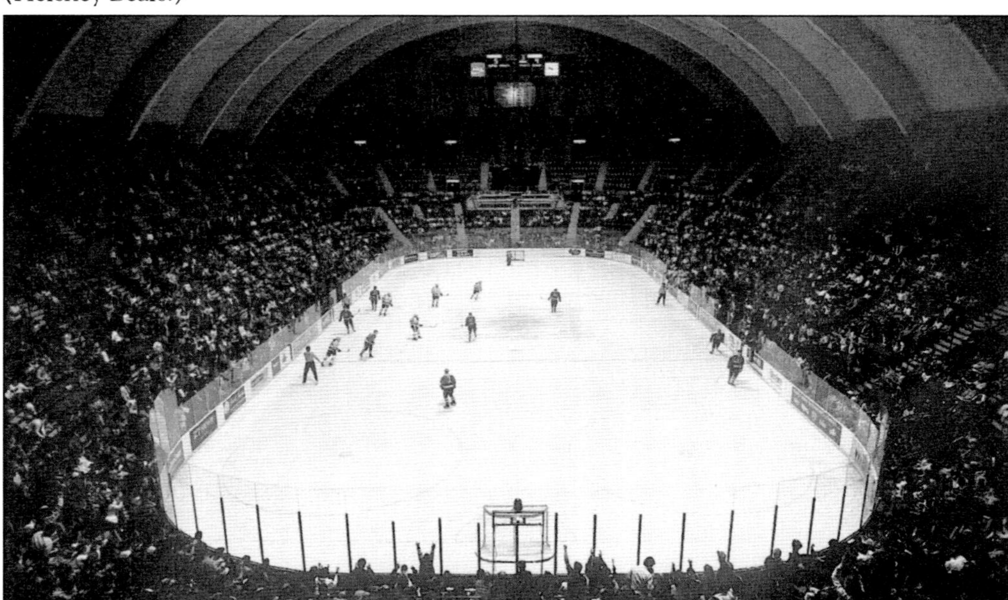

KEEPING SCORE. Hersheypark Arena's original scoreboard was replaced in 1963. The new scoreboard, with digital features replacing analog features, is visible in the background above. To limit the load on the arched roof, Hersheypark Arena never had an overhead scoreboard. (Hershey Bears.)

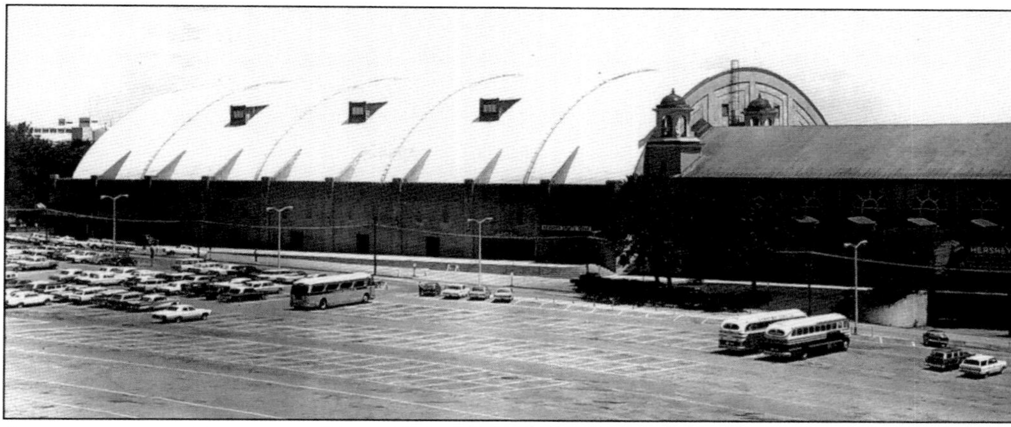

ARCHITECTURAL PARTNERS. The old Ice Palace (right) and Hersheypark Arena still stand side-by-side. The above shot was taken during the 1960s. (Hershey Bears.)

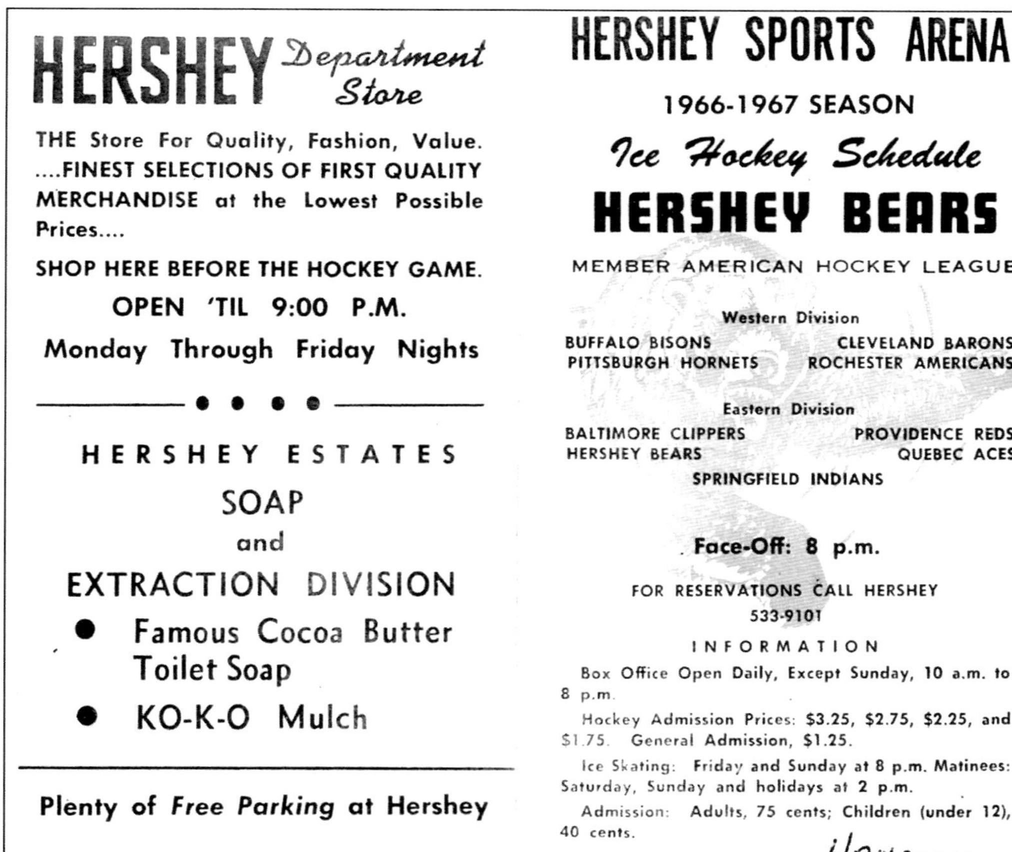

HERSHEY Department Store

THE Store For Quality, Fashion, Value. ....FINEST SELECTIONS OF FIRST QUALITY MERCHANDISE at the Lowest Possible Prices....

SHOP HERE BEFORE THE HOCKEY GAME.

OPEN 'TIL 9:00 P.M.

Monday Through Friday Nights

HERSHEY ESTATES

SOAP

and

EXTRACTION DIVISION

- Famous Cocoa Butter Toilet Soap
- KO-K-O Mulch

Plenty of *Free Parking* at Hershey

HERSHEY SPORTS ARENA

1966-1967 SEASON

Ice Hockey Schedule

HERSHEY BEARS

MEMBER AMERICAN HOCKEY LEAGUE

Western Division

BUFFALO BISONS — CLEVELAND BARONS
PITTSBURGH HORNETS — ROCHESTER AMERICANS

Eastern Division

BALTIMORE CLIPPERS — PROVIDENCE REDS
HERSHEY BEARS — QUEBEC ACES
SPRINGFIELD INDIANS

Face-Off: 8 p.m.

FOR RESERVATIONS CALL HERSHEY
533-9101

INFORMATION

Box Office Open Daily, Except Sunday, 10 a.m. to 8 p.m.

Hockey Admission Prices: $3.25, $2.75, $2.25, and $1.75. General Admission, $1.25.

Ice Skating: Friday and Sunday at 8 p.m. Matinees: Saturday, Sunday and holidays at 2 p.m.

Admission: Adults, 75 cents; Children (under 12), 40 cents.

HANCOCK

A BARGAIN RATE. This is a Bears pocket schedule from the 1966–1967 season. A ticket could be purchased for as little as $1.25 for general admission. The best seat in the house cost $3.25. Hershey went 38-24-10 for 86 points and won the Eastern Division championship that season but was beaten in the first round of the playoffs by Pittsburgh, the eventual Calder Cup champion. (Hershey Bears.)

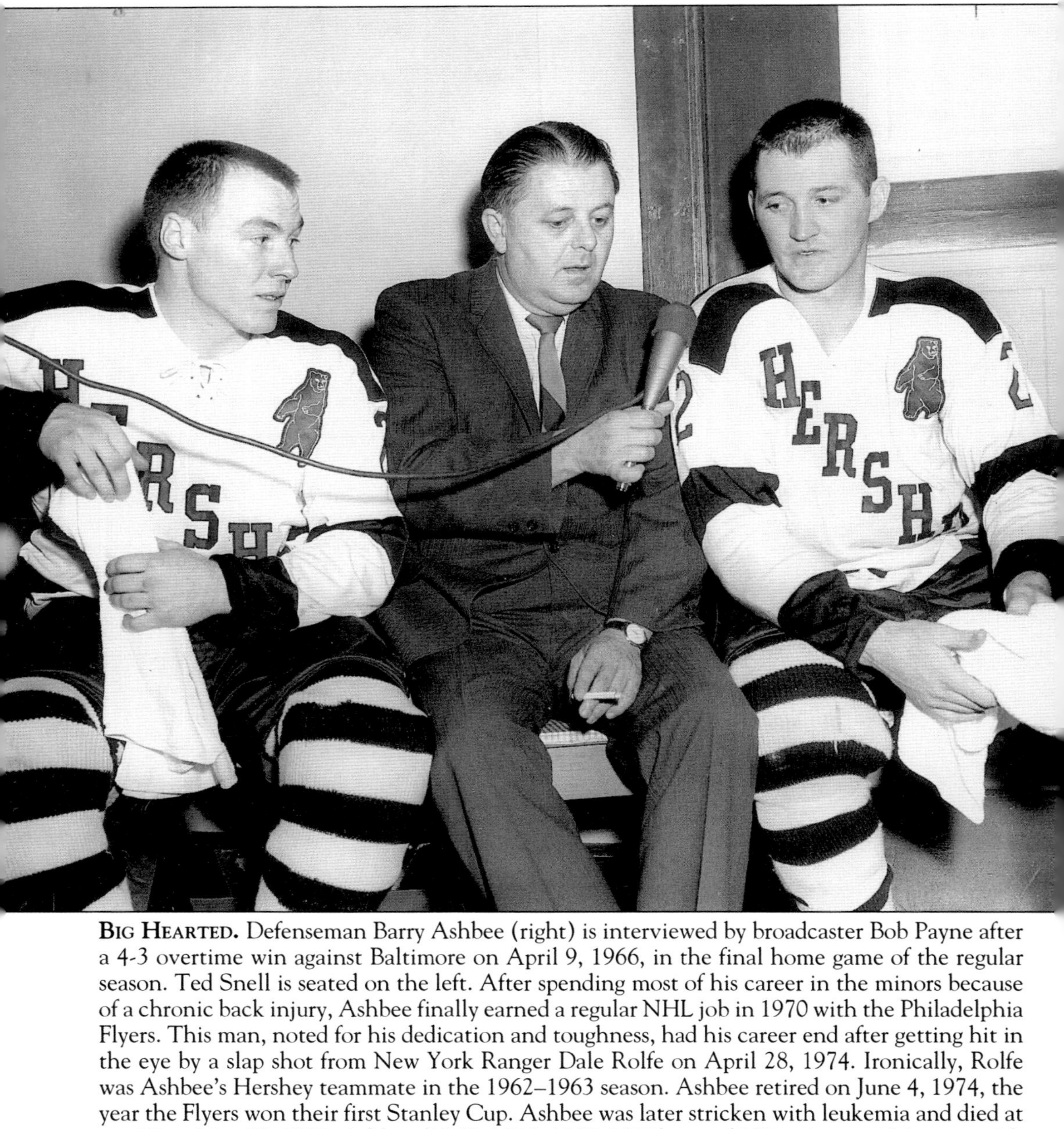

Big Hearted. Defenseman Barry Ashbee (right) is interviewed by broadcaster Bob Payne after a 4-3 overtime win against Baltimore on April 9, 1966, in the final home game of the regular season. Ted Snell is seated on the left. After spending most of his career in the minors because of a chronic back injury, Ashbee finally earned a regular NHL job in 1970 with the Philadelphia Flyers. This man, noted for his dedication and toughness, had his career end after getting hit in the eye by a slap shot from New York Ranger Dale Rolfe on April 28, 1974. Ironically, Rolfe was Ashbee's Hershey teammate in the 1962–1963 season. Ashbee retired on June 4, 1974, the year the Flyers won their first Stanley Cup. Ashbee was later stricken with leukemia and died at age 37 on May 12, 1977. Ashbee (1962–1966, 1967–1970) scored 137 points in 454 games with the Bears. Winger Snell (1965–1973, 1975–1976) scored 250 points in 470 Hershey games. (Hershey Bears.)

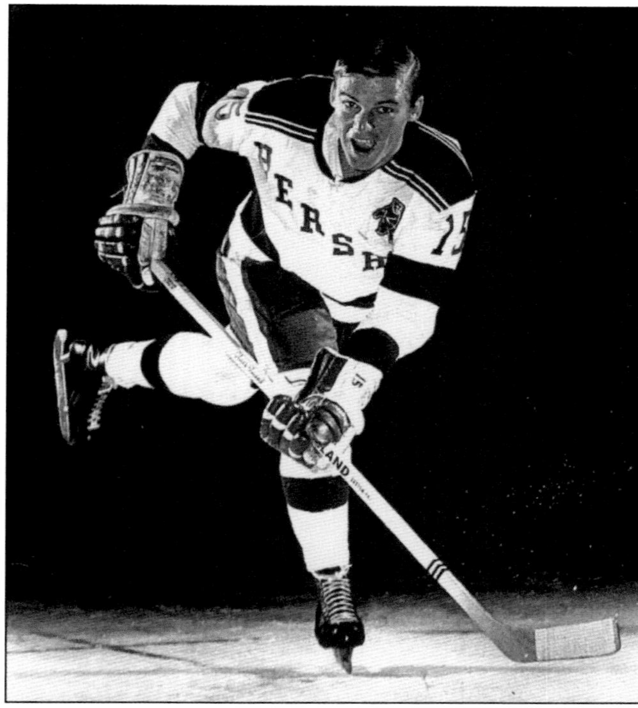

A Towering Tragedy. Garnet "Ace" Bailey, working as director of professional scouting for the Los Angeles Kings, was killed in the September 11, 2001, terrorist attacks. Headed to the Kings' camp, he was aboard United Flight 175 from Boston to Los Angeles that crashed into the World Trade Center's South Tower. Wayne Gretzky's future roommate played one season in Hershey, scoring 24 goals during the 1968–1969 Calder Cup campaign and was on Boston's 1972 Stanley Cup team. (Hershey Bears.)

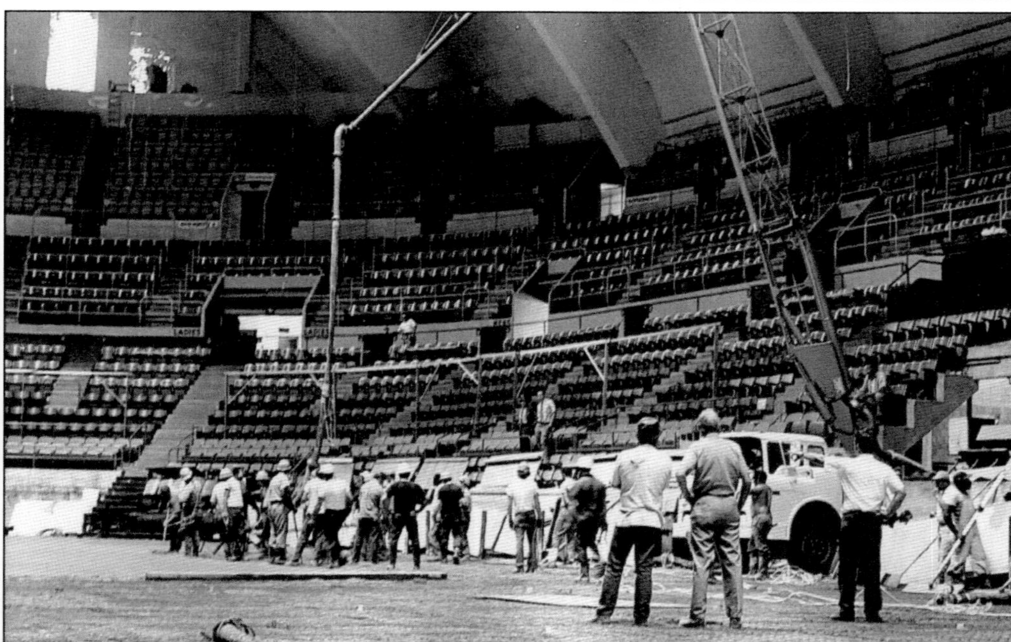

A Fresh Coat. Hersheypark Arena underwent a major renovation starting on June 13, 1971. Repainting the cork ceiling, which covers the inside surface of the concrete roof, took 2,000 gallons of white paint. In the top left corner of this photograph, taken in August 1971, is a seldom-seen view of arena windows stripped of paint. Sun rays had a warming effect on the ice, so the windows were painted over early in the arena's history. (Hershey Bears.)

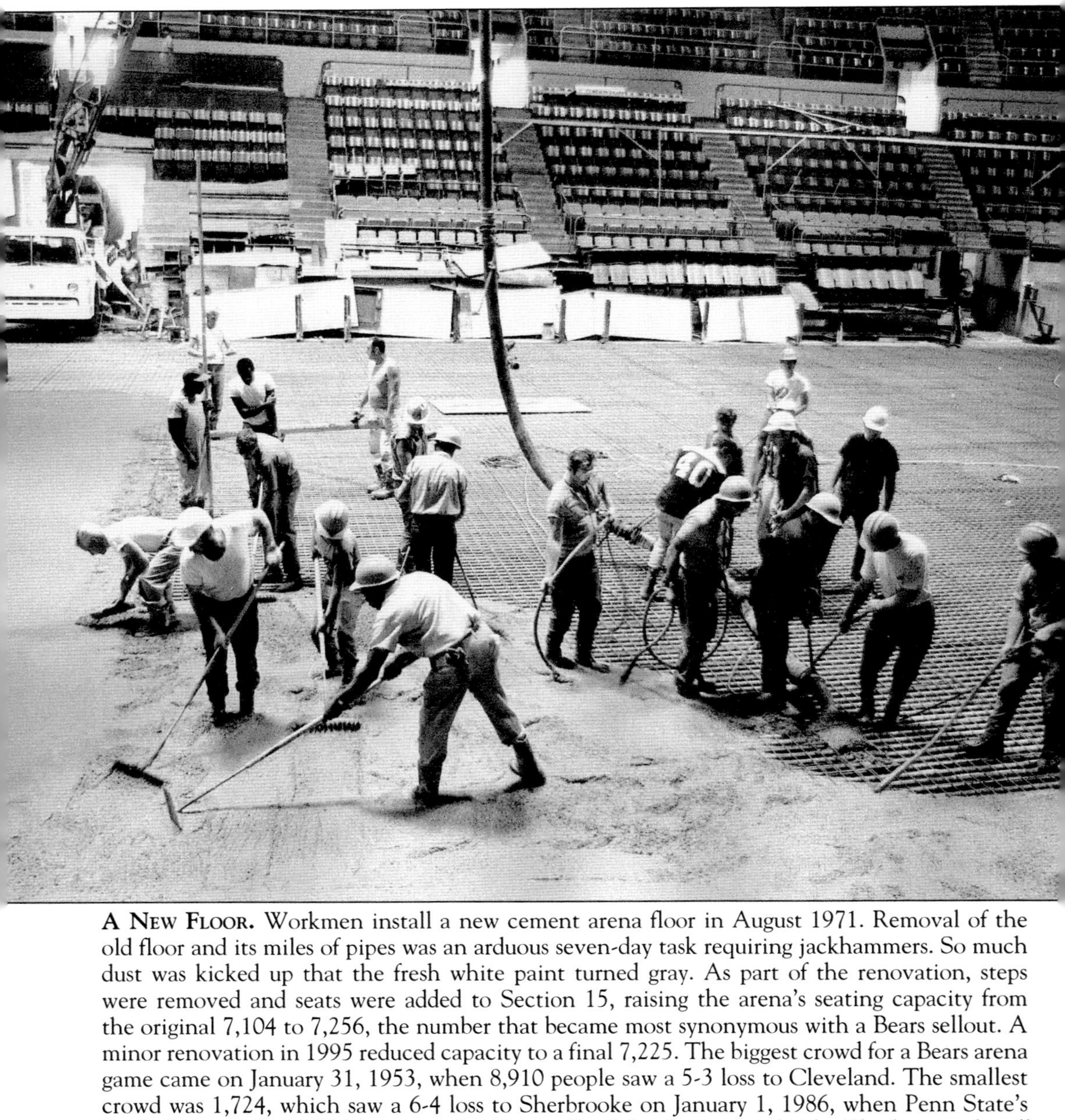

A New Floor. Workmen install a new cement arena floor in August 1971. Removal of the old floor and its miles of pipes was an arduous seven-day task requiring jackhammers. So much dust was kicked up that the fresh white paint turned gray. As part of the renovation, steps were removed and seats were added to Section 15, raising the arena's seating capacity from the original 7,104 to 7,256, the number that became most synonymous with a Bears sellout. A minor renovation in 1995 reduced capacity to a final 7,225. The biggest crowd for a Bears arena game came on January 31, 1953, when 8,910 people saw a 5-3 loss to Cleveland. The smallest crowd was 1,724, which saw a 6-4 loss to Sherbrooke on January 1, 1986, when Penn State's football team played Oklahoma in the Orange Bowl for the national title. The largest playoff crowd was on May 8, 1974, when 8,703 people watched the Bears clinch the Calder Cup with a 4-3 victory over Providence. (Hershey Bears.)

An NHL Exhibition Game. On October 5, 1974, the Bears played an exhibition game against the Minnesota North Stars. NHL preseason games were common events. The Boston Bruins held their training camp in Hershey in 1937. Hershey and its arena were so respected that in the 1970s, Hershey Entertainment chief Ken Hatt was approached about putting an NHL expansion franchise in Hershey. The NHL ultimately decided that the building and market were too small. (Hershey Bears.)

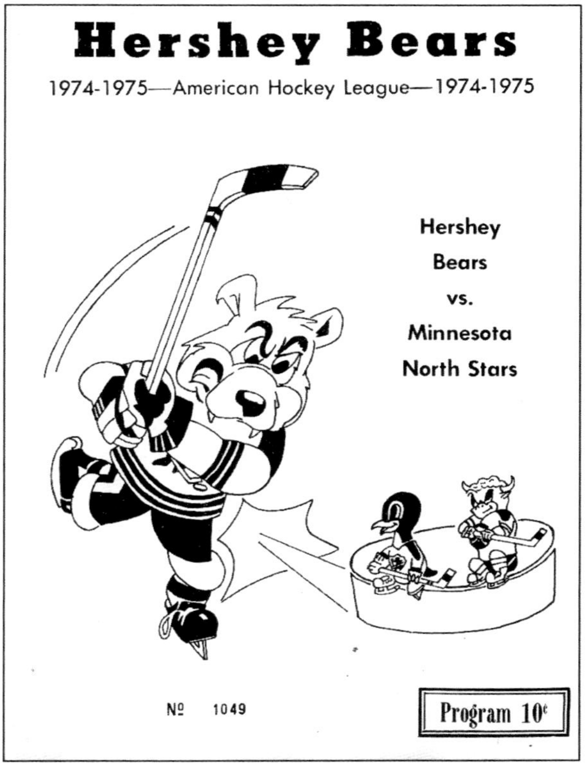

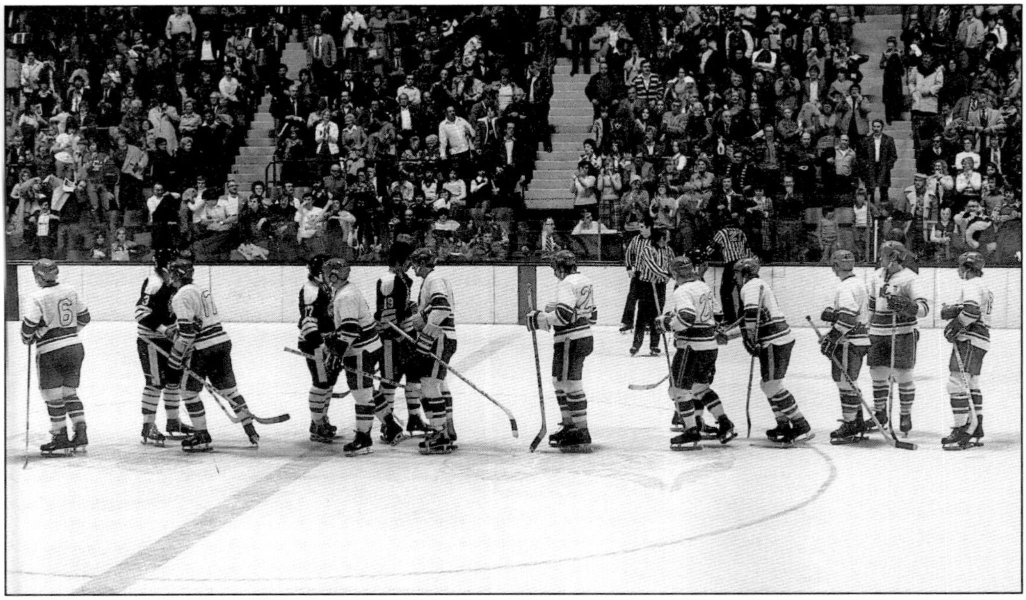

The Cold War. During the Cold War era, teams from the Soviet Union visited Hershey on four occasions. The Bears and Soviet Wings shake hands following Hershey's 10-7 win on January 5, 1975. Hershey and the Moscow Spartak tied 2-2 on January 9, 1976, as the Bears rallied from a 2-0 deficit in the final six minutes. The Moscow Dynamo beat Hershey 6-4 on December 30, 1977, and the Moscow Spartak beat Hershey 8-3 on December 9, 1986. (Hershey Bears.)

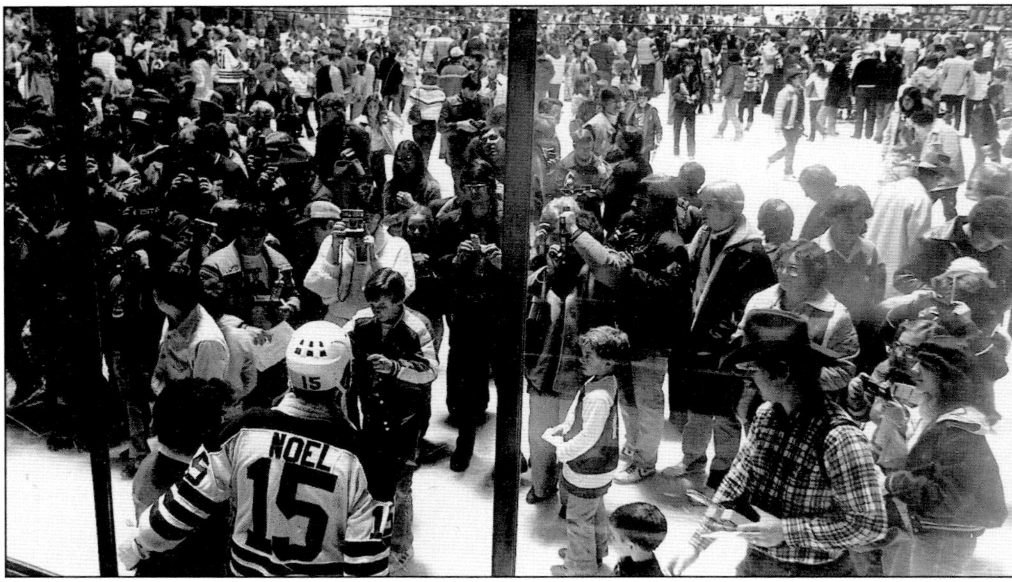

LIGHTS, CAMERA, ACTION. Picture night, when fans get to meet and take photos of their favorite players following a Bears game, is an annual tradition. Center Claude Noel (above), a Bear from 1976 to 1981, who twice led Hershey in scoring and was a member of the 1980 Calder Cup team, greets the public. Noel has gone on to a minor-league coaching career and has been a head coach in the East Coast Hockey League (ECHL), IHL, and AHL. (Hershey Bears.)

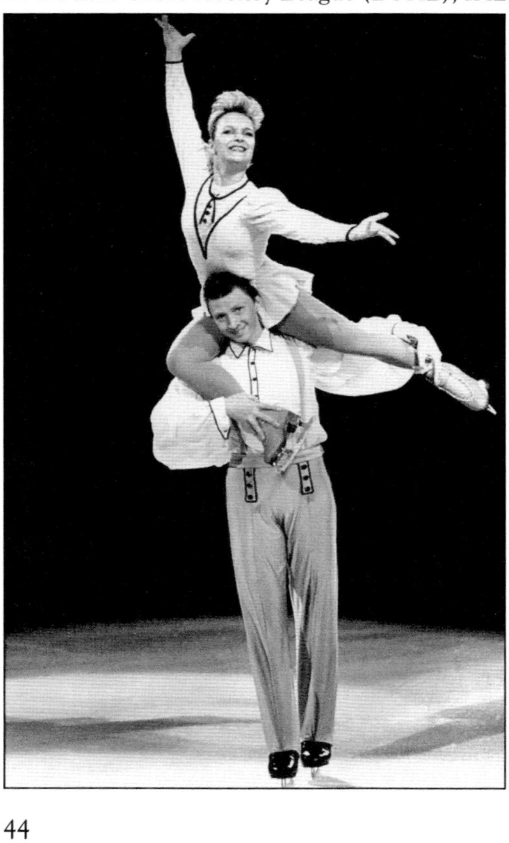

RINK BALLET. Russian pair Elena Valova and Oleg Vassiliev appear during a November 1992 Ice Capades show at the arena. The Ice Capades were invented in Hershey. On Valentine's Day in 1940, Hershey executive John B. Sollenberger, a brilliant sports entrepreneur, convened a meeting of arena owners at the Hotel Hershey who were looking for ideas to fill dates. The Ice Capades evolved from that meeting. (Hershey Bears.)

TURNPIKE AFFILIATION. Hershey's affiliation with the Philadelphia Flyers spanned 12 seasons (the longest in Bears history) and resulted in the 1988 Calder Cup. Hershey had formal affiliations with eight NHL clubs since 1967: Boston (1967–1971, 1983–1985), Pittsburgh (1971–1977), Buffalo (1974–1979), Washington (1977–1984), Philadelphia (1984–1996), Colorado (1996–present), Florida (2001–2002 partial), and Tampa Bay (2003–2004 partial). (Hershey Bears.)

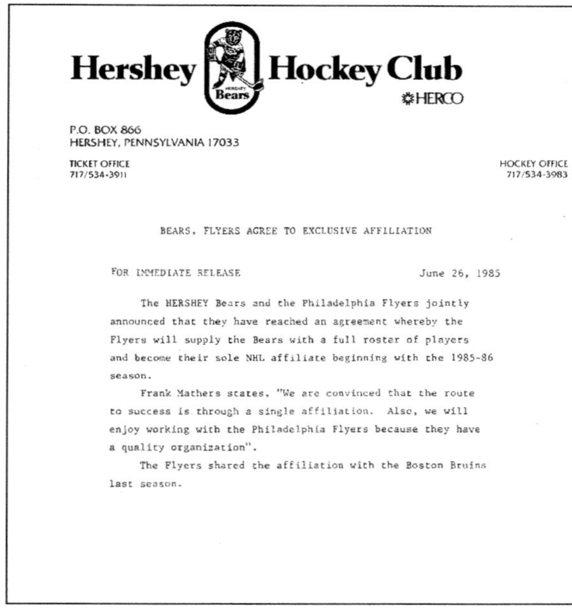

Hershey Hockey Club

HERCO

P.O. BOX 866
HERSHEY, PENNSYLVANIA 17033

TICKET OFFICE
717/534-3911

HOCKEY OFFICE
717/534-3983

BEARS, FLYERS AGREE TO EXCLUSIVE AFFILIATION

FOR IMMEDIATE RELEASE June 26, 1985

The HERSHEY Bears and the Philadelphia Flyers jointly announced that they have reached an agreement whereby the Flyers will supply the Bears with a full roster of players and become their sole NHL affiliate beginning with the 1985-86 season.

Frank Mathers states, "We are convinced that the route to success is through a single affiliation. Also, we will enjoy working with the Philadelphia Flyers because they have a quality organization".

The Flyers shared the affiliation with the Boston Bruins last season.

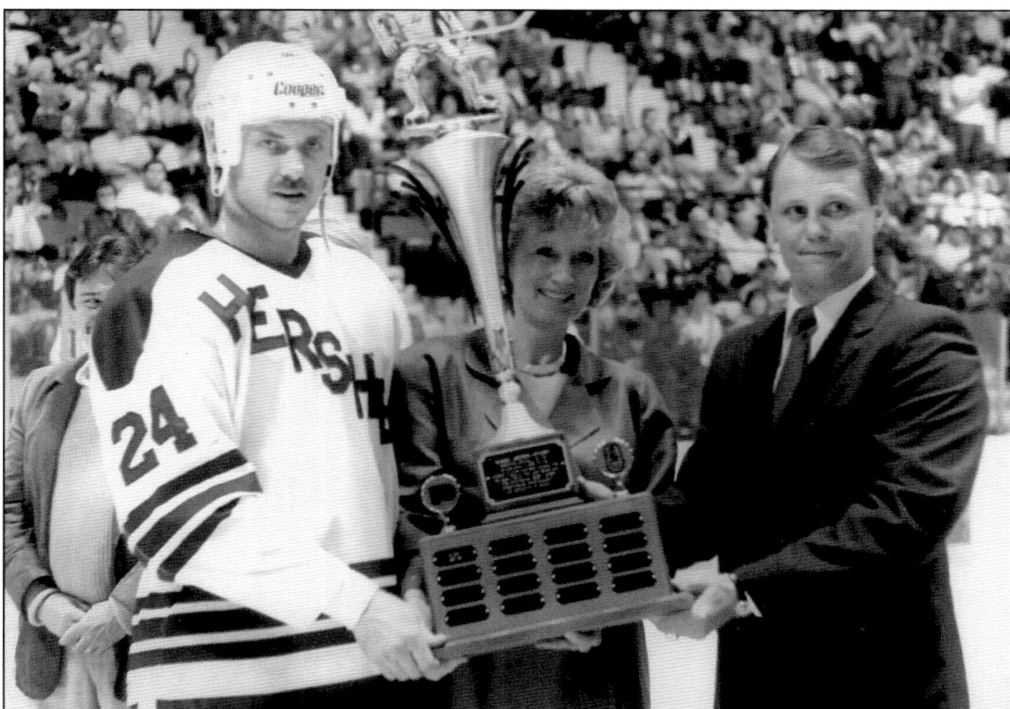

ALIVE IN MEMORY. Al Hill (left) is presented with the inaugural Barry Ashbee Award in 1988 by Donna Ashbee (Barry's widow) and Bill Barber. The award, given for dedication, was presented annually during the Flyers affiliation and has carried on with the Philadelphia Phantoms, who came into existence in 1996. Hill (1984–1989), now a Flyers scout, went on to serve as a Bears assistant coach and head coach of the Binghamton Rangers (1993–1995). (Hershey Bears.)

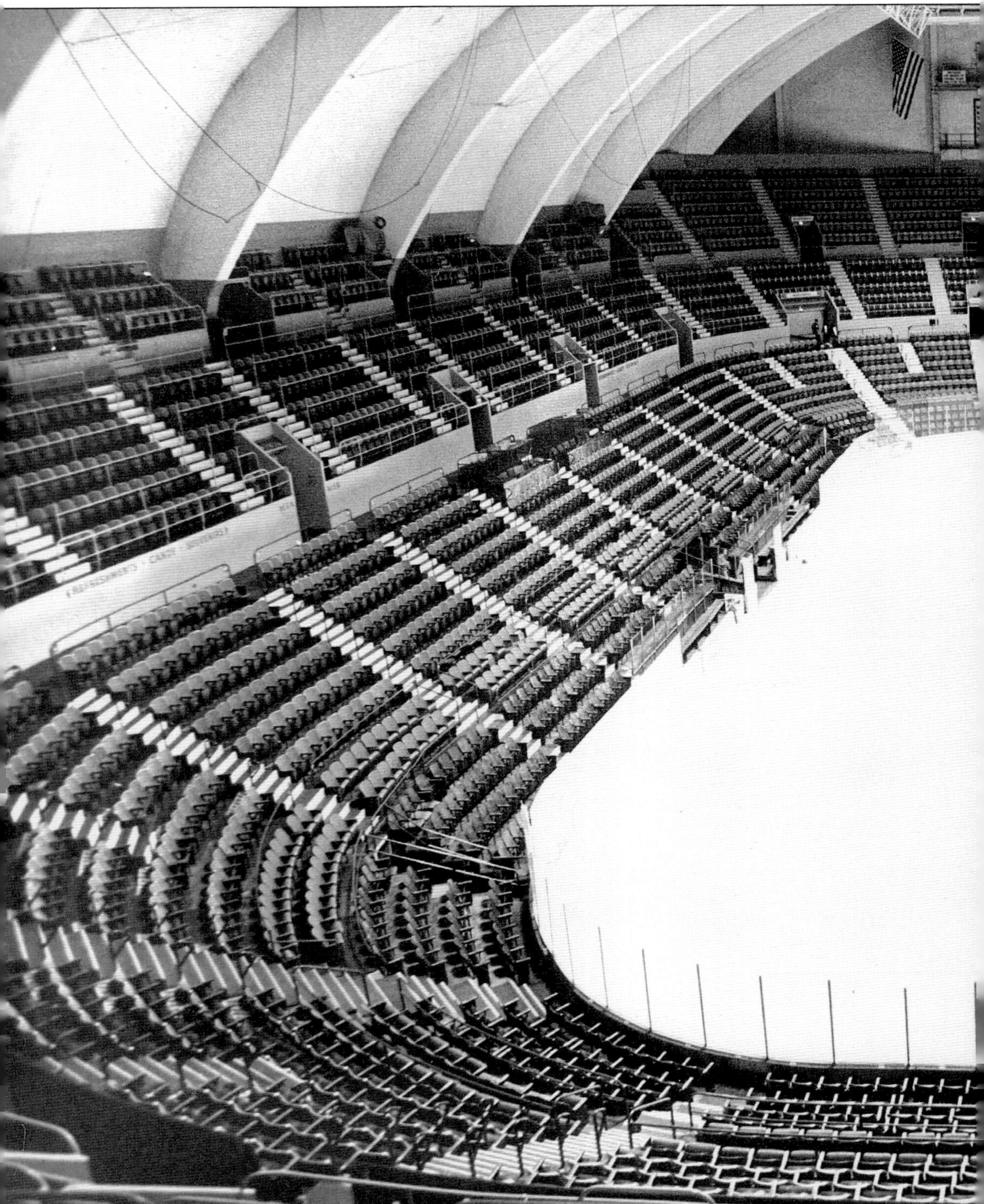

CLASSIC INTIMACY. There was not a bad seat in the house at Hersheypark Arena. On the far wall under the scoreboard, the AHL standings from the 1986–1987 season are visible. Keeping

league standings by hand was an arena tradition. (Hershey Bears.)

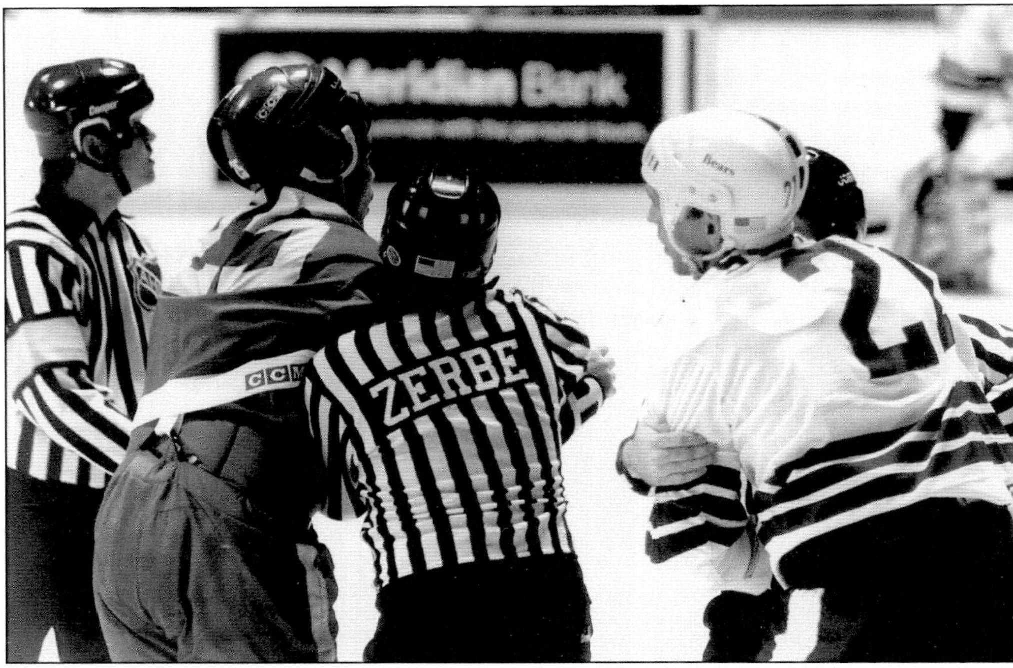

BATTLE STRIPES. Linesman Rich Zerbe was a Hersheypark Arena fixture until his retirement in the late 1990s. Here, he helps break up a fight between Hershey's Mike Stothers (right) and an unidentified Adirondack Red Wing. (Hershey Bears.)

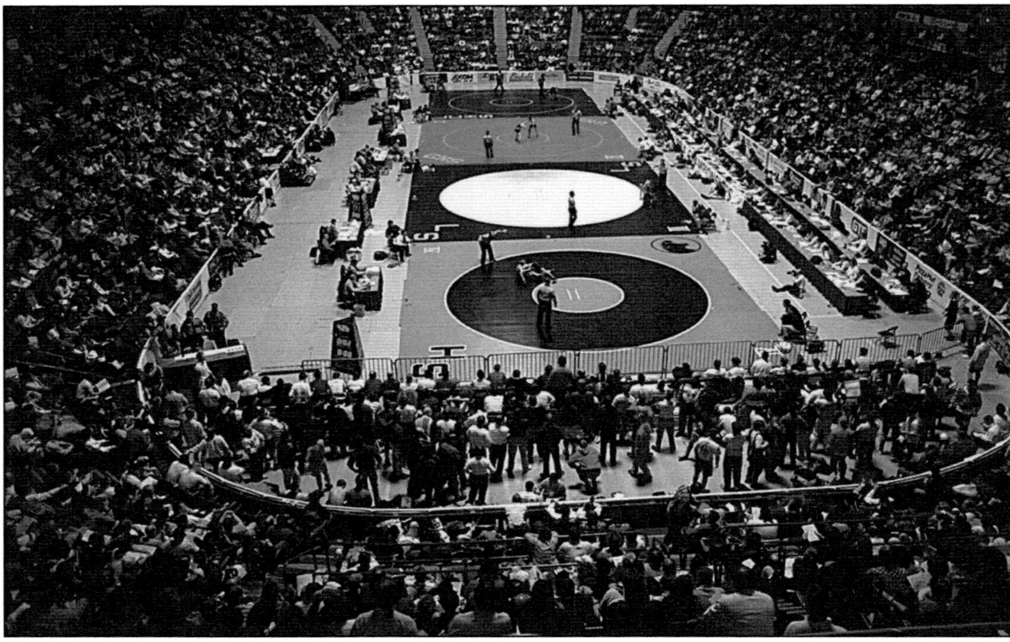

MAT MANIA. The Pennsylvania Interscholastic Athletic Association's state championship wrestling tournament grew into one of the nation's top high-school sports events. Attracting tens of thousands of fans annually, it was the first major stage for numerous wrestlers who went on to win NCAA, world, and Olympic championships. (Peter Taylor/*Patriot-News*.)

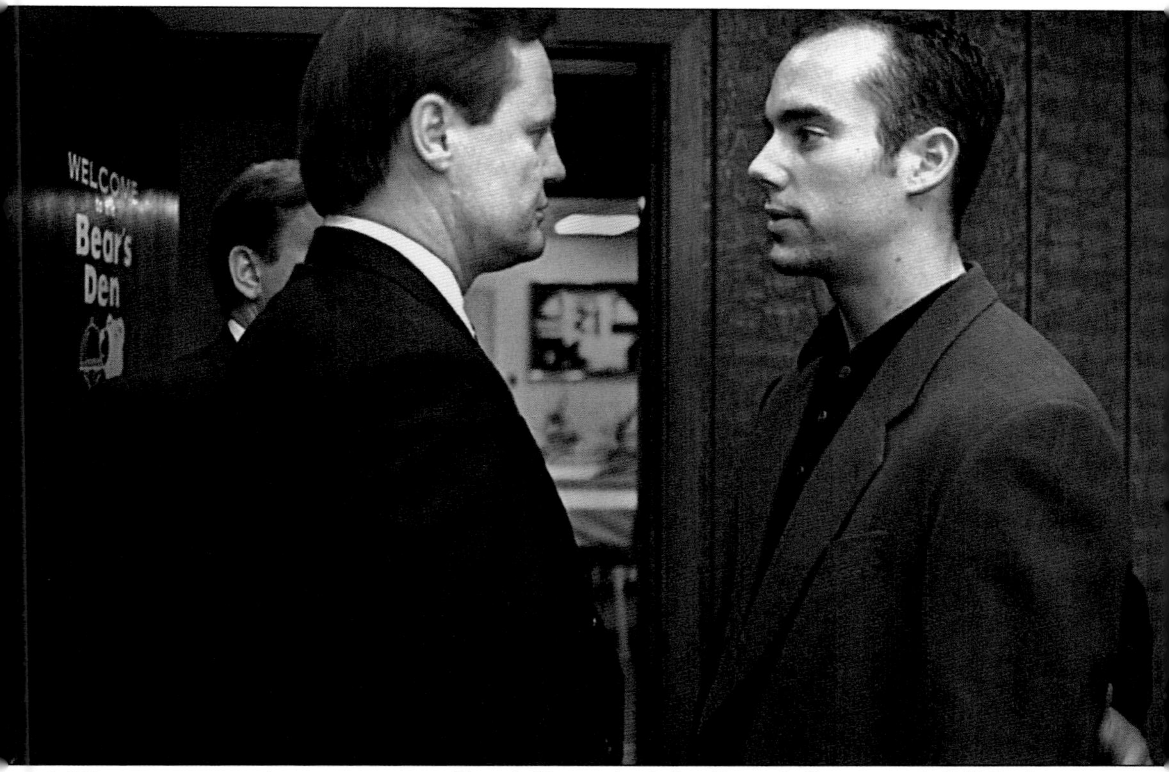

A Heartbreaking Announcement. Yanick Dupre (right) talks with Bears coach Bill Barber after announcing on April 12, 1996, that he had been diagnosed with leukemia. "I wouldn't be human if I said I wasn't scared," Dupre said. Barber had been a teammate of Barry Ashbee, who died from leukemia in 1977. Dupre's diagnosis was the lowest moment of a tumultuous 1995–1996 season that saw head coach Jay Leach fired and replaced by Barber and the end of the Hershey-Philadelphia affiliation. Dupre, Hershey's lone representative at the 1995 AHL All-Star Game in Providence, Rhode Island, died at age 24 in August 1997 in a Montreal hospital after a 16-month battle. The AHL's man of the year award, given for outstanding contributions to the local community and charitable organizations, is named the Yanick Dupre Award. Dupre scored 161 points in 207 Hershey games and also played 35 games for the Flyers. (Kristen Cortazzo/*Patriot-News*.)

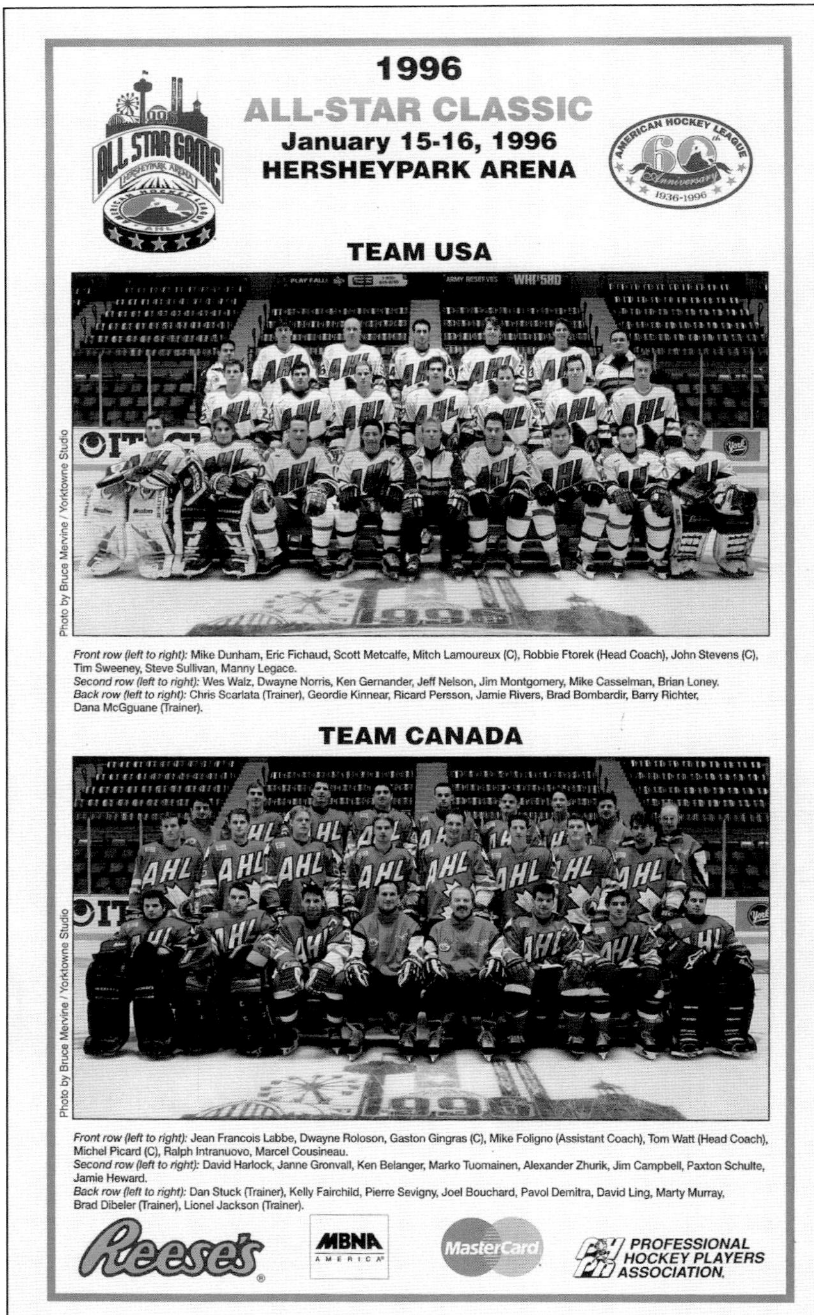

Stars on Ice. The AHL All-Star Game was played in Hershey on January 16, 1996. The United States beat Canada 6-5. Jim Montgomery, of the U.S. team, was Hershey's lone representative. There is plenty of future Bears' history in the Team Canada photograph. Cornwall's J.F. Labbe helped Hershey to the Calder Cup in the 1996–1997 season. St. John's assistant Mike Foligno was Hershey's head coach from 1998 to 2003. St. John's forward Kelly Fairchild was Hershey's captain in the 2001–2002 season. (Hershey Bears.)

A Historic Spot. Hershey Entertainment chief Scott Newkam (left) welcomes Hersheypark Arena's designation in 2002 as a historic Pennsylvania site for Wilt Chamberlain's 100-point game. On March 2, 1962, Chamberlain, playing for the Philadelphia Warriors, set the NBA single-game scoring record against the New York Knicks. Chamberlain, who lived in New York at the time, rode home with Knicks players after the game. (Bill Duh and Bruce Tyson/Just Sports.)

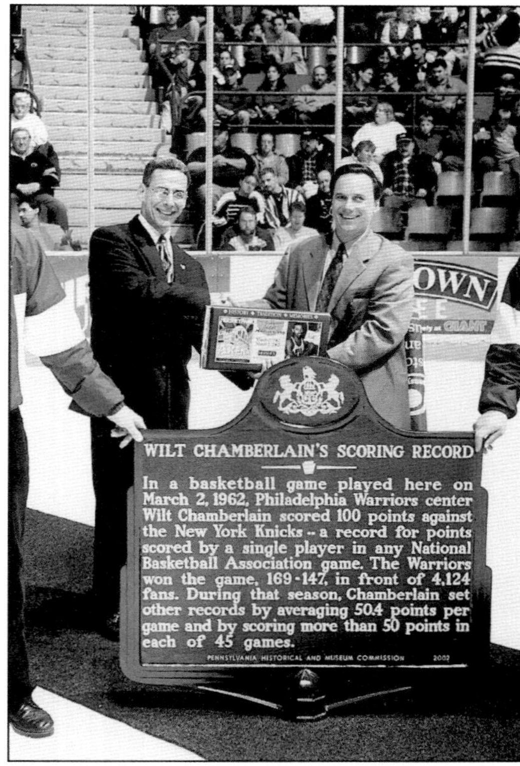

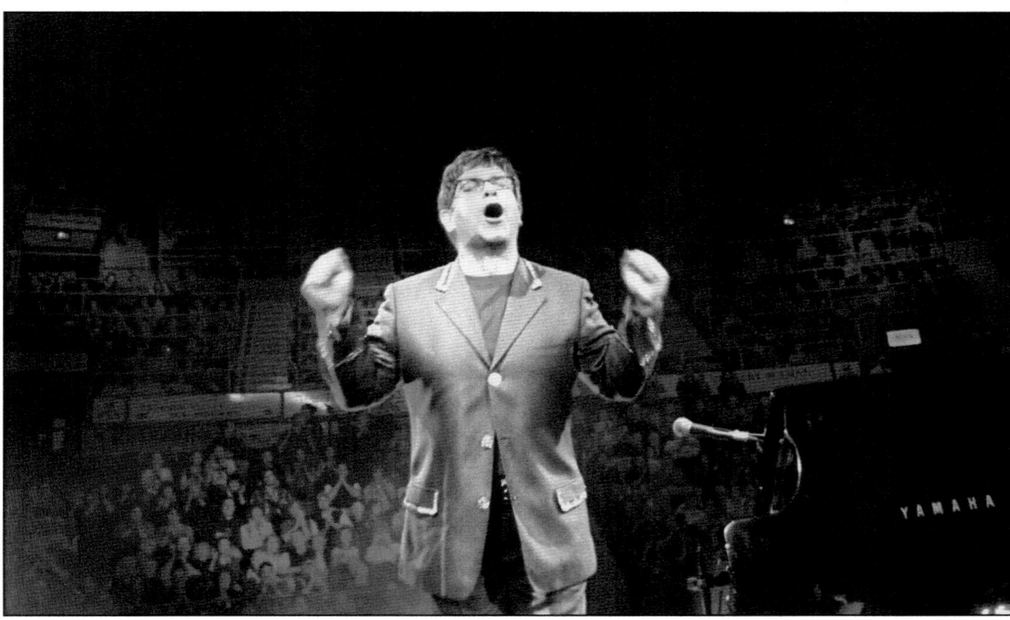

Crocodile Rock. Elton John, performing at Hersheypark Arena in 2000, is among hundreds of entertainers who played at the building. The long list also includes Frank Sinatra, Bill Cosby, Aerosmith, Reba McIntire, the Philadelphia Orchestra, the Harlem Globetrotters, and professional wrestlers. (Amiran White/*Patriot-News*.)

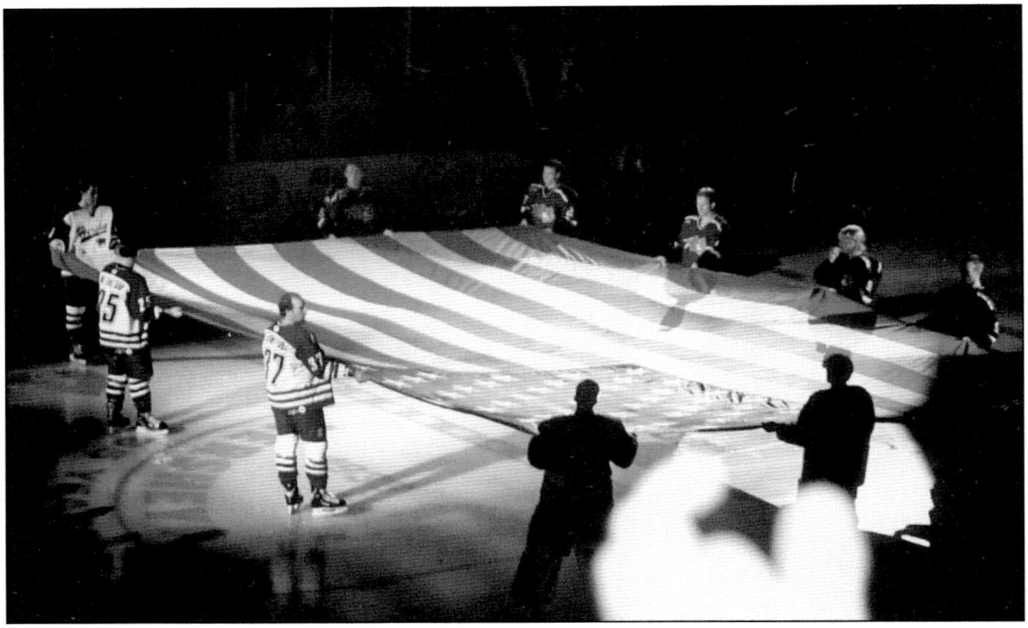

SHOWING COLORS. Members of the Bears and Worcester IceCats unfurl a giant U.S. flag as the final season at Hersheypark Arena begins on October 6, 2001. The September 11, 2001, terrorist attacks took place less than a month earlier. Worcester won the game 5-2 before a crowd of 6,331. (Hershey Bears.)

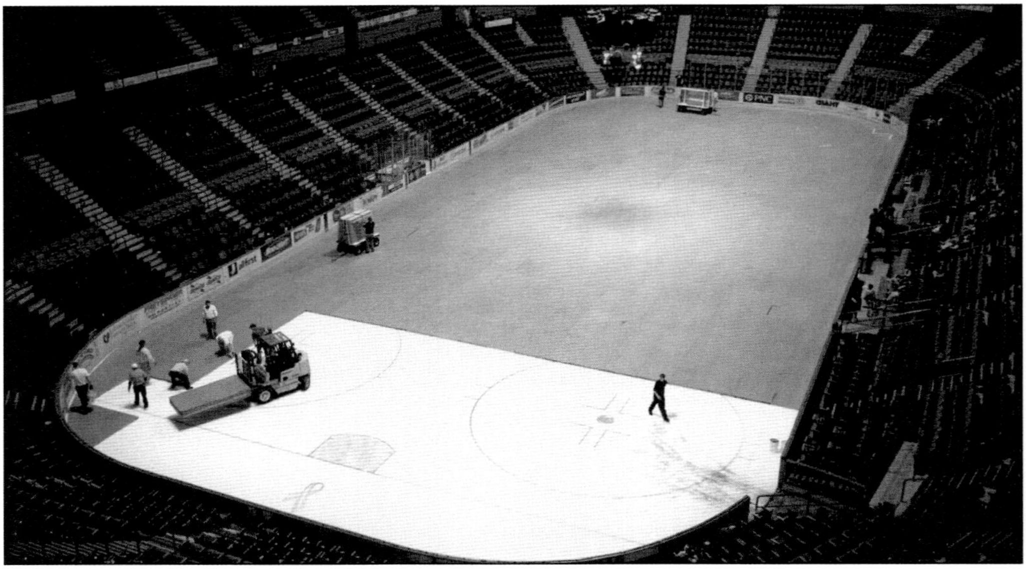

LION IN WINTER. This shot was taken on February 23, 2002, during Hersheypark Arena's final season as home of the Hershey Bears. The arena also served as an evacuation center for 150 people after the Three Mile Island nuclear emergency on March 28, 1979. With Three Mile Island officials downplaying the severity of the episode, the Bears played a regular home game against New Brunswick before a crowd of 3,252 the day the incident started. An April 3, 1979 game against the Philadelphia Firebirds was moved to the Capital Centre in Landover, Maryland. (John C. Whitehead/*Patriot-News*.)

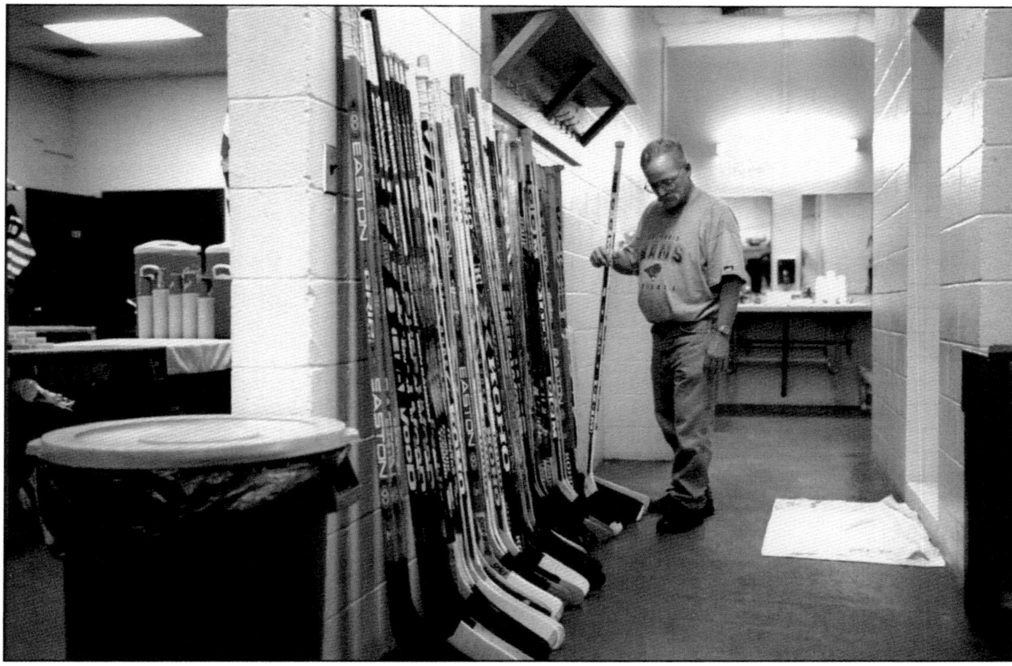

DRESSING ROOM GHOSTS. This is the visitors' locker room at Hersheypark Arena on February 9, 2002. The arena still hosts college hockey, youth hockey, and occasional Bears practices. (John C. Whitehead/*Patriot-News*.)

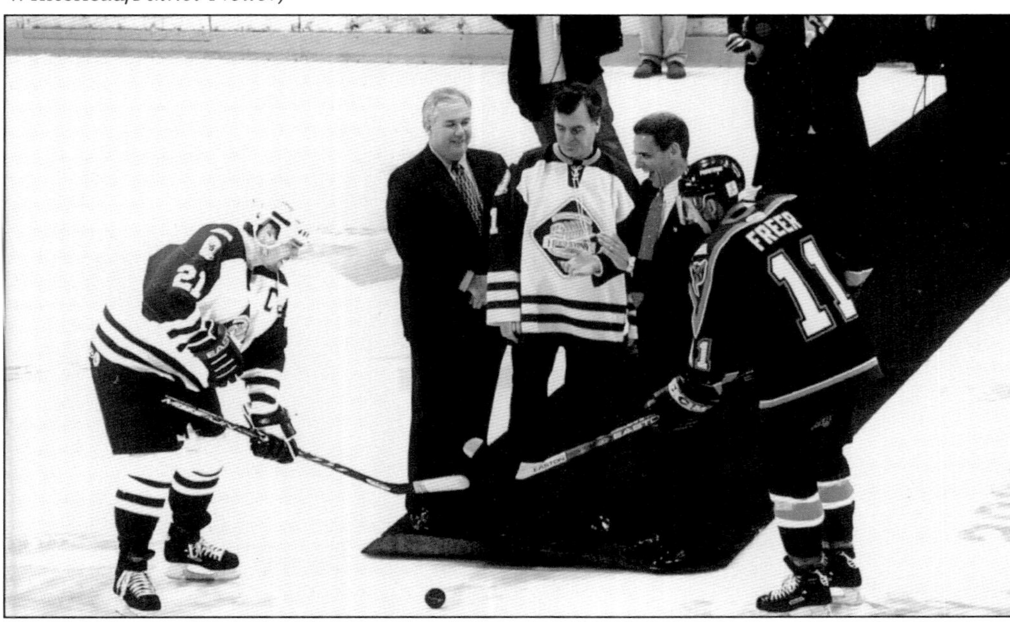

APRIL 7, 2002. Gov. Mark Schweiker (in the center wearing a commemorative Hersheypark Arena jersey) drops the puck for the ceremonial face-off prior to the final regular-season game in Hersheypark Arena history. Bears captain Kelly Fairchild (left) and Philadelphia Phantom Mark Freer, a once and future Bear, take the face-off. NHL broadcaster Mike Emrick served as master of ceremonies during pregame festivities. (Bill Duh and Bruce Tyson/Just Sports.)

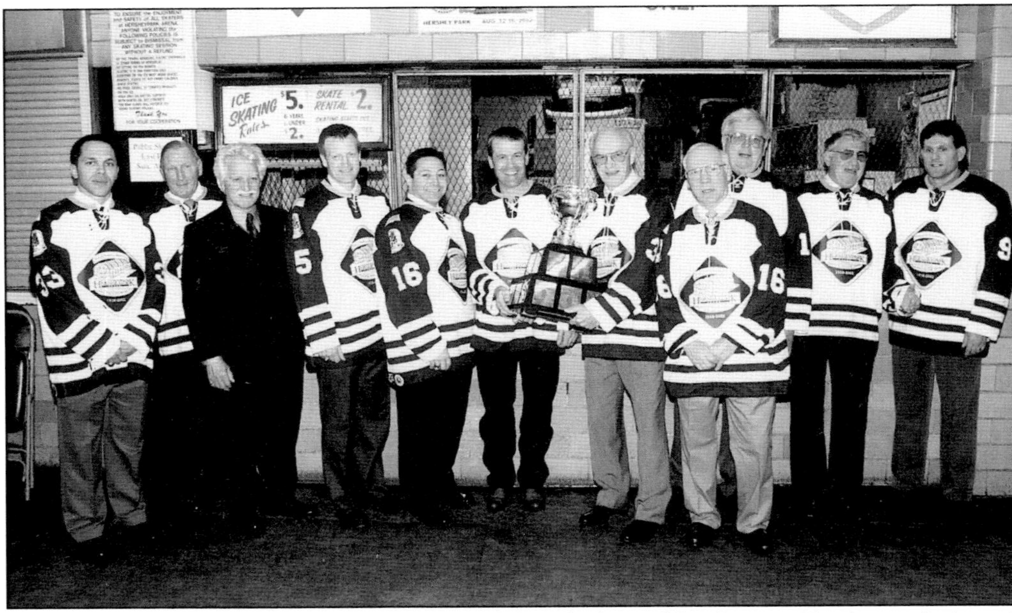

Home Again. Bears greats gather with an old friend, the Calder Cup, at Hersheypark Arena's last regular-season finale. From left to right, they are Mike McHugh, Paul Ronty, Ralph Keller, Dave Fenyves, Mitch Lamoureux, Bob Bilodeau, Frank Mathers, Willie Marshall, Obie O'Brien, Mike Nykoluk, and Tim Tookey. O'Brien scored 403 points in 481 Hershey games and was the team captain for the 1957–1958 season. (Bill Duh and Bruce Tyson/Just Sports.)

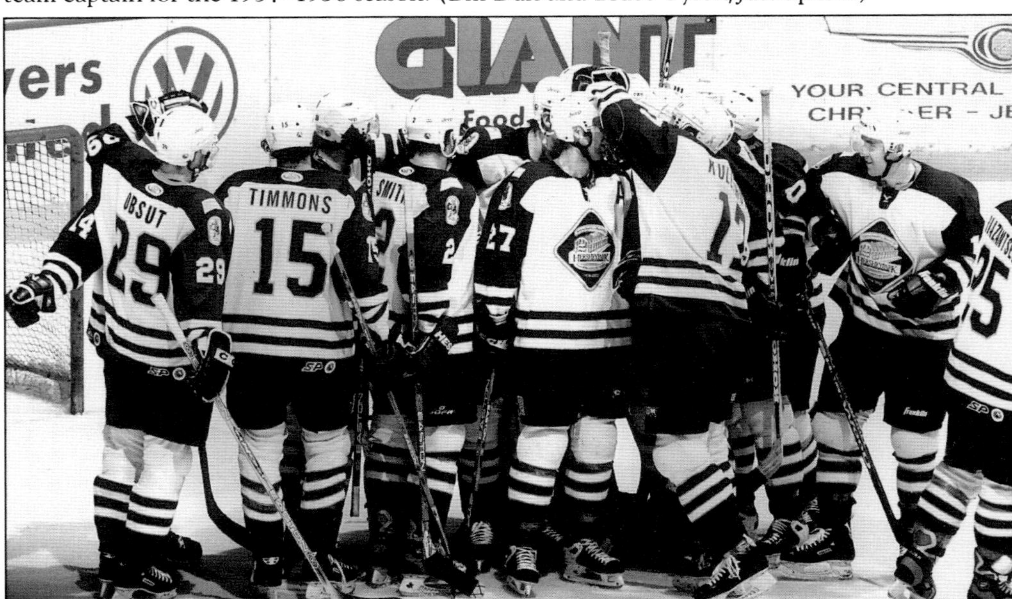

A Victory Exit. The Bears congratulate each other after beating Philadelphia 3-1 in Hersheypark Arena's last regular-season finale. Official attendance was 8,147, but, in reality, more than 8,700 packed the building. Goalie Phil Sauve earned the win. Mikhail Kuleshov, born in Perm, Russia, scored the final Bears game-winning regular-season goal in an arena built while Josef Stalin ruled the Soviet Union. (Bill Duh and Bruce Tyson/Just Sports.)

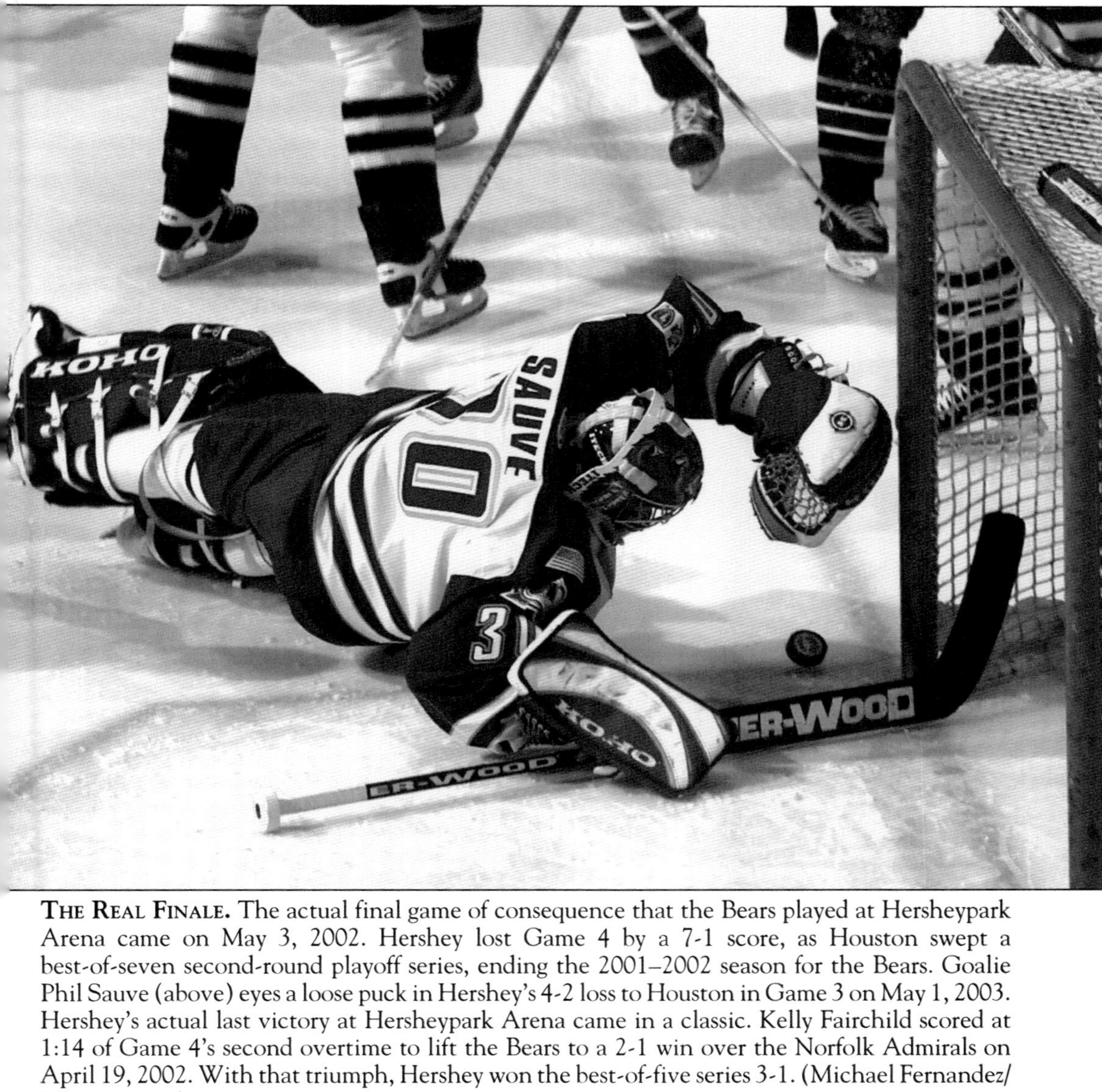

The Real Finale. The actual final game of consequence that the Bears played at Hersheypark Arena came on May 3, 2002. Hershey lost Game 4 by a 7-1 score, as Houston swept a best-of-seven second-round playoff series, ending the 2001–2002 season for the Bears. Goalie Phil Sauve (above) eyes a loose puck in Hershey's 4-2 loss to Houston in Game 3 on May 1, 2003. Hershey's actual last victory at Hersheypark Arena came in a classic. Kelly Fairchild scored at 1:14 of Game 4's second overtime to lift the Bears to a 2-1 win over the Norfolk Admirals on April 19, 2002. With that triumph, Hershey won the best-of-five series 3-1. (Michael Fernandez/ *Patriot-News*.)

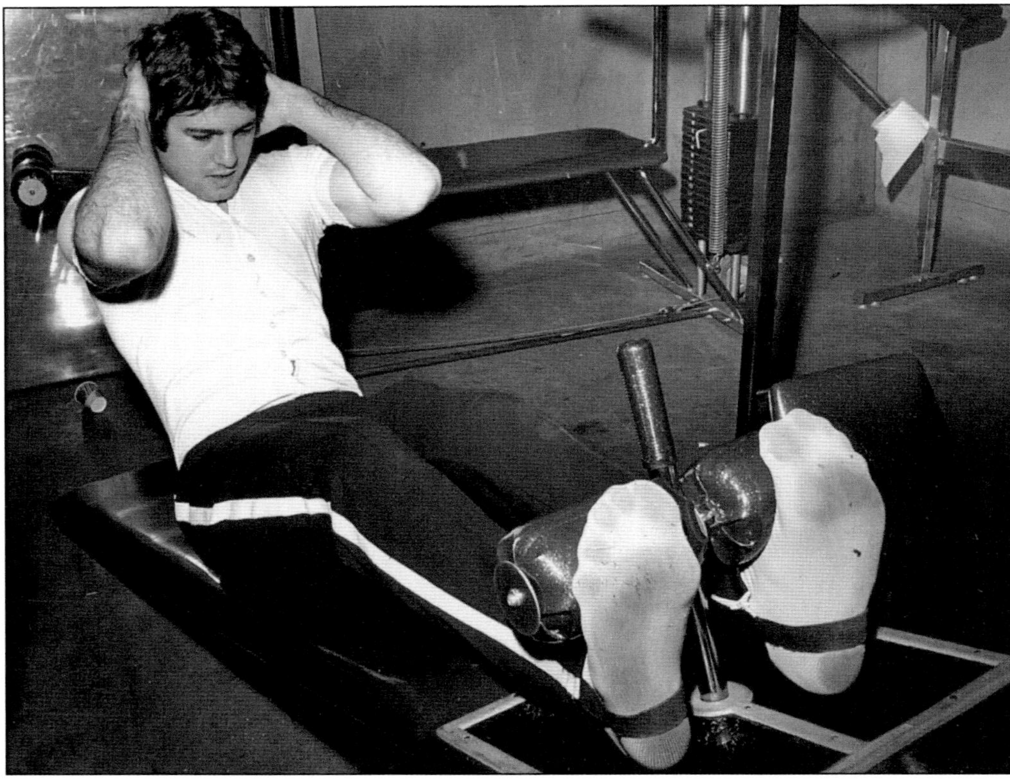

Crunch Time. Winger Morris Titanic (1974–1976, 1977–1978) works out in the Hersheypark Arena weight room. (Hershey Bears.)

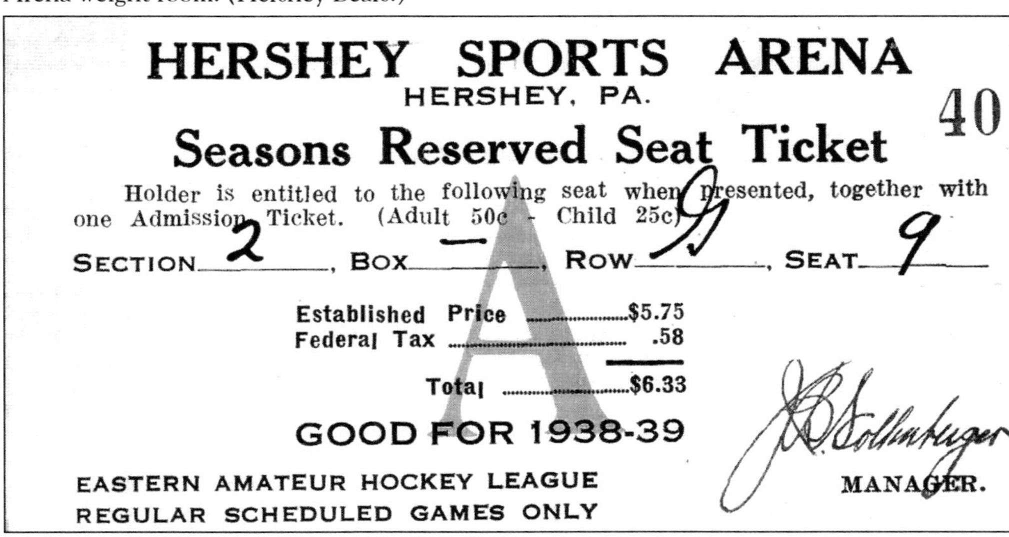

HERSHEY SPORTS ARENA

HERSHEY, PA.

40

Seasons Reserved Seat Ticket

Holder is entitled to the following seat when presented, together with one Admission Ticket. (Adult 50c - Child 25c)

SECTION 2, BOX —, ROW 9, SEAT 9

Established Price	$5.75
Federal Tax	.58
Total	$6.33

GOOD FOR 1938-39

EASTERN AMATEUR HOCKEY LEAGUE
REGULAR SCHEDULED GAMES ONLY

MANAGER.

Hersheypark Arena (1936–2002). The Bears played more than 2,600 regular-season and playoff games in minor-league hockey's grand cathedral. The arena still stands proudly in its unique location next to Hersheypark. Milton S. Hershey would have been pleased with the service the arena delivered to the community, except for maybe one thing: he did not approve of Sunday hockey games. (Bruce C. Cooper collection.)

Three

Calder Cup Champions

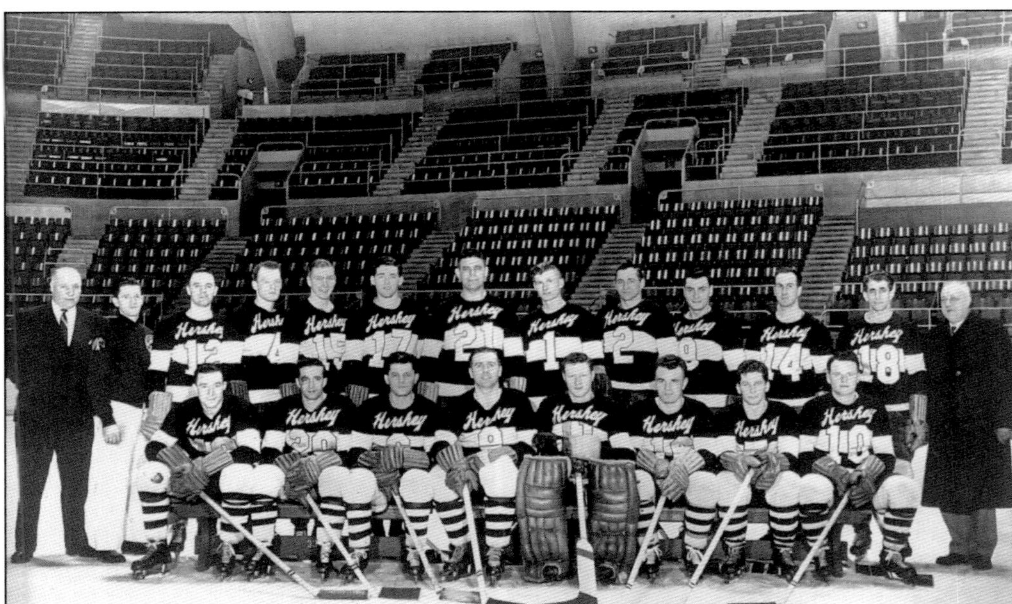

The 1946-1947 Calder Cup Champions. The 1946–1947 Calder Cup champions are shown here. They are, from left to right, as follows: (front row) Augie Herchenratter, Gino Rozzini, Frank Mario, Gordon Bruce, Gordon "Red" Henry, Pete Babando, Lloyd Gronsdahl, and Norm McAtee; (back row) coach Don Penniston, trainer Scotty Alexander, Armand Gaudreault, Andy Branigan, Paul Ronty, Johnny Peirson, Babe Pratt, Harvey Bennett, Pete Slobodian, Hy Buller, Herb Cain, Don Grosso, and general manager J.B. Sollenberger. (Hershey Bears.)

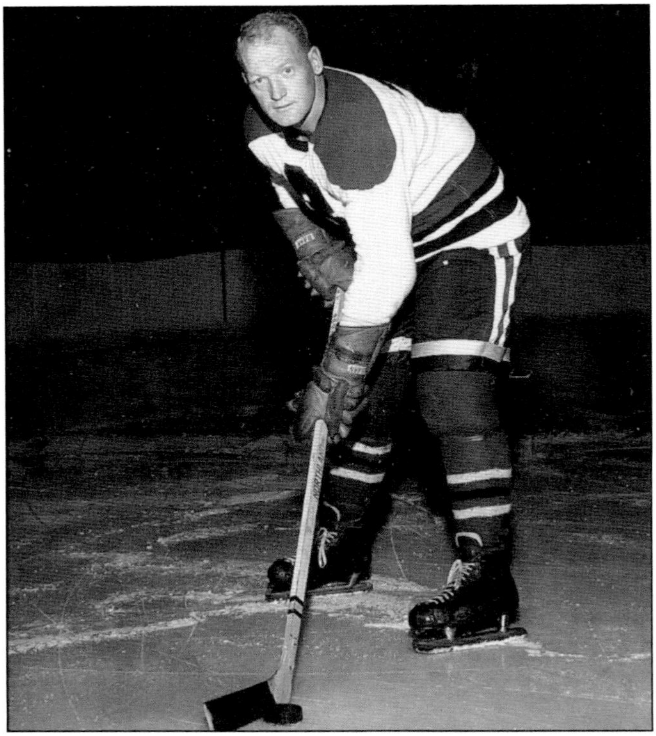

Andy Branigan (1946–1954). The 1946–1947 season was the first in Hershey for Andy Branigan, who would become one of the club's all-time great defensemen. One of five defensemen to play more than 500 games for Hershey, Branigan (508 games) ranks 11th in all-time scoring by Bears blue-liners (136 points). Hershey lost in the Calder Cup finals in the 1941–1942 season to Indianapolis and the 1944–1945 season to Cleveland before claiming the franchise's first AHL title. (Hershey Bears.)

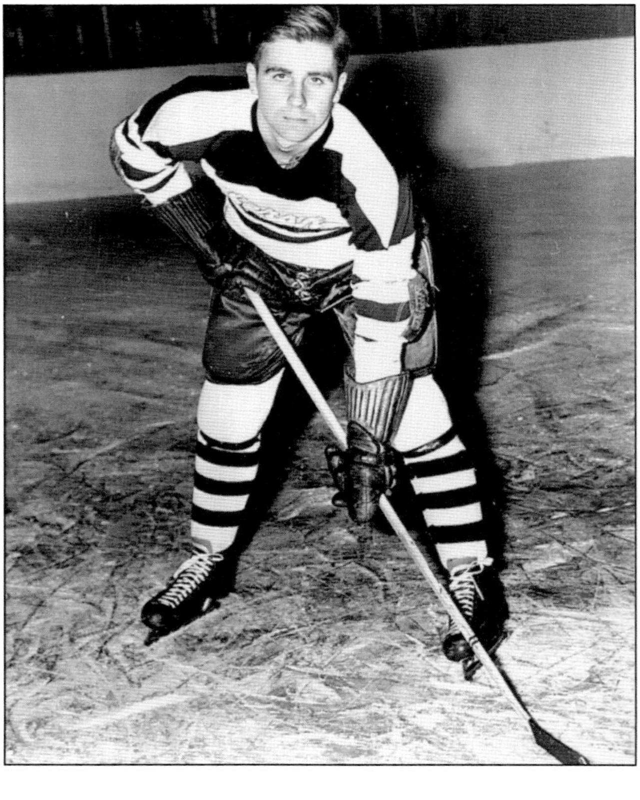

Gordie Bruce (1939–1942, 1946–1950). Left winger Gordie Bruce scored 35 goals for the 1946–1947 Bears, second on the team to Herb Cain (36). Despite playing with three cracked ribs, Bruce was second in the club in playoff scoring to AHL playoff scoring leader Frank Mario (18 points in 11 games). Bruce is tied for fifth in all-time Hershey playoff scoring (46 points in 41 games). (Hershey Bears.)

Harvey Bennett (1946–1947). Goalie Harvey Bennett was a second-team AHL All-Star his lone season in Hershey, going 34-15-11 with a 2.68 GAA. In the playoffs, he was supplanted by Gordon "Red" Henry, who had played just five regular-season games. Hershey swept Western Division champion Cleveland in the first round of the playoffs. Harvey Bennett Jr., Bennett's son, was a center who played for Hershey in the 1974–1975 season. (Hershey Bears.)

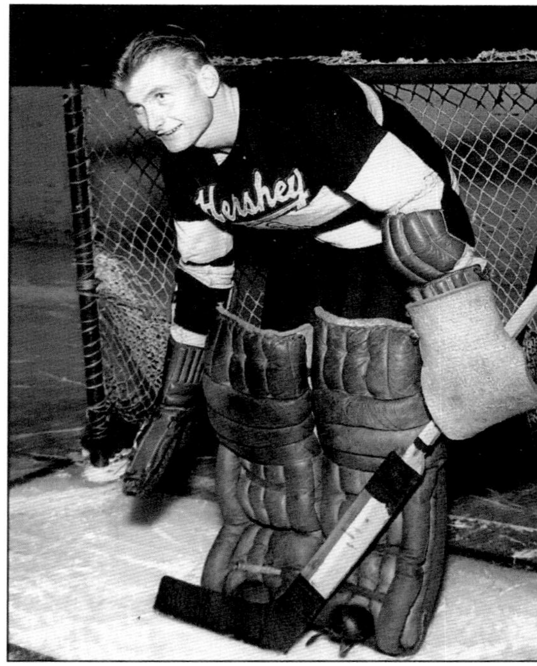

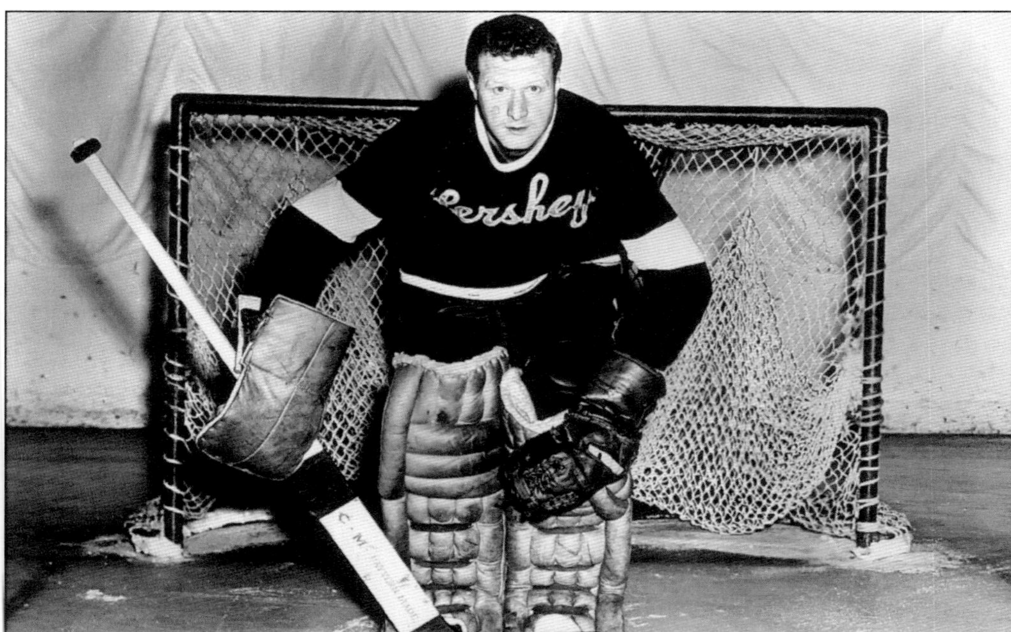

Gordon "Red" Henry (1945–1955). After falling behind Pittsburgh 3-1 in the Calder Cup finals, Henry allowed just one goal in the final three games. Hershey's all-time winningest goalie (226 wins) appeared in more games than any other Bears netminder. His 510 games played are 145 ahead of No. 2 Nick Damore. Henry holds the AHL record for most career playoff shutouts (8); five came in the 1947 playoffs. He is No. 6 on the AHL's all-time wins list. (Hershey Bears.)

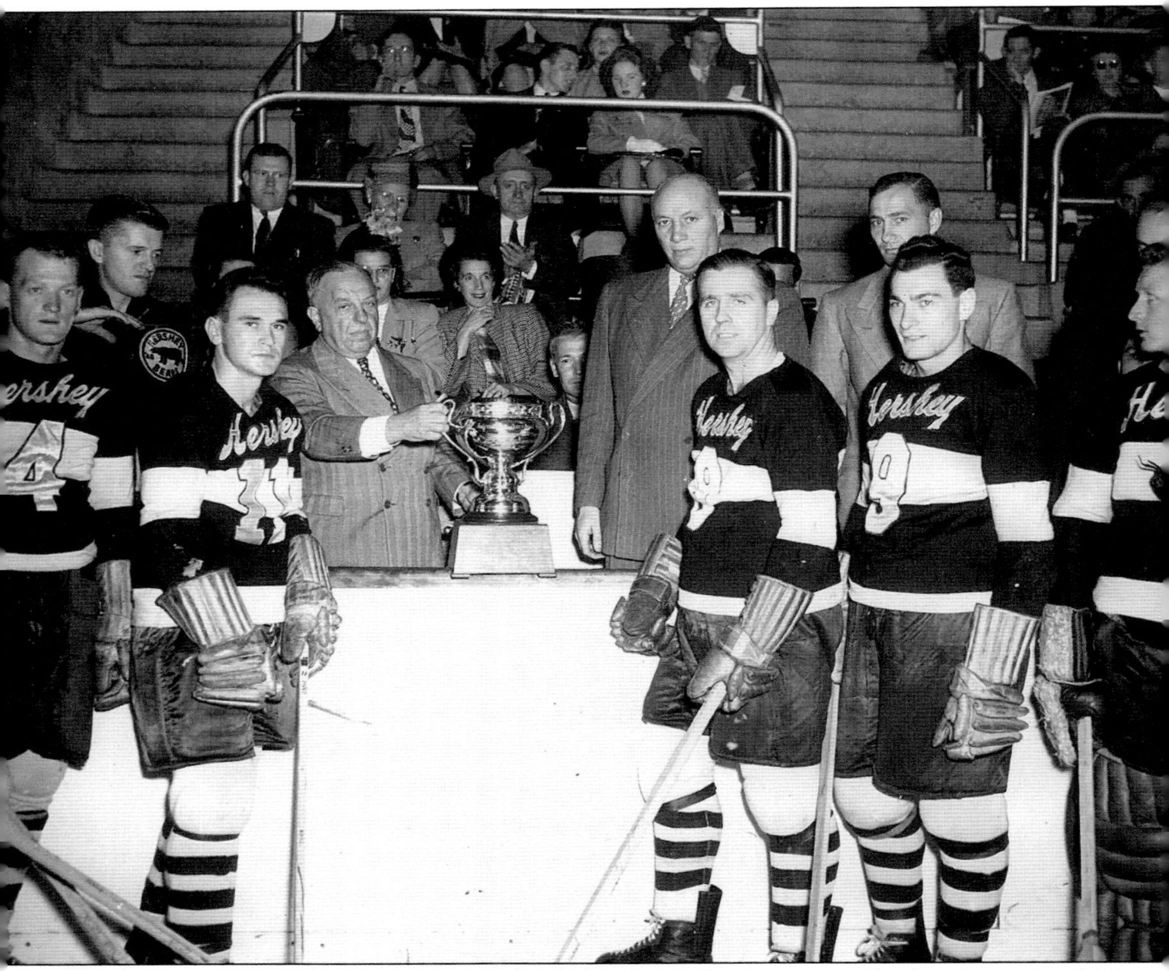

The 1947 Award Ceremony. Hershey's 5-0 Game 7 victory over Pittsburgh on April 15, 1947, at Hersheypark Arena clinched the Calder Cup. Hershey won Game 6 at Pittsburgh 2-1, staying alive by dealing the Hornets their first home loss since January 4, 1947. Frank Mario scored the opening goal at 8:30 of the first in a tough Game 7 for Pittsburgh goalie and future Hershey business manager Baz Bastien, whose name now is on the award that goes annually to the AHL's outstanding goalie. A turn-away crowd of 8,605 was in attendance. At the game's conclusion, the Hershey Orchestra played "My Hero," and fans stormed onto to the ice. Above, from left to right, Andy Branigan (No. 4), Frank Mario (No. 11), Gordie Bruce (No. 8), Hy Buller (No. 9), and "Red" Henry (No. 1) accept the Calder Cup. Coach Don Penniston stands behind Bruce. Mario (1941–1942, 1945–1952) ranks ninth in all-time Hershey points (424 in 453 games). (Hershey Bears.)

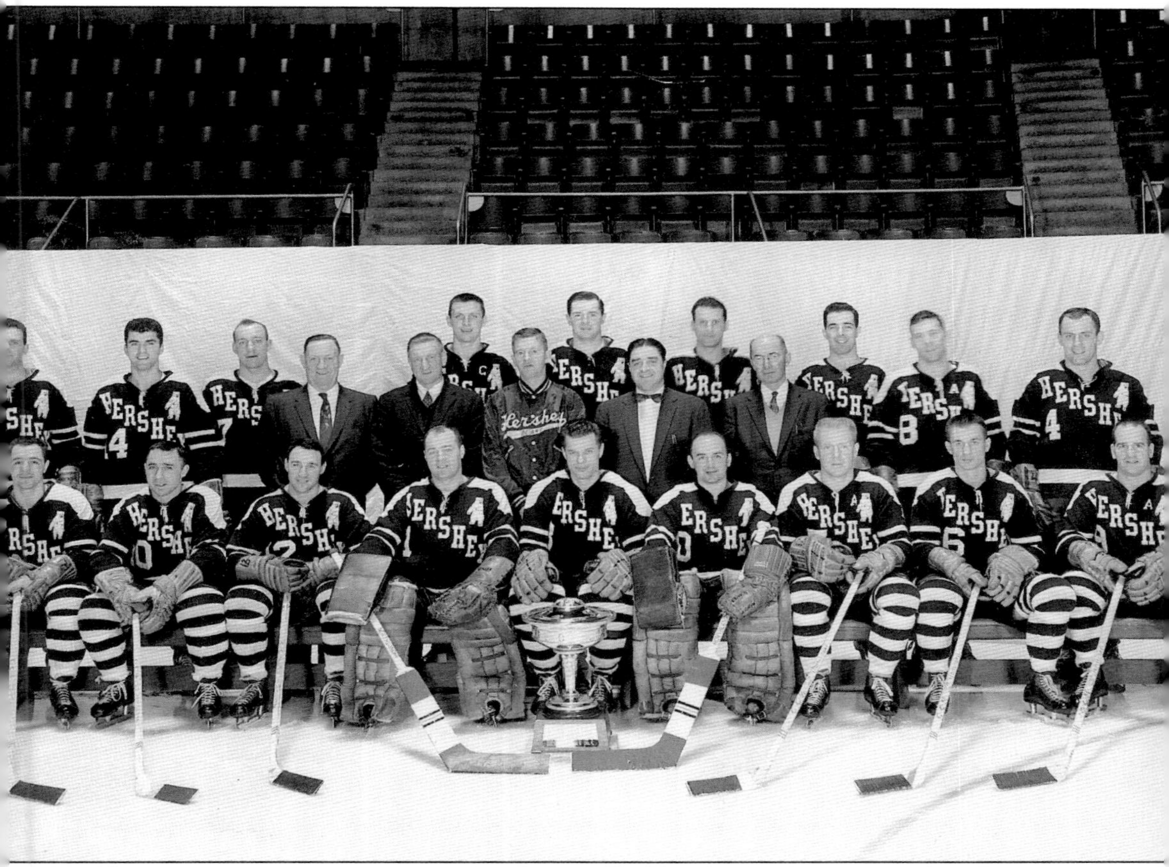

The 1957–1958 Calder Cup Champions. The 1957–1958 Calder Cup champions are pictured here. They are, from left to right, as follows: (front row) Ed Stankiewicz, Dunc Fisher, Len Haley, Bobby Perrault, player-coach Frank Mathers, Gil Mayer, Lorne Davis, Ed Panagabko, and Arnie Kullman; (middle row) scout Herb Mitchell, general manager Lloyd S. Blinco, trainer Scotty Alexander, business manager Baz Bastien, and arena manager George Bartles; (back row) Les Duff, Hec Lalande, Bob Solinger, Obie O'Brien, Al Dewsbury, Larry Zeidel, Bucky Hollingsworth, Willie Marshall, and Jack Price. The top line of Marshall, Fisher, and O'Brien produced 20 of the club's 36 playoff goals. The Calder Cup is named in honor of Frank Calder, who served as the NHL's first president from 1917 to 1943. During the 1920s, Calder guided hockey into major American cities—Boston, Detroit, New York, and Chicago—and later helped in the formation of the AHL. (Hershey Bears.)

(*Read instructions for completion and registration on reverse side.*)

STANDARD ASSIGNMENT AGREEMENT

(Uniform agreement for assignment of the rights to services of a player, amateur or professional, to or by a club.)

This Agreement made and entered into this 11th day of June 1956.,

BETWEEN: Pennsylvania Promotions, Inc. Pittsburgh Hockey Club
(Corporate name of the Company, Club or Association) PARTY OF THE FIRST PART

and: Hershey Estates, Inc. Hershey Hockey Club
(Corporate name of the Company, Club or Association) PARTY OF THE SECOND PART

WITNESSETH: The party of the First Part hereby assigns to the Party of the Second Part its rights to services of

PLAYER(s) FRANK MATHERS

under {Standard Contract, ~~XXXXXXB~~" / ~~XXXXXXXXXXXXXXXX~~"} upon the following terms and conditions:
Strike out inappropriate parts

SOLD OUTRIGHT TO HERSHEY HOCKEY CLUB FOR THE SUM OF FIVE THOUSAND ($5,000.00) DOLLARS.

CENTRAL REGISTRY SEEN REC'D JUL 9 10 35 AM '56 ACTION

WAIVER CERTIFICATE:

The transferor hereby certifies: (***strike out*** (*1*) ***or*** (*2*) ***below***)

(1) The Player(s) is a(n) ~~XXXX~~ prof. player for whom League waivers are not required.

(2) ~~XXXXXXXXXXXXXXXXXXXXXXXXXXXXXXXXXXXXXXXXXXXXXXXXXXXXXXXXXXXXXX (3) XXXXXXXXXXXXXXXXXXXXXXXXXXXXXXXXXd.~~

IN WITNESS WHEREOF the parties hereto have subscribed through our respective Presidents or authorized agents, witnessed on the date set out above.

PENNSYLVANIA PROMOTIONS? INC.
PITTSBURGH HOCKEY CLUB
CLUB

M. Green
WITNESS

BY James D. ...
(Party of the First Part)

HERSHEY ESTATES, INC.
HERSHEY HOCKEY CLUB
CLUB

Anna M. Kuntz
WITNESS

BY J.B. Sollenberger
(Party of the Second Part)

A LANDMARK TRANSACTION. Pittsburgh folded in 1956 when Duquesne Gardens was torn down. J.B. Sollenberger and Lloyd Blinco, running a franchise that won one Calder Cup in its first 19 seasons, seized a chance to upgrade. They acquired seven Hornets—Frank Mathers, Gil Mayer, Willie Marshall, Les Duff, Bob Solinger, Jack Price, and Bob Hassard—and business manager Baz Bastien. Above is the June 11, 1956, $5,000 purchase agreement for Mathers. (Hershey Bears.)

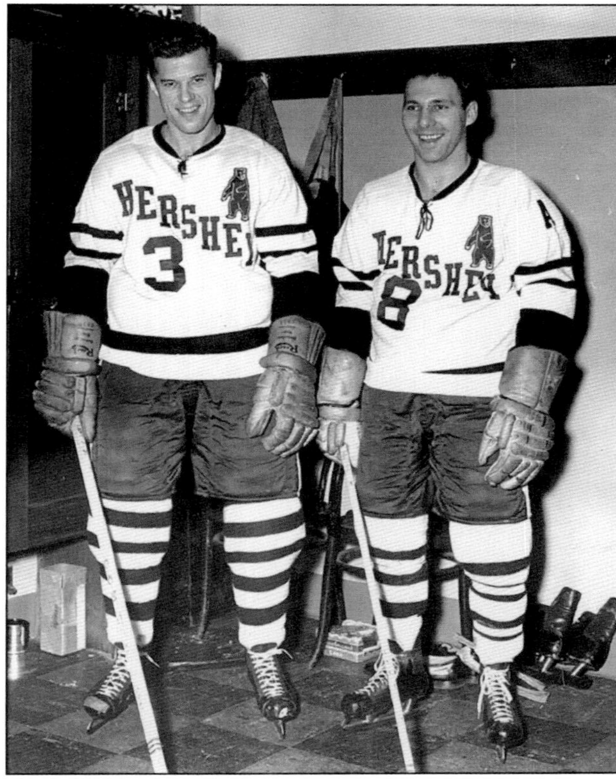

THE DYNAMIC DUO. Frank Mathers (left) and Willie Marshall, first-team All-Star teammates in Pittsburgh, teamed up again in Hershey with title results. The pair was named to the AHL's All-Century Team in 1999. Mathers, a five-time All-Star in Pittsburgh, became the most towering figure in Bears history. "There's one thing I won't buy, and that's a loser," J.B. Sollenberger said of the seven-player deal that brought the two from the Hornets. (Hershey Bears.)

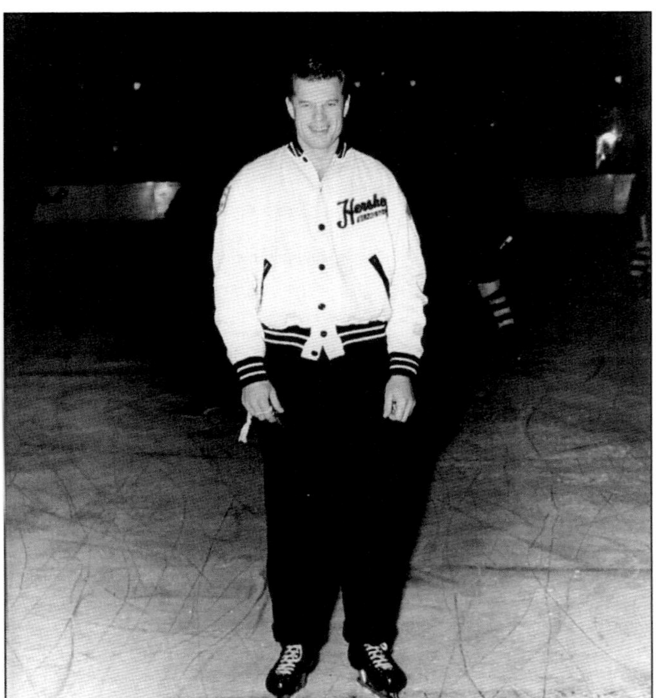

TWO HATS, ONE WHISTLE. Defensemen Johnny Crawford (1950–1952) and Murray Henderson (1952–1956) preceded Frank Mathers (left) as player-coaches in Hershey. Mathers continued both roles until retiring as a player following the 1961–1962 season. His first Hershey team in the 1956–1957 season went 32-28-4, with 68 points, and finished fourth before losing a seven-game series in the first round of the playoffs to eventual Calder Cup champion Cleveland. (Hershey Bears.)

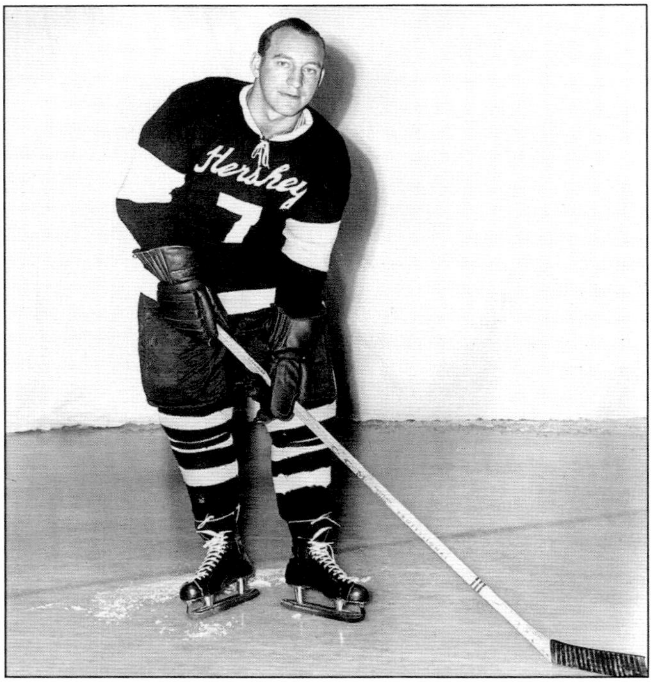

A Five-Time Winner. Bob Solinger, 1947–1948 AHL Rookie of the Year, also was part of the epic seven-player deal with Pittsburgh. The left winger played in Hershey from 1956 to 1960. Solinger, Bears teammate Les Duff (1956–1963), Fred Glover, and Mike Busniuk share the AHL record for most Calder Cups won by a player (five). Solinger ranks fourth in all-time AHL playoff scoring (92 points in 97 games). (Hershey Bears.)

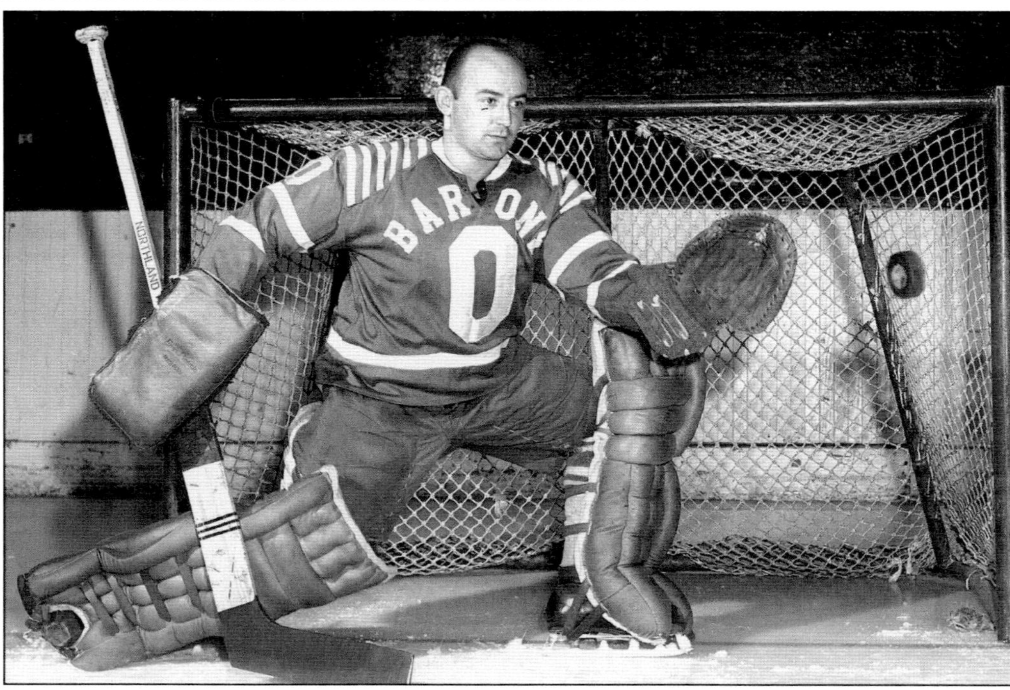

Net Gain. Gil Mayer (above as a Cleveland Baron) and Bobby Perrault gave Hershey the best goalie tandem in the AHL. Perrault (2.72 GAA) and Mayer (2.82 GAA) respectively finished second and third in the league in goals-against average for the 1957–1958 season. Perrault played all 11 playoff games. Mayer (346) is ranked second in all-time AHL wins to Johnny Bower (359), but incomplete records do not reflect all of his appearances. (Hershey Bears.)

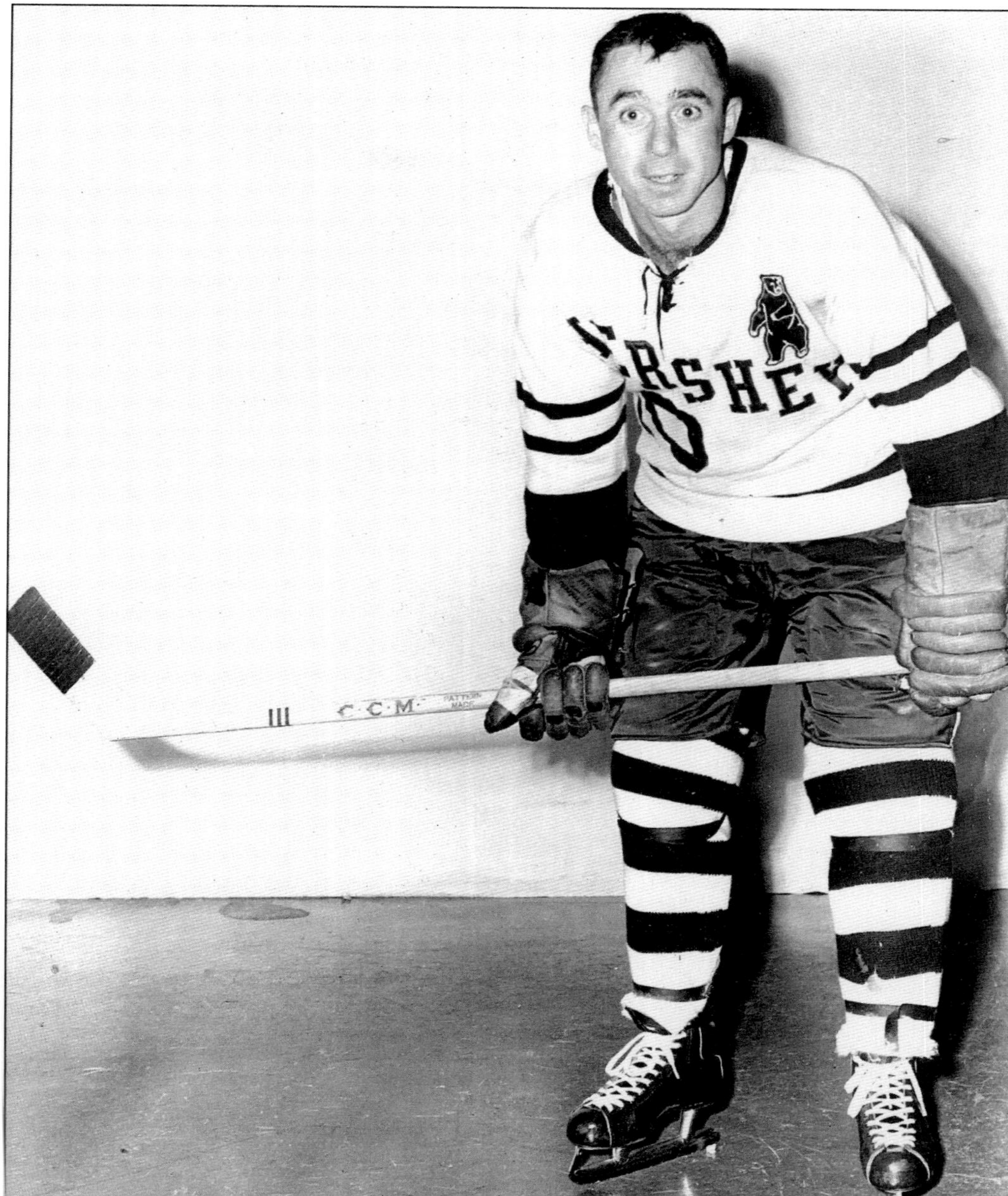

A One-Two Punch. While line mate Willie Marshall (104 points) led the AHL in scoring in the 1957-1958 season, Dunc Fisher (above) finished second with 88 points. Fisher (561 points in 511 games) ranks sixth in all-time Hershey scoring and first in goals (260). Fisher (1952–1960) was a five-time AHL All-Star. The right winger played 275 NHL games for New York, Boston, and Detroit. Fisher had a hand in both goals of the Game 6 clincher at Springfield. (Hershey Bears.)

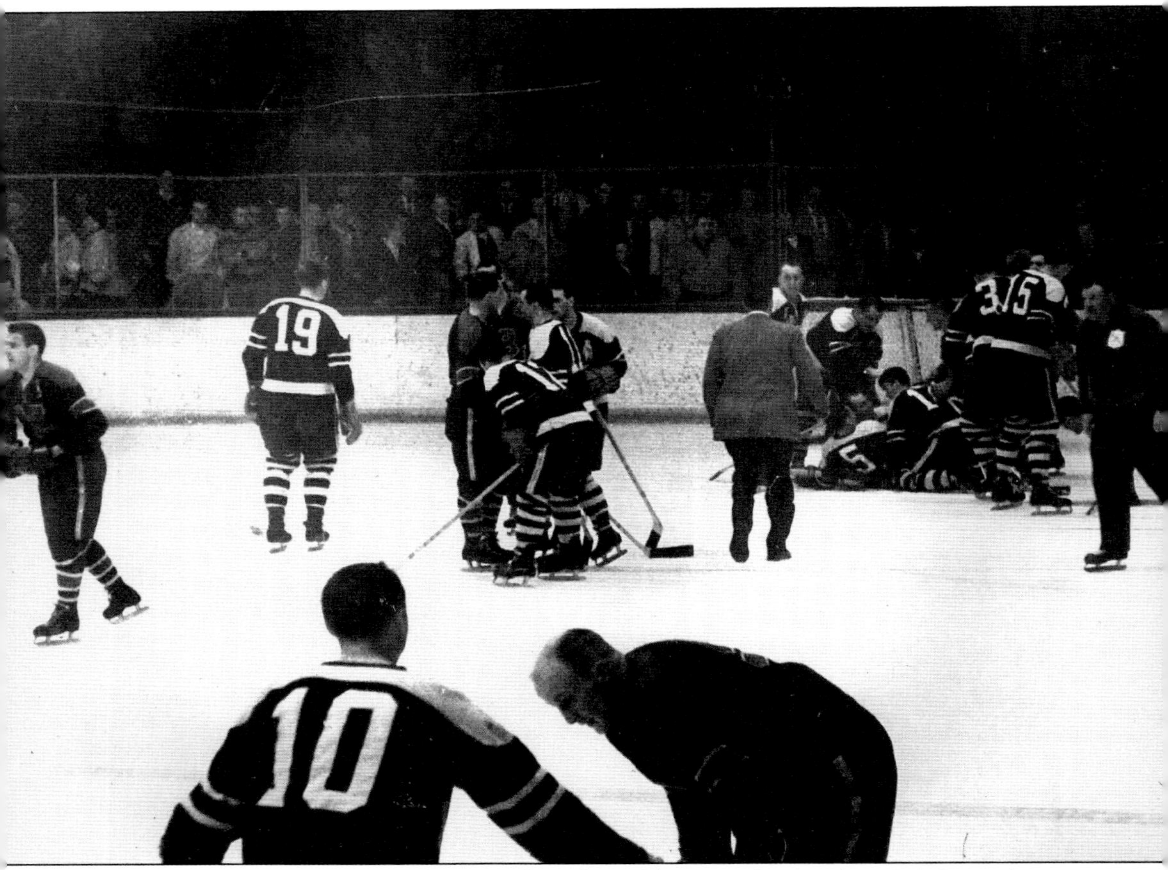

A Cup Celebration. Bears players mob goalie Bobby Perrault after their 2-1 Game 6 victory on April 20, 1958, in Springfield. Hershey (39-24-7, 85 points) finished first overall in the regular season and beat Providence in five games in the first round to advance to the finals against the Indians. A 7-6 Game 4 win in Springfield on April 16 gave the Bears a 3-1 lead, but the Indians won Game 5 in Hershey 4-2 to earn a trip back home. A standing-room crowd of 5,920 at the Springfield Civic Center saw the Indians take a 1-0 lead in the first eight minutes, but Dunc Fisher tied it 1-1 early in the second period. Willie Marshall scored the game-winning goal with 3:05 remaining on a 20-foot backhander past goalie Claude Evans. Perrault finished with 25 saves, and Marshall (19 points) was the leading playoff scorer. Hershey came from behind to win six times during the 1958 playoffs. Each Bear pocketed an estimated $1,300 playoff share. (M. Jaffe/Hershey Bears.)

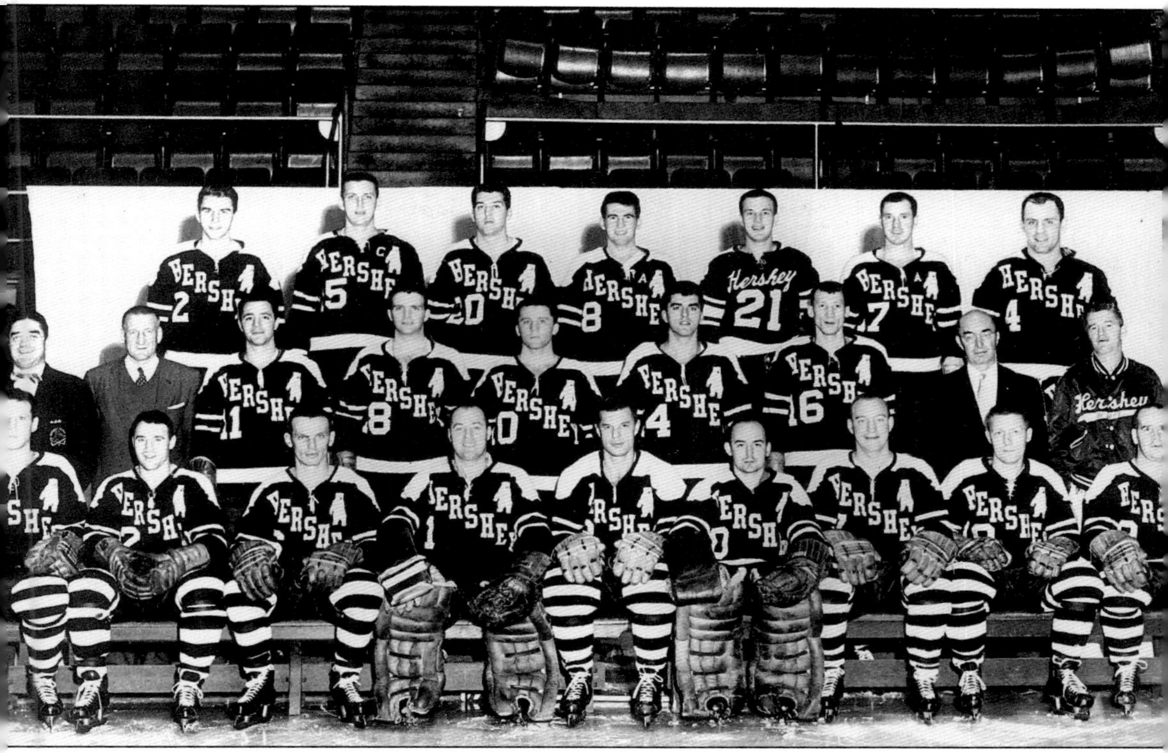

THE 1958–1959 CALDER CUP CHAMPIONS. The 1958–1959 Calder Cup champions are shown here. They are, from left to right, as follows: (front row) Larry Zeidel, Len Haley, Howie Yanosik, Bobby Perrault, player-coach Frank Mathers, Gil Mayer, Bob Solinger, Ron Hurst, and Arnie Kullman; (middle row) business manager Baz Bastien, general manager Lloyd Blinco, Ed Stankiewicz, Les Duff, Wally Boyer, Hec Lalande, Jacques Gagnon, arena manager George Bartels, and trainer Scotty Alexander; (back row) Gordon Strate, Obie O'Brien, Tom McCarthy, Mike Nykoluk, Jack Hendrickson, Don Poile, and Jack Price. The 1958–1959 Bears certainly did not take an easy road to become the only back-to-back champions in club history. They began the season without Willie Marshall, who was traded to Toronto in the off-season for 23-year-old Mike Nykoluk. Marshall demanded a trade back to Hershey after playing 19 games for Rochester. Nykoluk (53 points) led the team in scoring. (Hershey Bears.)

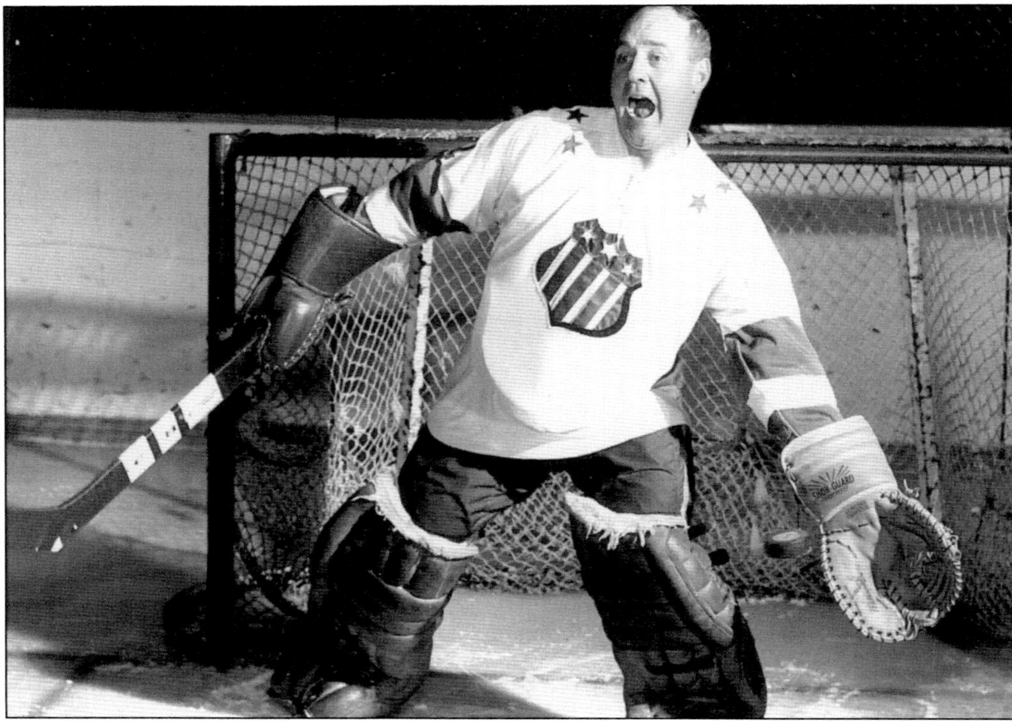

Bobby Perrault (1957–1962). Goalie Bobby Perrault (above as a Rochester American) led the AHL with a 2.68 GAA in the 1958–1959 season and became the first Bear to win the Harry "Hap" Holmes Memorial Award for outstanding team goaltending. Perrault ranks fourth in Hershey history in goalie games played (279) and fifth in AHL history in wins (229, though incomplete records do not include all of his appearances). (Hershey Bears.)

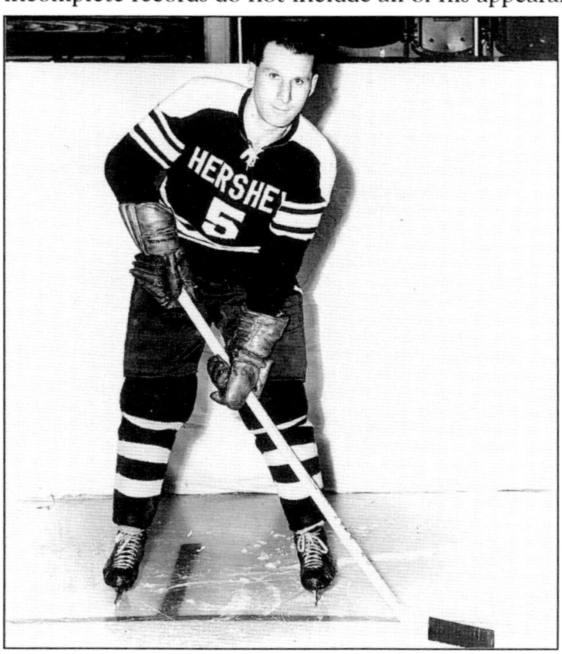

Hammer Time. Tough defenseman Larry Zeidel (1955–1963) led Hershey in penalty minutes seven times. He ranks second in all-time Hershey penalty minutes (1,335) and accumulated 1,632 career AHL minutes (18th in league annals). Zeidel ranks third in all-time Hershey scoring for defensemen (218 points in 517 games). Teammates say he got so angry in Cleveland once that he tore the penalty box door off its hinges and threw it on the ice. (Hershey Bears.)

Howie Yanosik (1957–1967). After playing just 22 games in the 1957–1958 season, Yanosik enjoyed a breakout season in the 1958–1959 season en route to becoming one of Hershey's all-time great defensemen. He ranks second in all-time points by a Hershey defenseman (272) and fourth in all-time Hershey games played (605). He is also third in all-time Hershey playoff appearances (68). (Hershey Bears.)

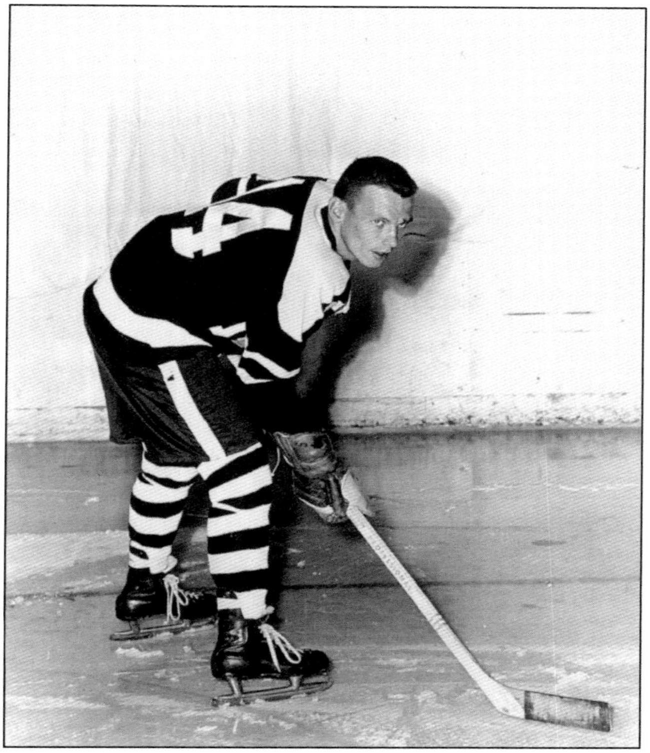

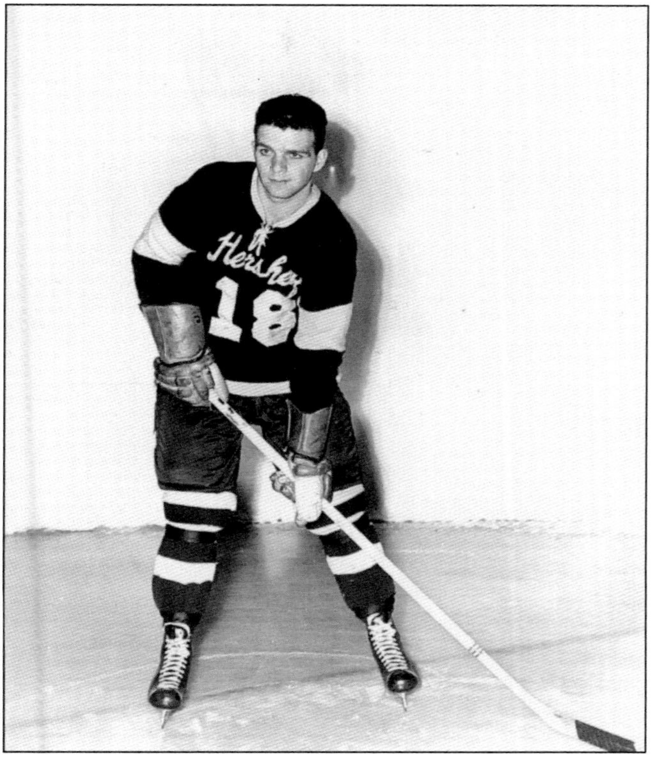

A Hearty Character. Les Duff (1956–1963) was the only Bear to play all 140 regular-season games in the back-to-back Calder Cup seasons of 1957–1958 and 1958–1959. The left winger played 467 career games for the Bears and amassed 238 points. (Hershey Bears.)

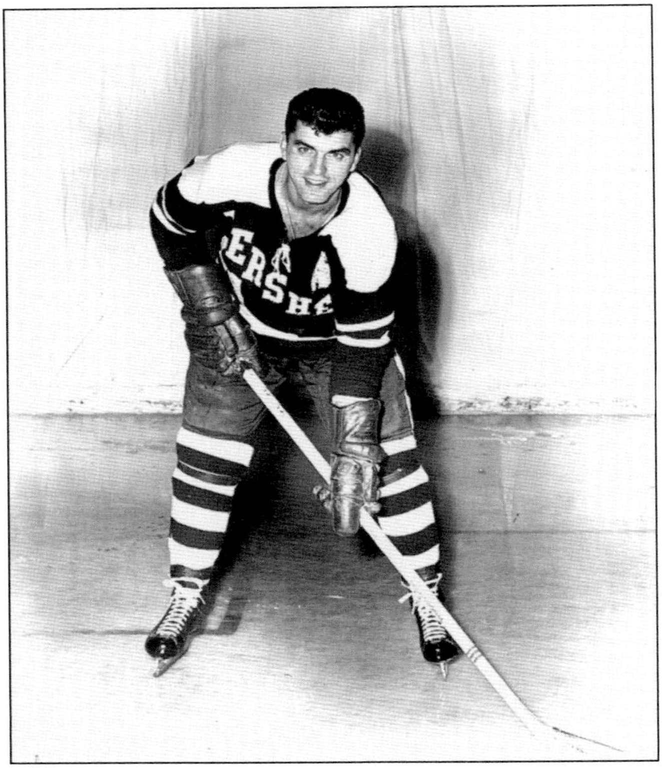

Fight Night. A second-period fight between Hec Lalande (left) and the notorious Fred Glover, second in all-time AHL scoring and third in all-time penalty minutes, sparked Hershey to a 4-3 win in Cleveland in Game 7 of the Calder Cup semifinals. "We had a real party that game," Lalande recalled. "It exploded, that's what it did. They thought they could push us around. . . . There was a little flare-up there and we put them back in their place." (Hershey Bears.)

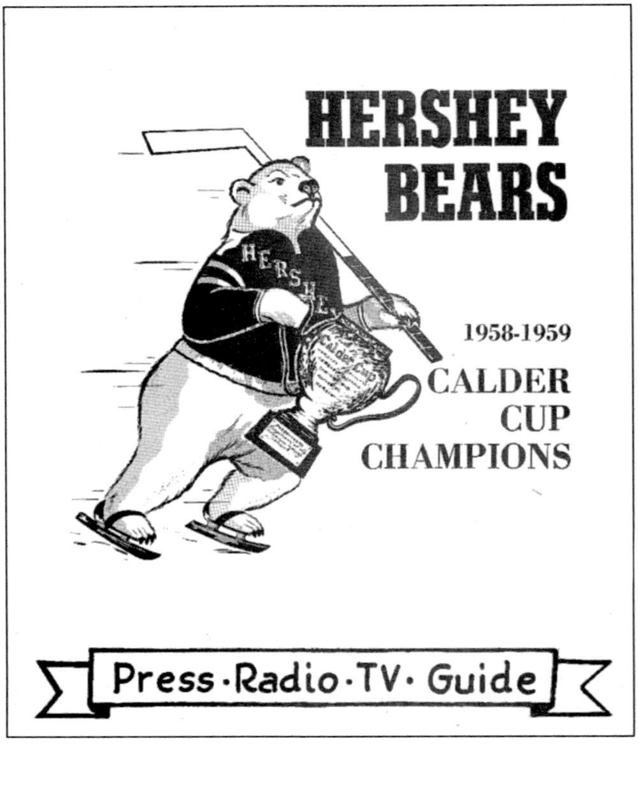

A Rough Road. Hershey finished the regular season in fourth place after going winless in its last 10 games (nine losses). Frank Mathers, age 35, was lost as a player for the playoffs after suffering a broken right hand in Game 3 against Cleveland. Hershey brought in defenseman Bud MacPherson, a seven-year NHL veteran with Montreal, as an emergency replacement. Mathers concentrated on his coaching duties. (Hershey Bears.)

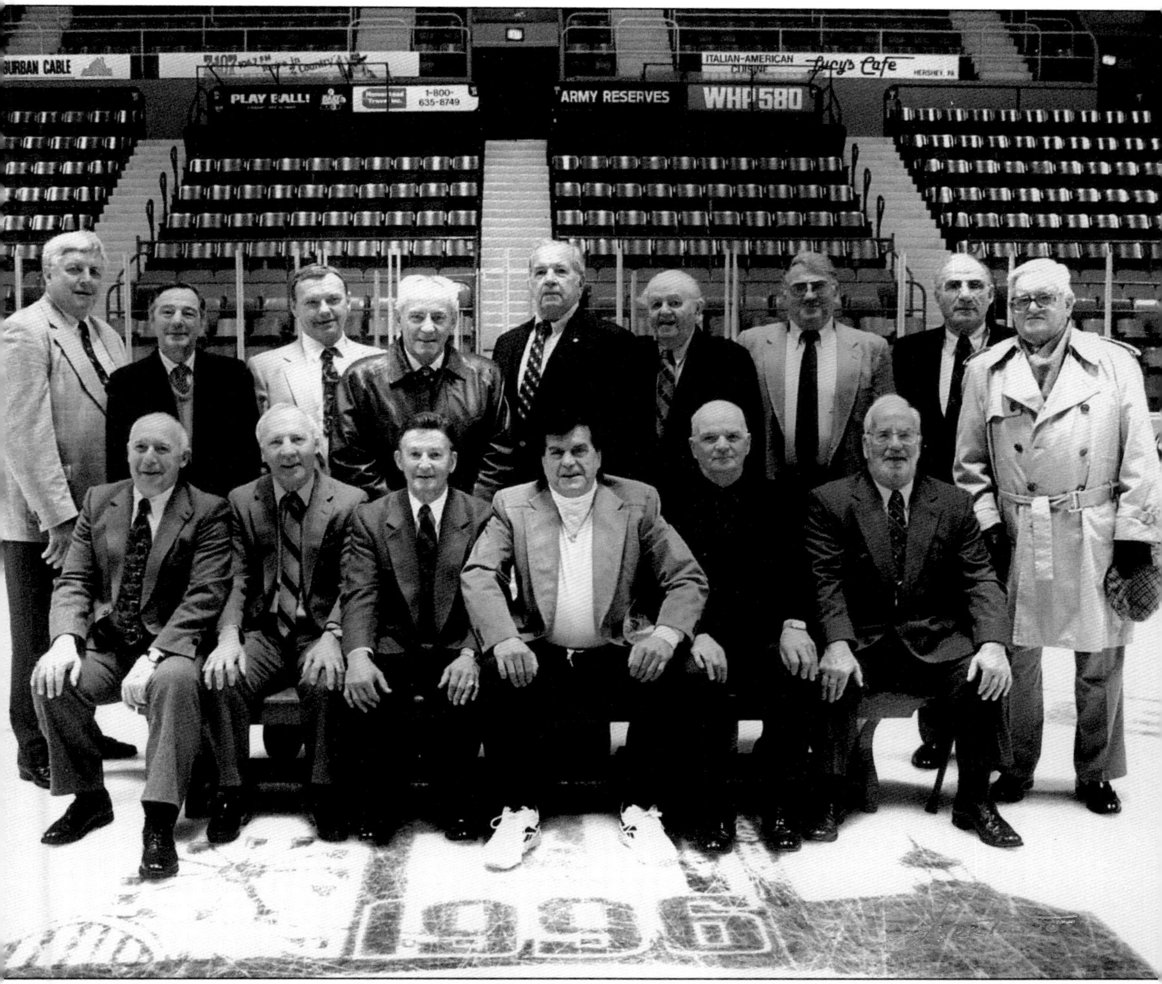

A CHAMPIONSHIP REUNION. Members of the 1958 and 1959 Calder Cup teams returned when Hersheypark Arena hosted the 1996 AHL All-Star Game. From left to right are the following: (front row) Gil Mayer, Willie Marshall, Ed Stankiewicz, Hec Lalande, Les Duff, and Arnie Kullman; (back row) Obie O'Brien, Dunc Fisher, Howie Yanosik, Jack Price, bus driver Gardner Gutshall, broadcaster Bob Payne, Mike Nykoluk, Larry Zeidel, and trainer Scotty Alexander. Hershey clinched the 1959 championship with a 5-2 win in Game 6 over Buffalo on April 28, 1959. Following a 9-4 loss in their first chance to clinch the championship in Game 5 at Buffalo, the Bears got the job done at home despite a stunning 75-foot, one-bounce Bill Dineen goal that gave Buffalo a 2-1 lead. Eddie Stankiewicz's goal at 2:20 of the third period broke a 2-2 tie and stood as the game-winner. A crowd of 7,014 produced a thunderous ovation and hurled cups and programs at the ice. (Hershey Bears.)

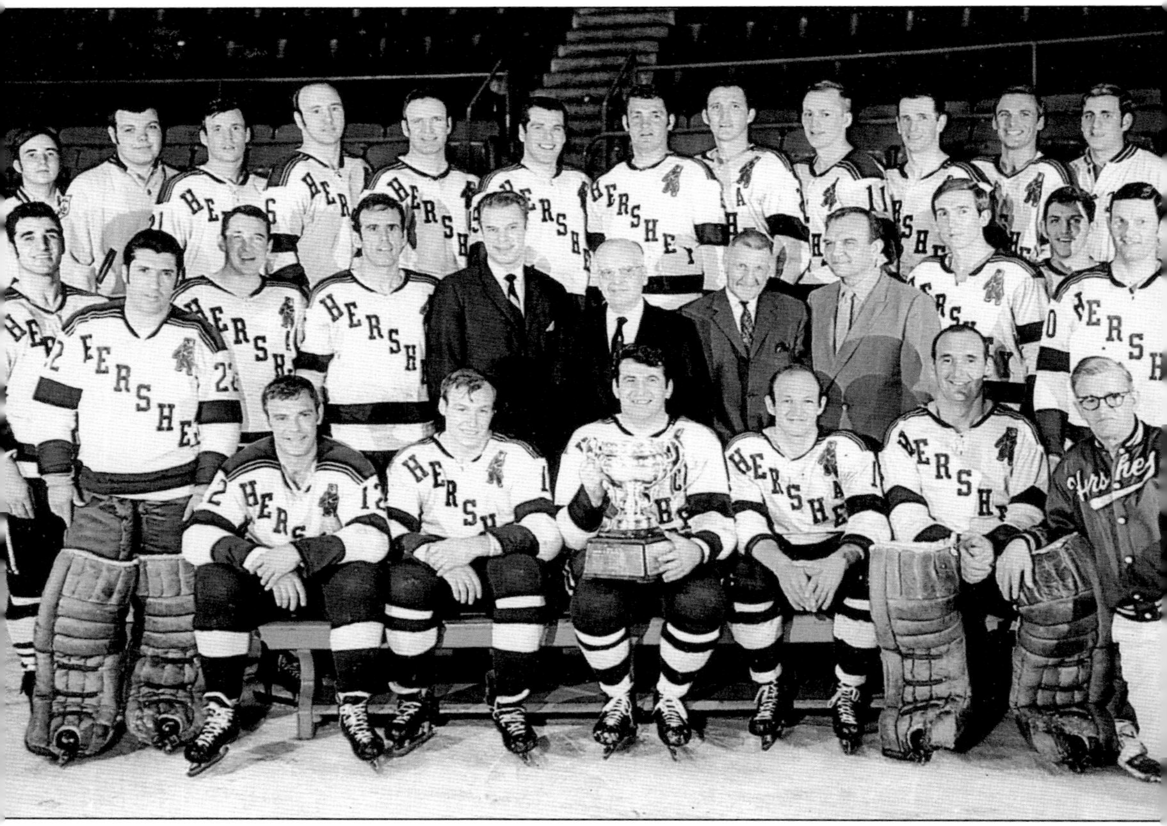

The 1968–1969 Calder Cup Champions. The 1968–1969 Calder Cup champions are shown here. They are, from left to right, as follows: (front row) Roger DeJordy, Ted Snell, Mike Nykoluk, Bob Leiter, John Henderson, and trainer Scotty Alexander; (middle row) Ralph Keller, Andre Gill, Gil Gilbert, Michel Harvey, general manager-coach Frank Mathers, Hershey Entertainment chief Arthur Whiteman, president Lloyd Blinco, team physician Dr. D. Lee Backenstose, Bud Debrody, Ray Adduono, and Colin McCormick; (back row) stick boy Jack Kegerreis, stick boy Barney Peters, Bob Barber, Larry McNabb, Mike Mahoney, Don Marcotte, Pete Ford, Barry Ashbee, Stan Gilbertson, Chuck Hamilton, Garnet "Ace" Bailey, and stick boy Bob Trenn. This is the last team Frank Mathers coached to the Calder Cup. The Bears won 8 of 11 playoff games. "There's no question this is the greatest Hershey team I coached," Mathers said. "They broke a bundle of records during the season and they could do so many things other teams couldn't." (Hershey Bears.)

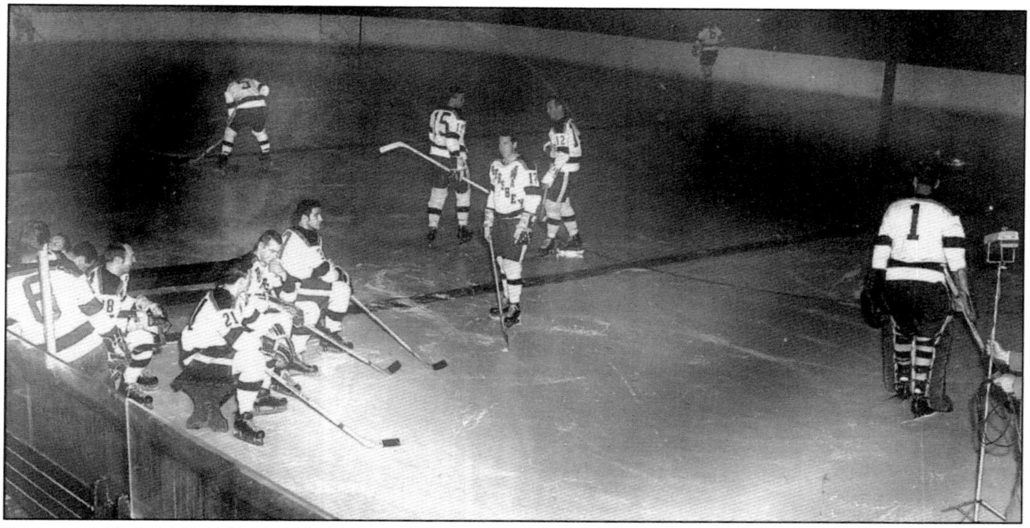

PICTURE DAY. The Bears gather on Christmas Day 1968 for a team photograph session. A powerhouse offense, featuring Gil Gilbert, Michel Harvey, Chuck Hamilton, Mike Nykoluk, Bob Leiter, Ace Bailey, Don Marcotte, Roger DeJordy, and Stan Gilbertson, scored a then-club-record 307 goals. Eight Bears scored more than 20 goals. Hershey went 41-27-6, with 88 points, and placed first in the Eastern Division, winning 6 of its last 7 regular-season games. (Hershey Bears.)

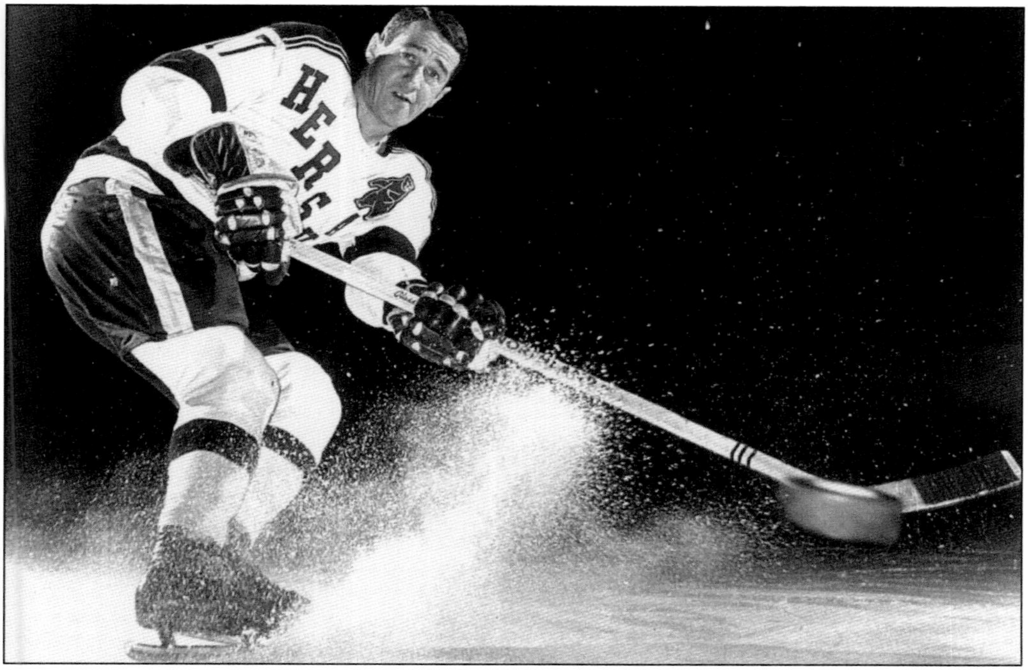

SCORING CHAMPION GIL GILBERT. Gil Gilbert's 100-point season (35 goals, 65 assists) led the AHL in scoring. Gilbert headed a parade of three first-team Hershey All-Stars that also included Michel Harvey and Ralph Keller. Gilbert (1965–1973) ranks fourth in all-time Hershey scoring (595 points in 551 games). The center finished his professional career in 1975 with the Quebec Nordiques in the upstart World Hockey Association. (Hershey Bears.)

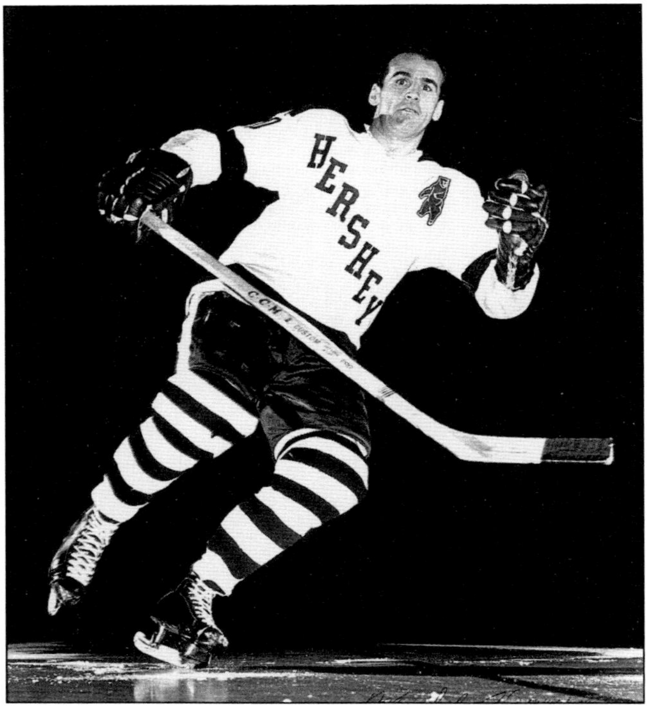

Michel Harvey (1963–1965, 1966–1971). Center Michel Harvey finished second to Gil Gilbert in AHL scoring, the second of two times in club history that the Bears have finished as No. 1 and No. 2 in league scoring. Harvey led Hershey with 41 goals in the 1968–1969 season and ranks 14th in all-time team scoring (393 points in 452 games). (Hershey Bears.)

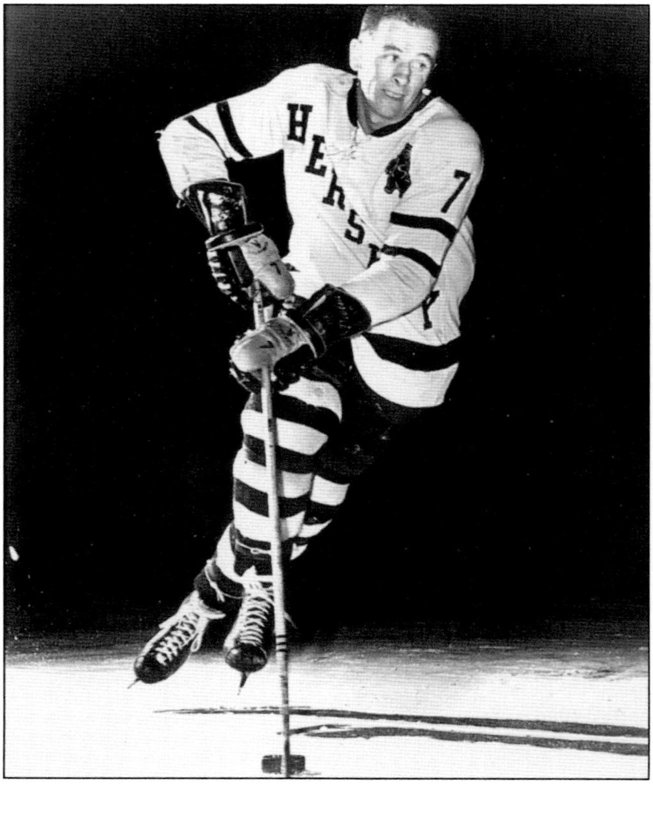

A Coach in Waiting. Forward Chuck Hamilton (1963–1970) was Hershey's No. 3 scorer in the 1968–1969 season (74 points). During this championship season, Frank Mathers added the title of general manager to his head coaching duties when Lloyd Blinco relinquished the role. In the 1973–1974 season, Hamilton assumed the mighty task of succeeding Mathers as head coach. (Hershey Bears.)

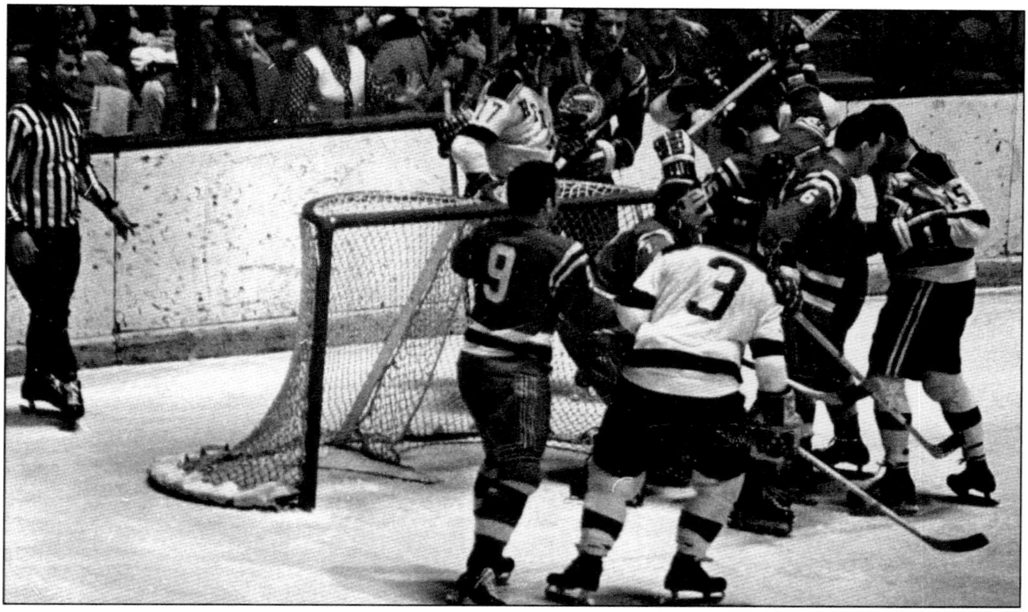

Rush Hour. Traffic gathers around Buffalo goalie Gilles Villemure, the AHL MVP for the 1968–1969 season, during a 5-1 Bisons victory over the Bears on March 29, 1969, at Hersheypark Arena. In an odd playoff format, Eastern Division champion Hershey and Western Division champion Buffalo, the top two teams in the league, played in the first round while the other four playoff qualifiers dueled for a berth in the finals. Hershey eliminated Buffalo in six games. (Hershey Bears.)

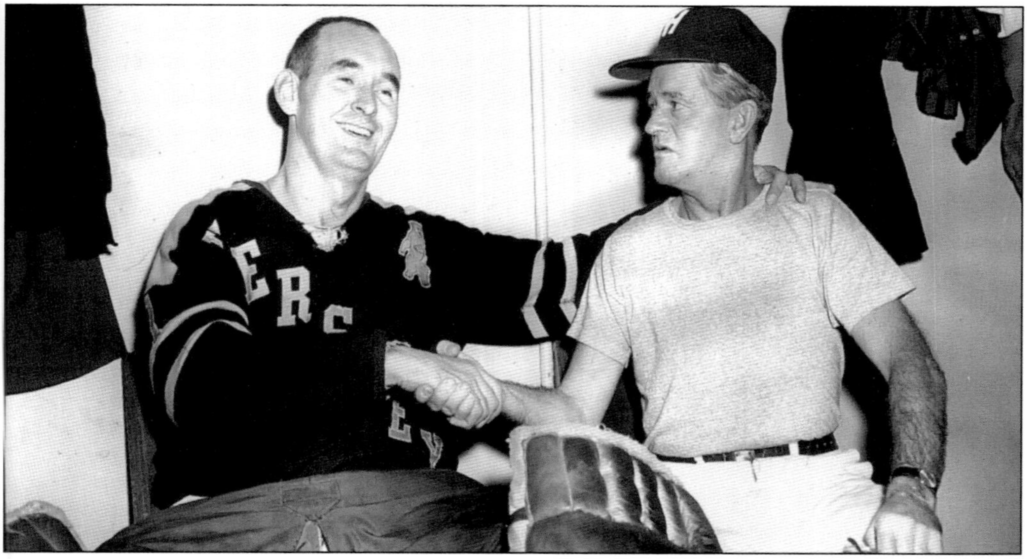

Main Man John Henderson. Even with estimable Andre Gill on the roster, John Henderson (1954–1956, 1966–1970) was Hershey's No. 1 netminder. The six-foot-five-inch tall Henderson went 23-14-3 with a 2.95 GAA that ranked second in the AHL. Henderson, being congratulated by Scotty Alexander after a regular-season game (above), shut out the Quebec Aces 3-0 in Game 5 of the Calder Cup finals at Hersheypark Arena to clinch the championship. He made 27 saves. (Hershey Bears.)

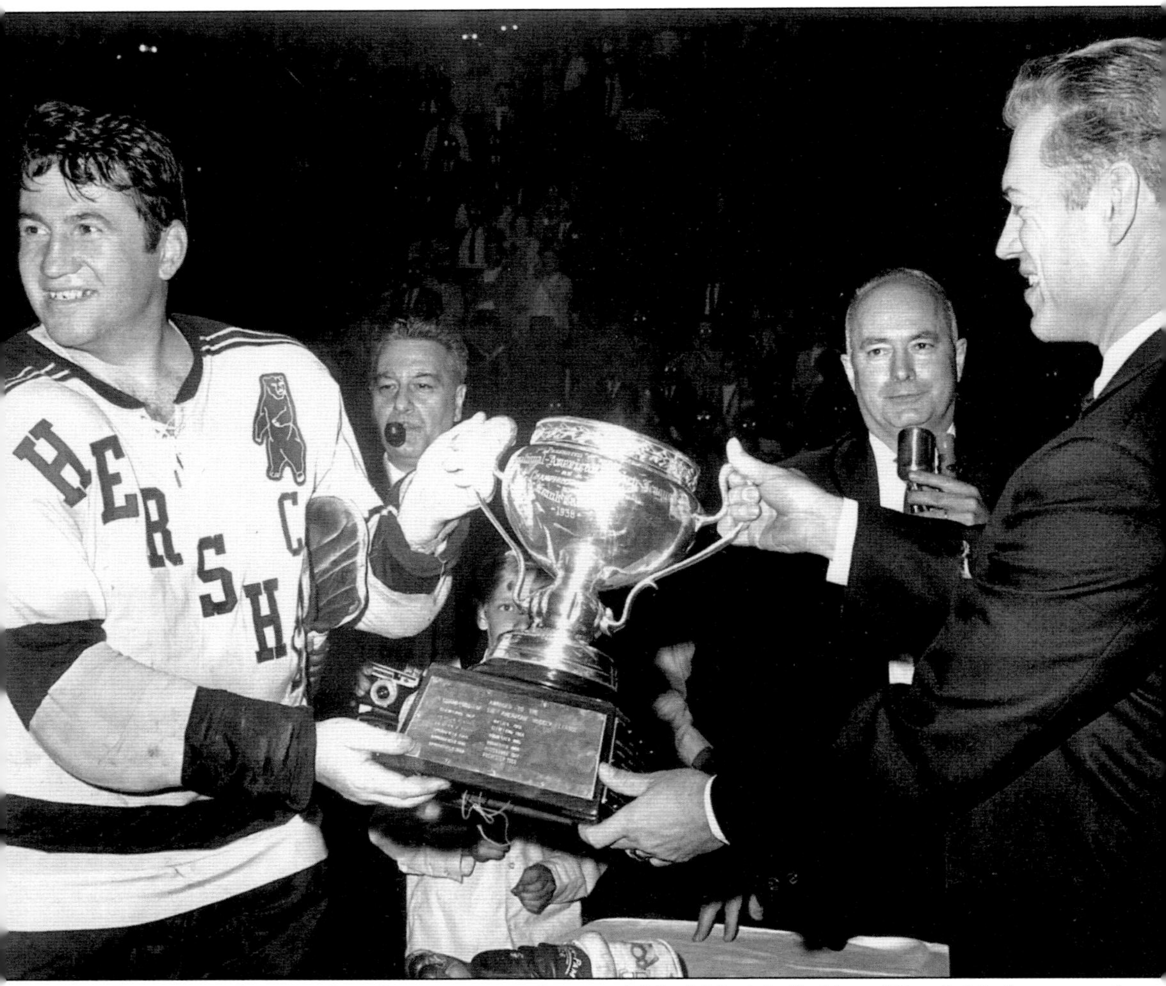

The 1969 Calder Cup Celebration. Captain Mike Nykoluk (left) and Frank Mathers, coach and general manager, hoist the Calder Cup on May 7, 1969, after eliminating Quebec in five games. After a 10-season Calder Cup drought, hungry fans littered the ice with debris and forced delays after each Hershey goal in the finale. Don Marcotte, Ted Snell, and Barry Ashbee all scored on goalie Dunc Wilson. The crowd of 6,425 began a standing ovation with 30 seconds left. Many fans rushed onto the ice to congratulate the club after the final buzzer. Each Bear collected a $2,000 check for winning the Calder Cup. This technically was Mathers's first Calder Cup won solely in an off-ice role, but a broken hand sidelined him in the 1959 playoffs and forced him into a coaching role during that Calder Cup run. Mathers won the Louis A.R. Pieri Memorial Award as AHL Coach of the Year. (Hershey Bears.)

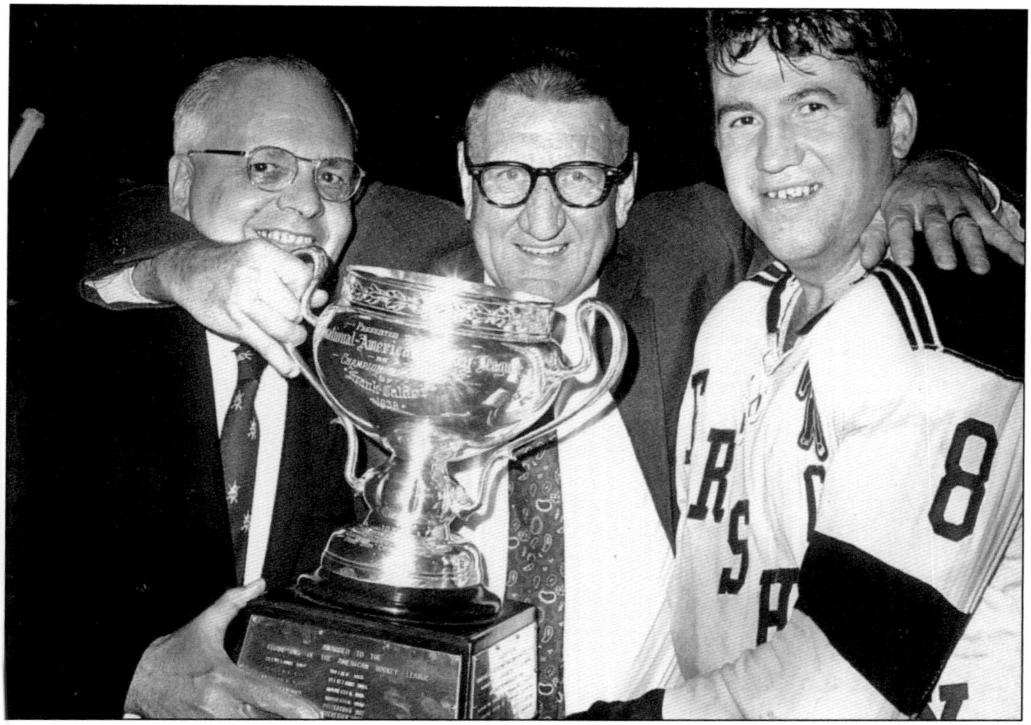

A Silver Gleam. Hershey Entertainment chief Arthur R. Whiteman (left), president Lloyd S. Blinco (center), and Mike Nykoluk (right) enjoy the Calder Cup. Blinco won the 1968–1969 James C. Hendy Memorial Award as the AHL's outstanding executive. Whiteman later won the Hendy Award in 1974. (Hershey Bears.)

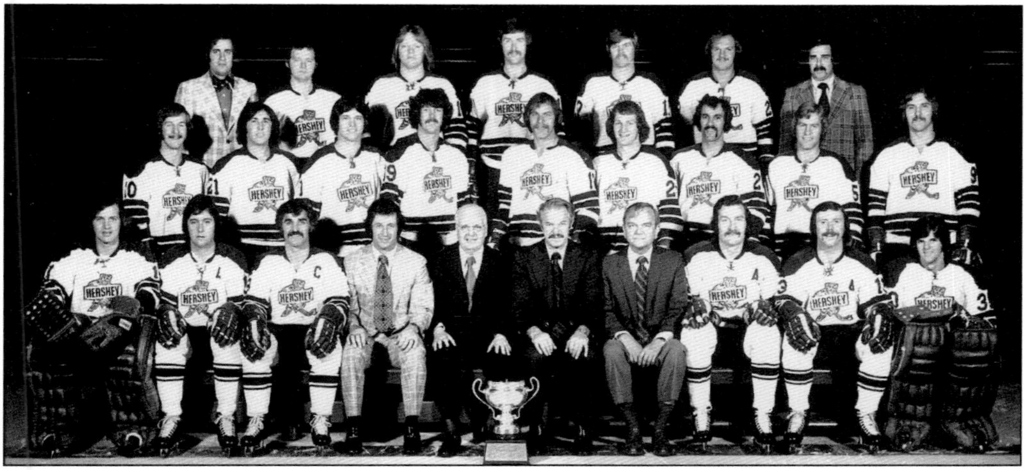

The 1973–1974 Calder Cup Champions. Seen here are, from left to right, the following: (front row) Bob Johnson, Hugh Harvey, Ralph Keller, coach Chuck Hamilton, Hershey Entertainment chief Arthur A. Whiteman, president-general manager Frank S. Mathers, team physician Dr. D. Lee Backenstose, Duane Rupp, Robin Burns, and Denis Herron; (middle row) Don Seiling, Jim Hrycuik, Jim Pearson, Dean Sheremeta, Hank Nowak, Dennis Owchar, Yvon Labre, Gerry Methe, and Terry Ewasiuk; (back row) trainer Bob Trenn, Wayne Ego, Guido Tenesi, Jim Wiley, Ron Jones, Steve Andrascik, and assistant trainer Chuck Trenn.

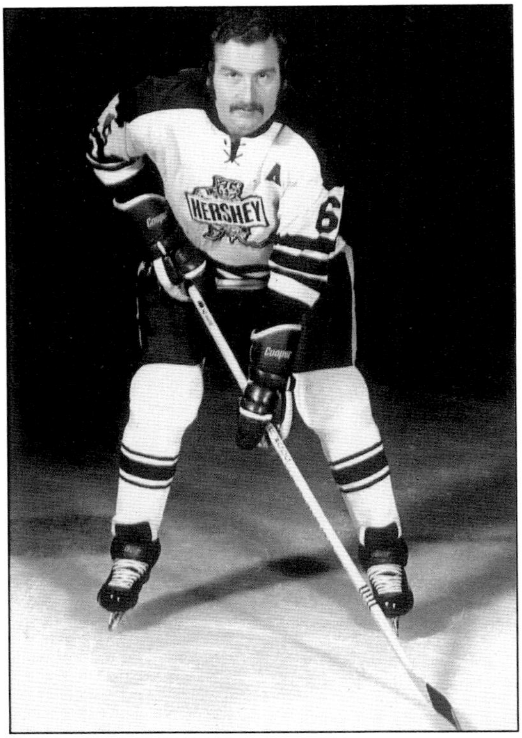

THE LONE ALL-STAR. Defenseman Duane Rupp (1971–1972, 1973–1974), a second-teamer, was Hershey's lone All-Star selection in 1973–1974. Rupp, who scored seven goals and added 27 assists, was a veteran of 374 NHL games. He later coached the Rochester Americans (1976–1979). (Hershey Bears.)

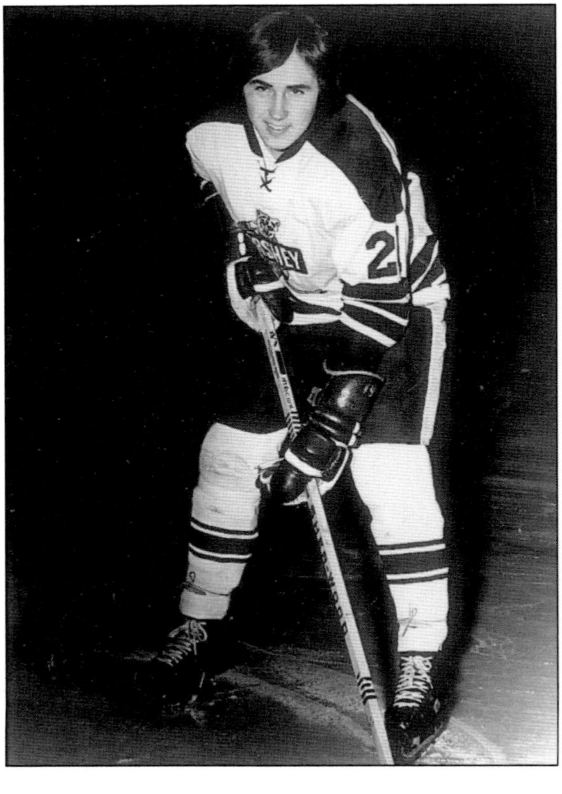

A BALANCED ATTACK. The 1973–1974 Bears featured nine players who scored 20 or more goals, a club record. Jim Hrycuik (right) was the leading scorer, producing 75 points during his lone season in Hershey. The nine-rookie team came to be known as the "Comeback Kids" for its propensity to rally to victory. All five games of the finals against Providence were decided by one goal. They pocketed playoff checks of $3,800 apiece after winning the Calder Cup. (Hershey Bears.)

Future Foe Jim Wiley. Jim Wiley (1972–1974) scored 54 points during the regular season and was the AHL's leading playoff scorer (16 points in 14 games). The Bears played five playoff overtime games. They won four, including Wiley's Game 3 winner at 1:40 of overtime for a 4-3 victory and a 3-0 lead over Providence in the finals. The center later became head coach of the San Jose Sharks and also the Kentucky Thoroughblades, a fierce Hershey rival in the 1990s. (Hershey Bears.)

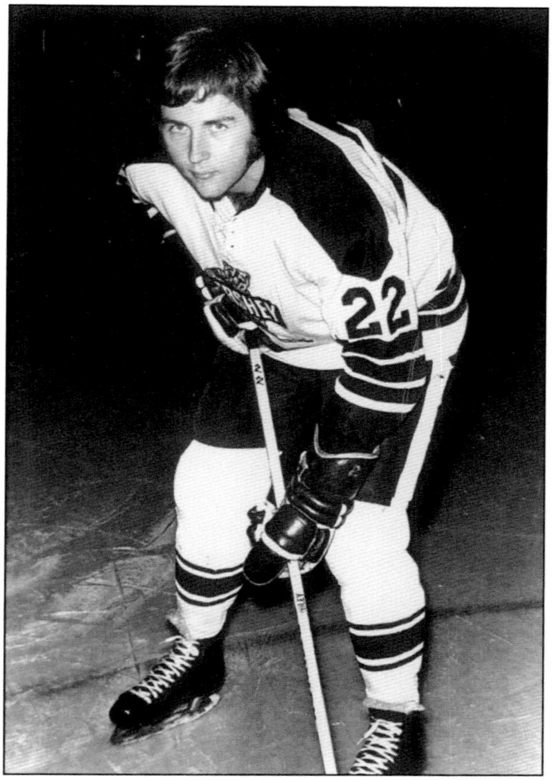

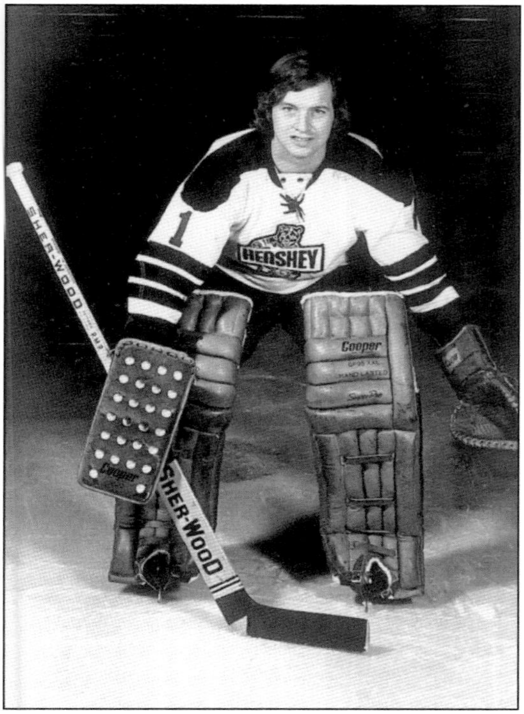

On a Roll. The 1973–1974 Bears lost just two of their final 14 regular-season games. They kept rolling in the playoffs, beating Cincinnati 4-1, Baltimore 4-0, and Providence 4-1 and winning 10 straight during one playoff stretch. Hershey clinched the championship on May 8, 1974, with a 4-3 Game 5 victory preserved by late acrobatic saves from goalie Bob Johnson (left). A crowd of 8,703, a record for playoff games at home, jammed Hersheypark Arena. (Hershey Bears.)

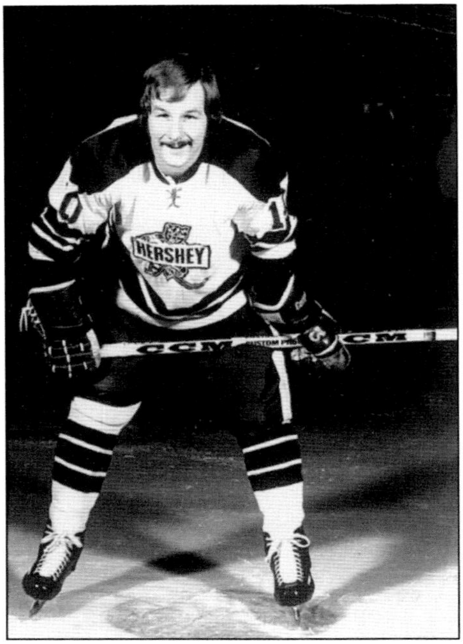

Miracle Goal. Hershey led 3-2 in the third period of Game 5 when Don Seiling (left) scored a stunning unassisted goal at 6:56. Stealing the puck at mid-ice, the left winger fired a breakaway shot that Reds goalie Peter McDuffe kicked to the corner. But the "Scooter" pounced on his own rebound, shooting a 20-footer from a near-horizontal angle that deflected off McDuffe's leg and into the net to send the standing-room crowd into a frenzy. (Hershey Bears.)

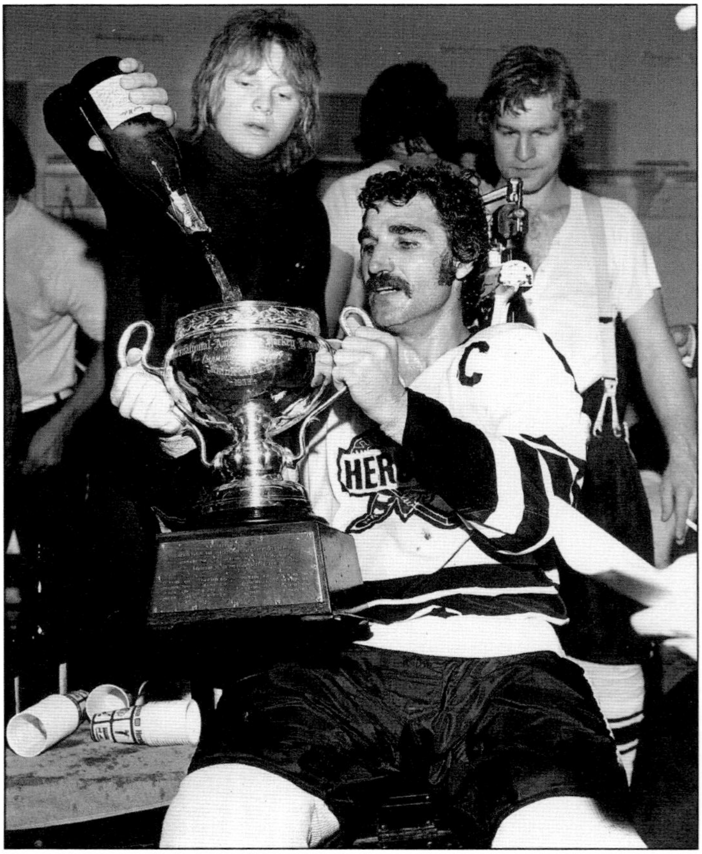

A Quenched Captain. Great defenseman Ralph Keller drinks from the Calder Cup for the second time. Organist Mitch Grand played "The Impossible Dream" in the final moments of the Game 5 clincher. The most poignant moment of the celebration came when Keller, who had played his last game after announcing his retirement, was hoisted on the shoulders of his teammates. Holding the Cup in one hand, he waved to the cheering crowd with the other. (Hershey Bears.)

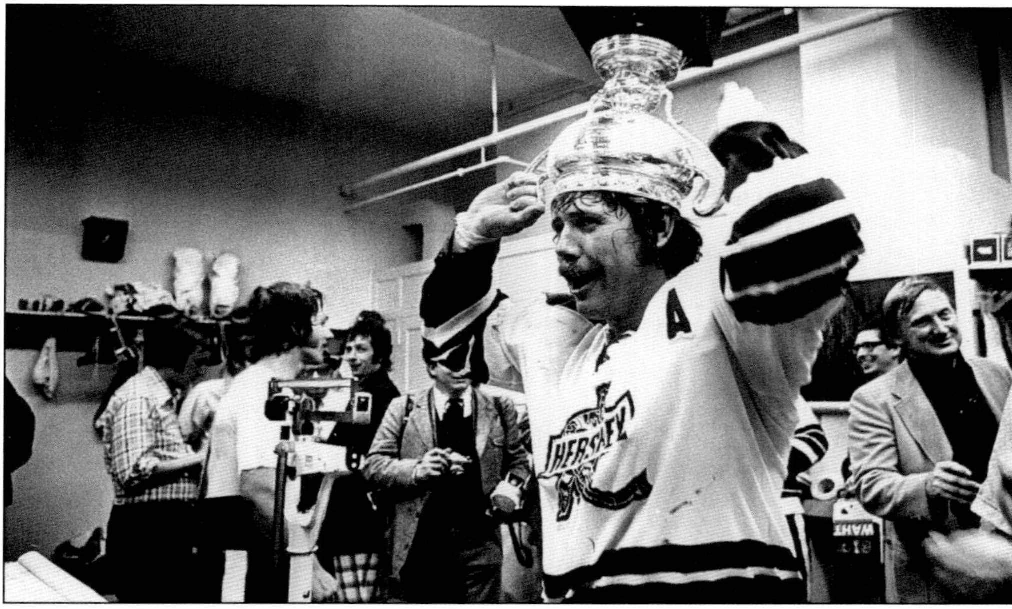

CROWNING GLORY. Alternate captain Robin Burns enjoys a moment with the cup. The Bears won 12 of 14 playoff games, coming from behind in 9 of them, and went 8-0 at home. The top line of Jim Wiley, Hank Nowak, and Jim Pearson produced 23 points in the finals against Providence. Chuck Hamilton (wearing plaid pants in the background to the left of Burns's right arm) led the Bears back to the finals in the 1975–1976 season, but they lost to Nova Scotia 4-1. During a five-plus-season run, Hamilton compiled a 187-199-52 record, second only to Frank Mathers in wins and games coached. (Hershey Bears.)

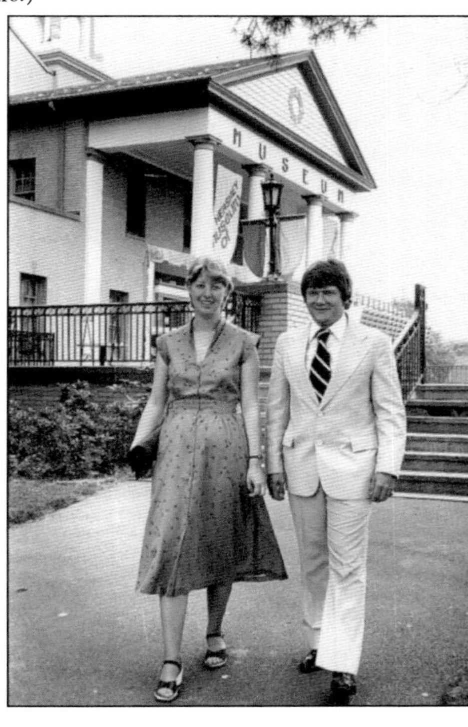

A SHORT REIGN. Gary Green (right with wife, Sharon, outside Hershey Museum on July 10, 1979) replaced Fred Stanfield as Hershey's head coach in 1979. He spent only 14 games behind the bench before being promoted to replace Dan Belisle as head coach of the Washington Capitals at age 26. Green, the 1978–1979 Ontario Hockey League (OHL) Coach of the Year with Peterborough, was himself replaced as Caps head coach in 1981 by another Bears coach, Bryan Murray (1980–1981). (Peter R. Rekus/*Patriot-News*.)

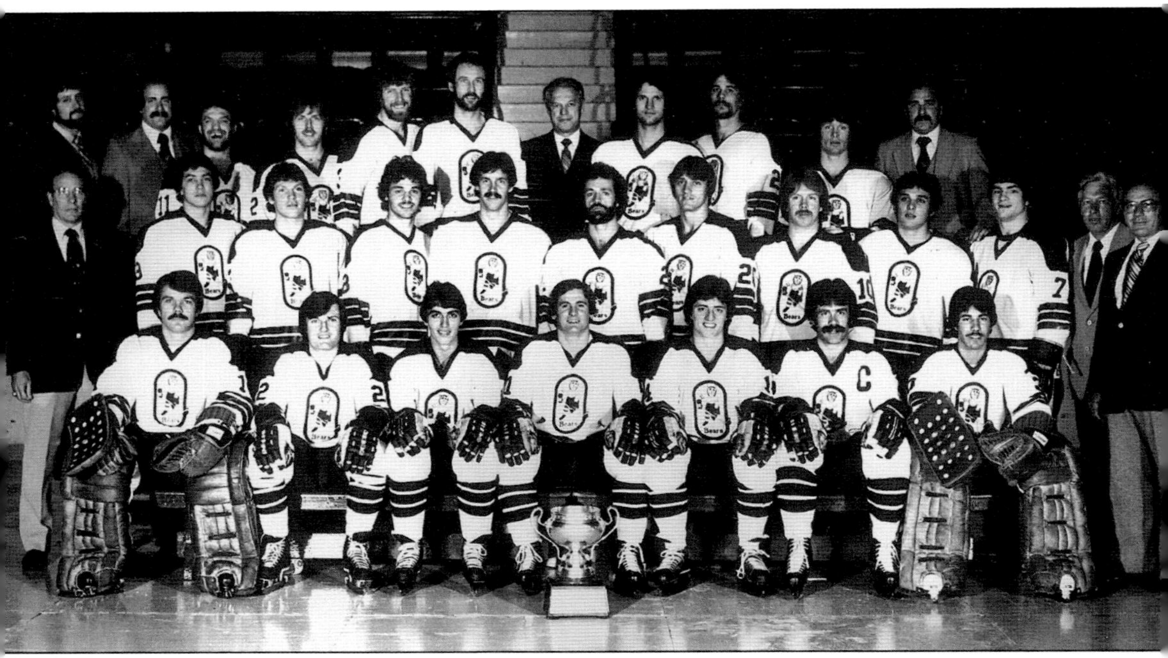

The 1979–1980 Calder Cup Champions. The 1979–1980 Calder Cup champions are shown here. They are, from left to right, as follows: (front row) Gary Inness, Ron Lalonde, Claude Noel, player-coach Doug Gibson, Tony Cassolato, Bob Bilodeau, and Dave Parro; (middle row) HERCO chairman Edward Book, Jim McTaggert, Greg Theberge, Lou Franceschetti, Harvey Pocza, Bob Girard, Tim Coulis, Cam MacGregor, Errol Rausse, Jay Johnston, HERCO vice president J. Bruce McKinney, and HERCO president Ken Hatt; (back row) broadcaster J.D. Mathers, trainer Bob Trenn, Gary Rissling, Eddy Godin, Roger Lemelin, Ray McKay, president-general manager Frank Mathers, Steve Clippingdale, Randy Stover, Mike Haworth, and assistant trainer Chuck Trenn. In the Calder Cup finals, the Bears and New Brunswick Hawks played Game 5 on May 16, 1980, at New Brunswick and flew a special charter immediately after the game to Hershey, where they played deciding Game 6 on May 17. (Hershey Bears.)

A Multi-Tasker. Center Doug Gibson assumed the role of player-coach when Gary Green left. Frank Mathers, general manager and president, became his assistant coach. Hershey went 35-39-6 for 76 points during the regular season but upset New Haven (101 points) and New Brunswick (96 points) en route to the Calder Cup. Gibson, AHL MVP with Rochester in 1975 and 1976, was named AHL Coach of the Year for the 1979–1980 season. He finished his playing career in Germany (1980–1983). (Hershey Bears.)

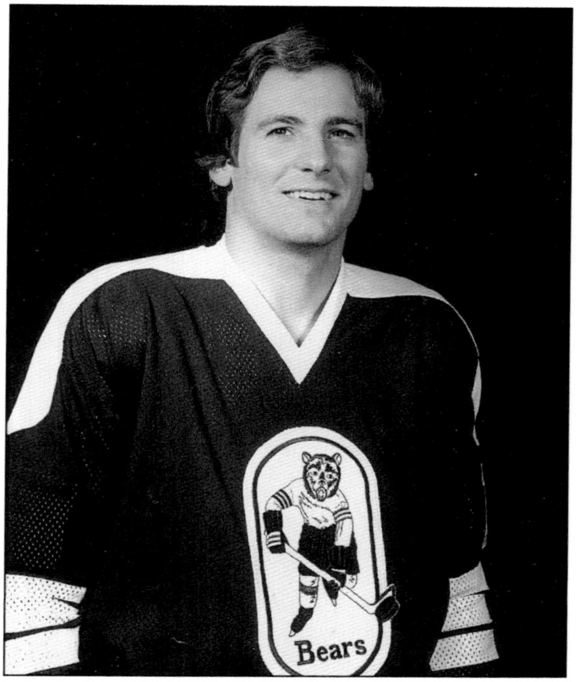

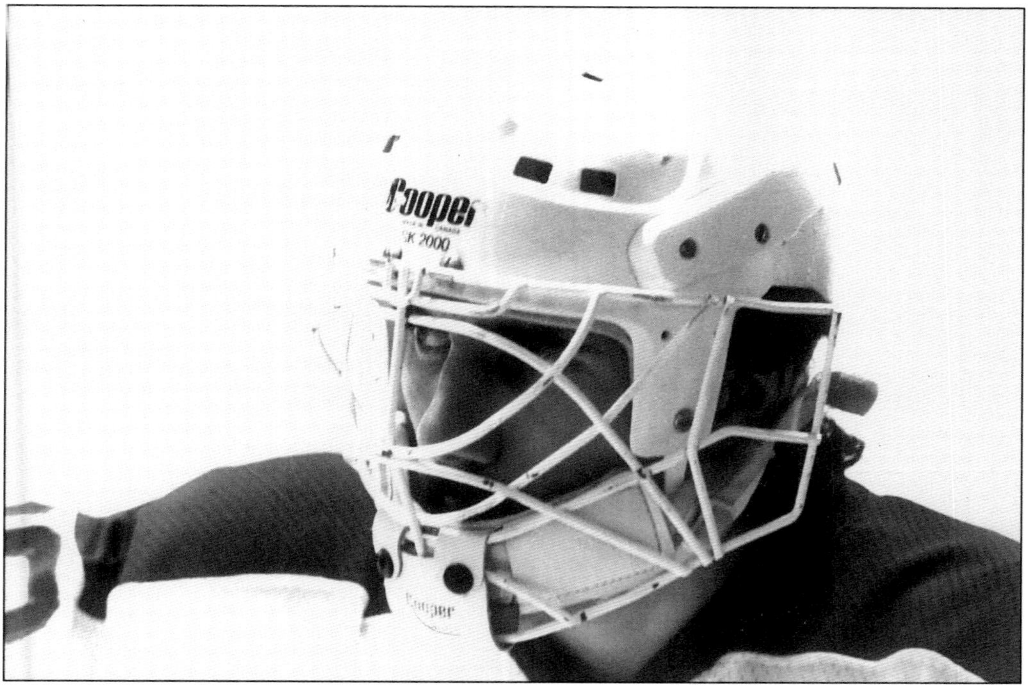

Crease Comfort. Dave Parro (above) and Gary Inness went a combined 12-3 in net during the 1980 playoffs. Future Bears coach Inness (1981–1984) went 6-1 and Parro went 6-3. The club hit stride in mid-March and went 9-4-2 in its final 15 regular-season games. Parro (1979–1981, 1982–1984) is tied with Phil Sauve for sixth in all-time games played by a Hershey goalie (157). (Hershey Bears.)

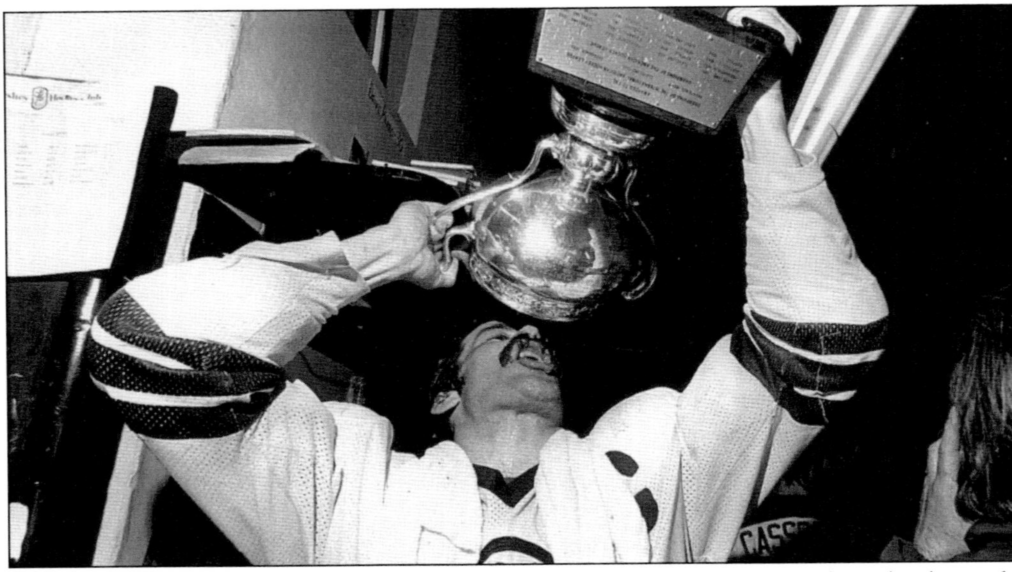

Bottom's Up. Bob Bilodeau, captain, drinks from the Calder Cup after clinching the championship with a 7-4 victory over New Brunswick. Hershey won two double-overtime games in the finals. Steve Clippingdale's goal at 10:01 of the second overtime gave Hershey a 5-4 Game 2 victory. Doug Gibson, who had 21 points in 16 playoff games, delivered a 3-2 victory in Game 4 at 7:44 of the second overtime. That triumph gave Hershey a 3-1 series lead. (Hershey Bears.)

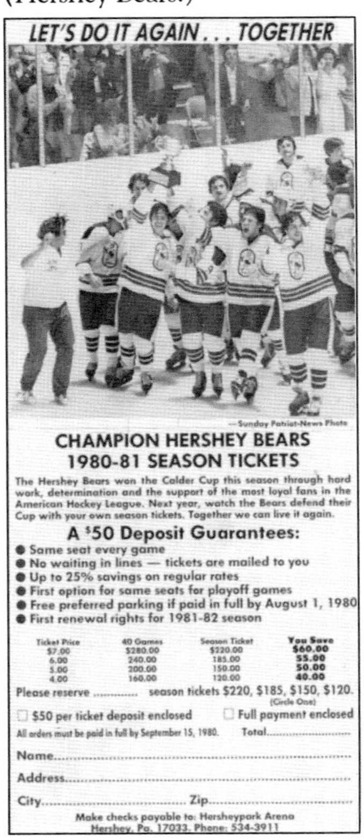

Sweet Home. Hershey, powered by Claude Noel's hat trick, overcame deficits of 1-0, 3-1, and 4-3 in Game 6 before a crowd of 6,745. The last time the Bears won the Calder Cup at home was in 1980. They also won it at Hersheypark Arena in 1947, 1959, 1969, and 1974 and three times on the road in 1958, 1988, and 1997. The 1980 celebration was used in the club's 1980–1981 marketing campaign (left). (Hershey Bears.)

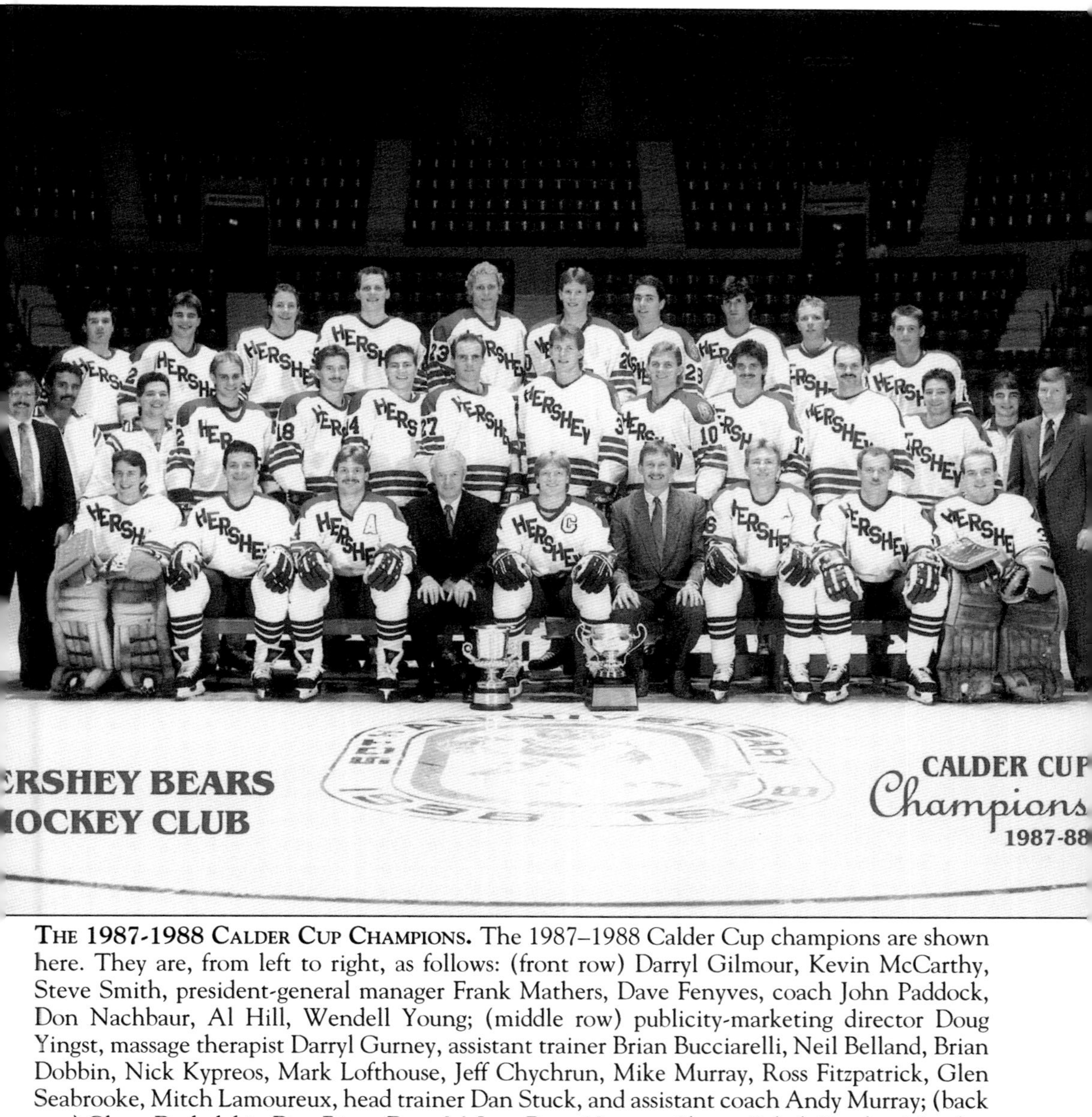

The 1987-1988 Calder Cup Champions. The 1987–1988 Calder Cup champions are shown here. They are, from left to right, as follows: (front row) Darryl Gilmour, Kevin McCarthy, Steve Smith, president-general manager Frank Mathers, Dave Fenyves, coach John Paddock, Don Nachbaur, Al Hill, Wendell Young; (middle row) publicity-marketing director Doug Yingst, massage therapist Darryl Gurney, assistant trainer Brian Bucciarelli, Neil Belland, Brian Dobbin, Nick Kypreos, Mark Lofthouse, Jeff Chychrun, Mike Murray, Ross Fitzpatrick, Glen Seabrooke, Mitch Lamoureux, head trainer Dan Stuck, and assistant coach Andy Murray; (back row) Cleon Daskalakis, Don Biggs, Dave McLay, Dave Hanson, Shawn Sabol, Gordon Murphy, John Stevens, Magnus Roupe, Kevin Maxwell, and Ray Allison. John Stevens went on to win Calder Cups with Springfield (1991) and Philadelphia (1998) before succeeding Bill Barber as head coach of the Phantoms in 2000. (Hershey Bears.)

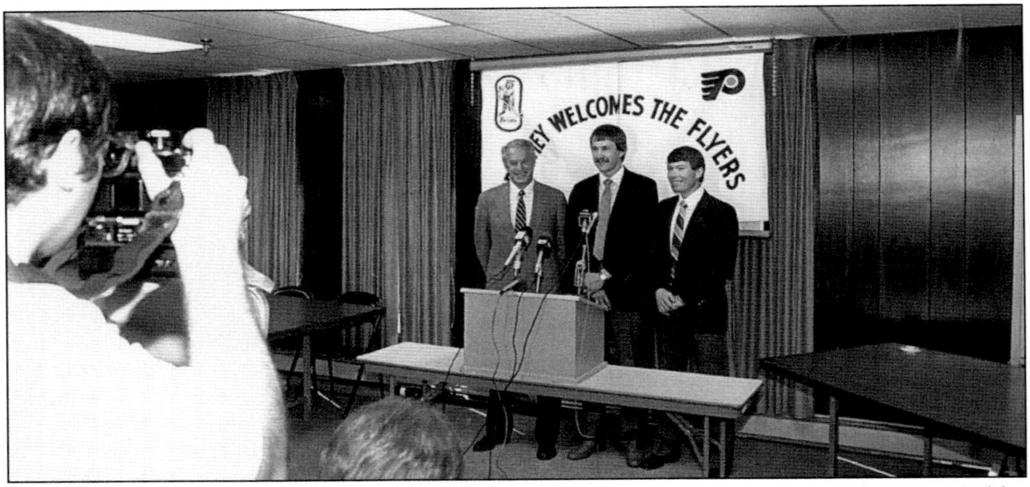

A TALL TASK. On June 26, 1985, John Paddock (center), an NHL veteran who won Calder Cups as a player in Maine in 1978 and 1979, was introduced as Hershey's head coach by Frank Mathers (left) and Philadelphia Flyers general manager Bobby Clarke (right). The greatest four-year regular-season run in Bears history ensued. Paddock, who averaged 45.3 victories, is the only Bears coach to win 40 or more games every season in Hershey. (Barry Ford/Hershey Bears.)

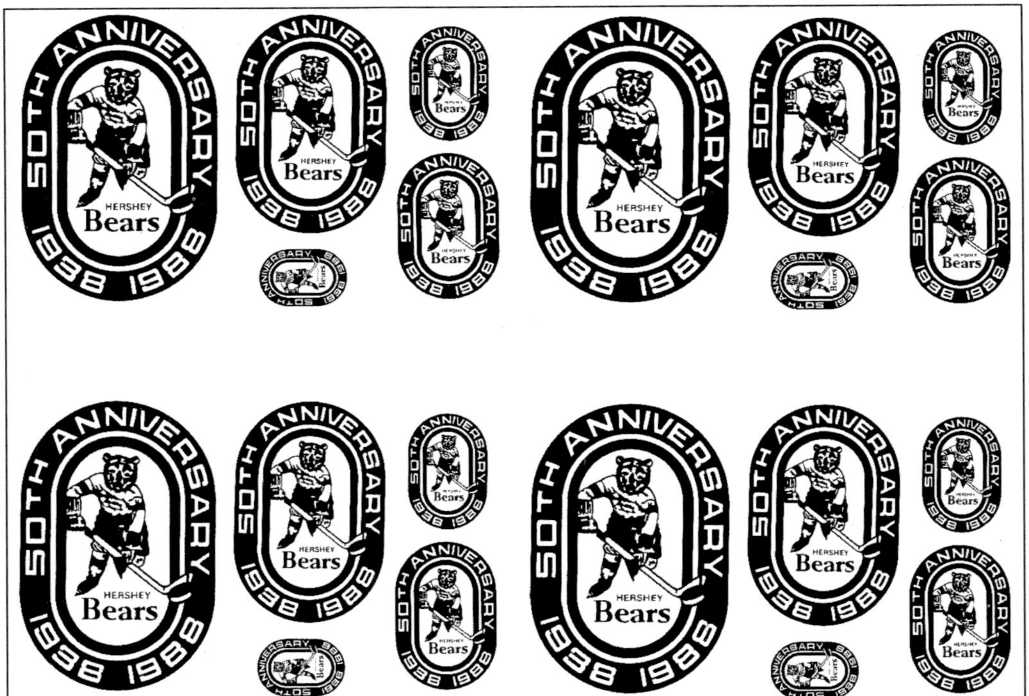

THE BEARS' GOLDEN ANNIVERSARY. Hershey celebrated its 50th anniversary season in the AHL during the 1987–1988 season by winning a club-record 50 games. The Bears went 50-25-3-2 for 105 points to place first in the Southern Division and the league. Mitch Lamoureux (87 points) led a balanced attack that featured five players with more than 70 points and produced a league-high 343 goals. Wendell Young (33-15-1, 2.77 GAA) was named the AHL's outstanding goalie. (Hershey Bears.)

Championship Captain Dave Fenyves. Dave Fenyves is the only player in AHL history to captain two different teams to the Calder Cup in back-to-back years. In the 1986–1987 season, Fenyves and the Rochester Americans won the Cup. The following season, after moving from the Buffalo organization to Philadelphia, Fenyves tasted from the cup again. Fenyves (1987–1993) ranks third in all-time scoring by Hershey defensemen (217 points in 359 games). (Hershey Bears.)

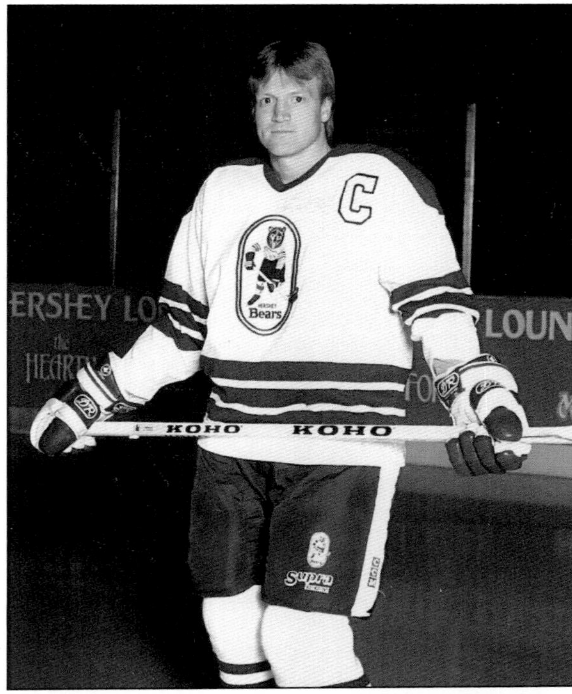

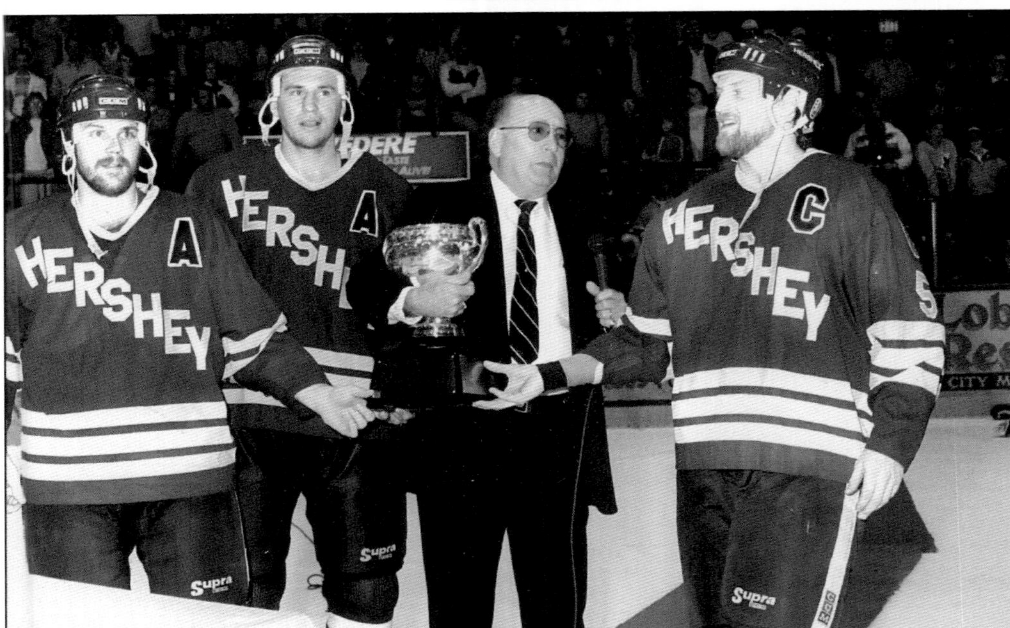

An Amazing 12-0 Playoff Run. Steve Smith (far left), Don Nachbaur (second from the left), and Dave Fenyves (far right) are presented the Calder Cup by Jack Butterfield after beating host Fredericton 4-2 in Game 4 on May 12, 1988. The triumph completed an unprecedented 12-0 playoff run. Hershey swept Binghamton, Adirondack, and Fredericton to become the first team in professional hockey history to go unbeaten in three best-of-seven series en route to a title. (Dorothy Scott/Hershey Bears.)

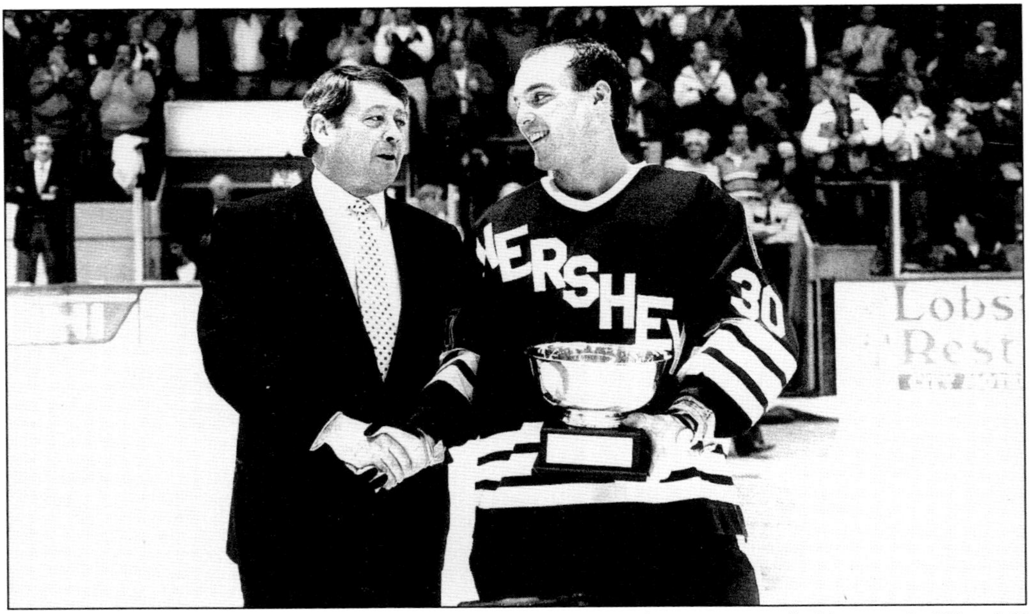

CUP COLLECTOR WENDELL YOUNG. AHL executive Gordie Anziano (left) awards Wendell Young the Jack Butterfield Trophy as playoff MVP. Young went 12-0 and allowed just 2.33 goals per game. The goalie won all four of North America's major hockey championships: the Memorial Cup (Kitchener Rangers), the Calder Cup (Hershey), the Stanley Cup (Pittsburgh Penguins), and the Turner Cup (Chicago Wolves). (Dorothy Scott/Hershey Bears.)

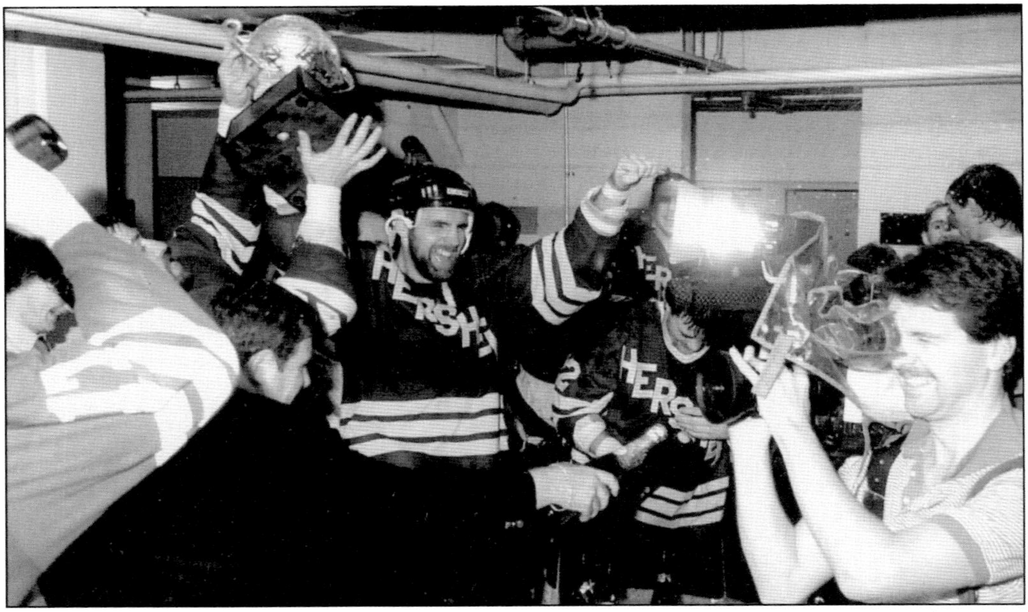

A BUBBLY SHOWER. Champagne flows in Hershey's locker room in Fredericton. The Bears outscored the Express, which finished the regular season with 95 points and led the AHL with 370 goals, 18-5 in the finals. During the playoffs, Hershey outscored its foes 60-28. The Bears went 3-0 in overtime and won every regulation game by at least two goals. The celebration continued back home in Hershey with a victory parade. (Hershey Bears.)

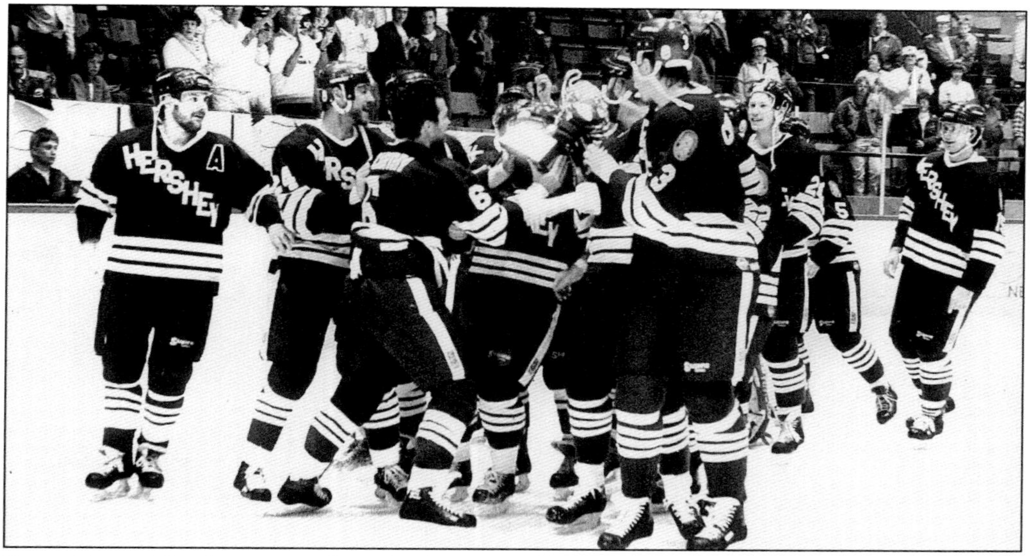

Road Rave. The Bears won their final two regular-season games, which means they finished the 1987–1988 season with a 14-0 run. Hershey also won its 1988–1989 season opener against Rochester, giving it 15 straight wins in games of consequence. The Bears also won their first two playoff games in 1989 against Utica to stretch their playoff streak to 14 straight, which stands as the club postseason record. The regular-season record for consecutive wins is 10 (2001–2002). (Dorothy Scott/Hershey Bears.)

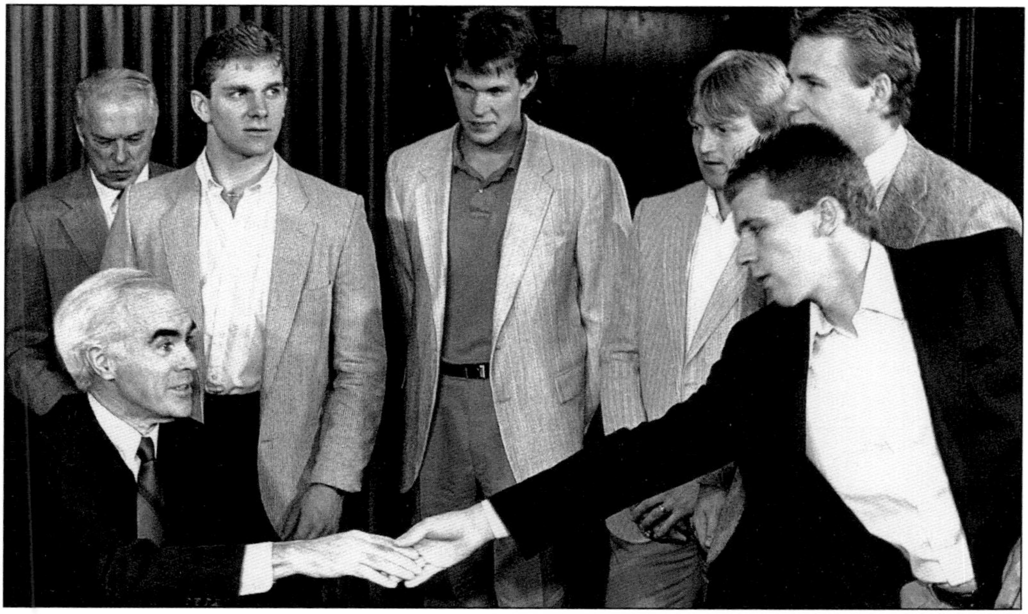

State Recognition. Gov. Robert P. Casey (seated) shakes hands with Kevin Maxwell on May 20, 1988, at a state reception for the Bears. From left to right in the background are Frank Mathers, Mike Murray, Jeff Chychrun, Dave Fenyves, and Don Nachbaur. Fenyves was named the AHL's Outstanding Defenseman for the 1987–1988 season and repeated the honor in the 1988–1989 season. John Paddock was named AHL Coach of the Year in 1988. (Peter R. Rekus/ *Patriot-News*.)

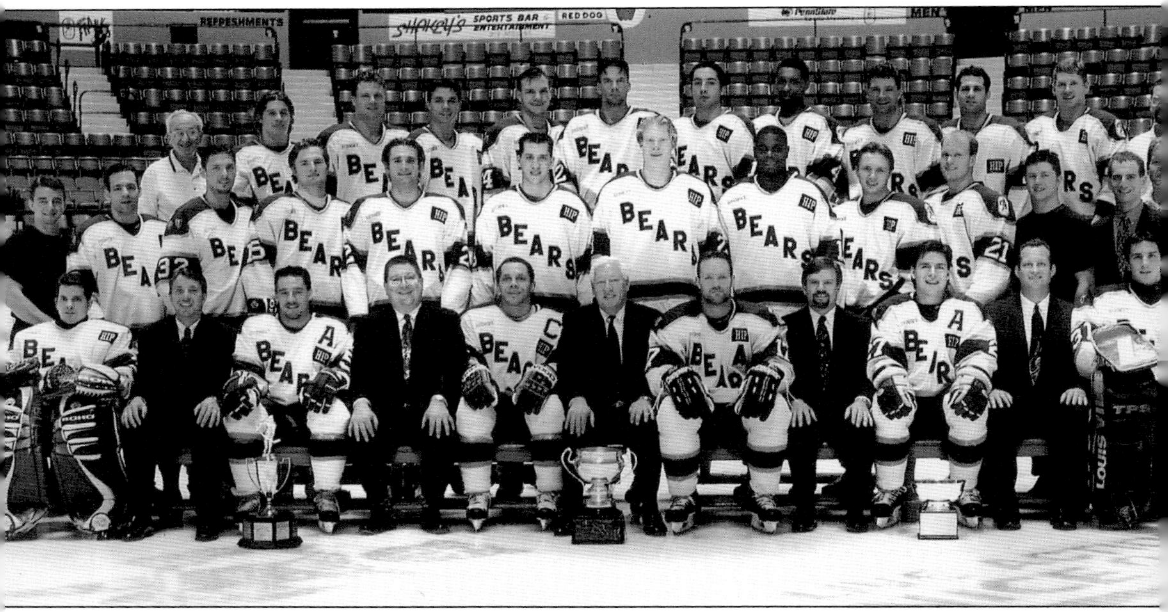

The 1996–1997 Calder Cup Champions. The 1996–1997 Calder Cup champions are shown here. They are, from left to right, as follows: (front row) J.F. Labbe, coach Bob Hartley, Eric Veilleux, president Jay Feaster, Mike McHugh, Hershey Entertainment chairman and chief executive officer J. Bruce McKinney, Doug Friedman, general manager Doug Yingst, Blair Atcheynum, assistant coach Bob McGill, and Marc Denis; (middle row) trainer Dan Stuck, Cory Banika, Sinuhe Wallinheimo, Josef Marha, Rich Brennan, Eric Messier, Wade Belak, Roger Maxwell, Pascal Trepanier, Steffon Walby, assistant trainer Brad Dibeler, broadcaster Dave Mishkin, and bus driver Roger Hull; (back row) attendant Bob Arehart, Rob Shearer, Bob Woods, Christian Matte, Kurt Miller, Dan Smith, Hugues Gervais, Paul Jerrard, Kevin MacDonald, Mike Hartman, Steve Lingren, and attendant Mike Mesaric. (Hershey Bears.)

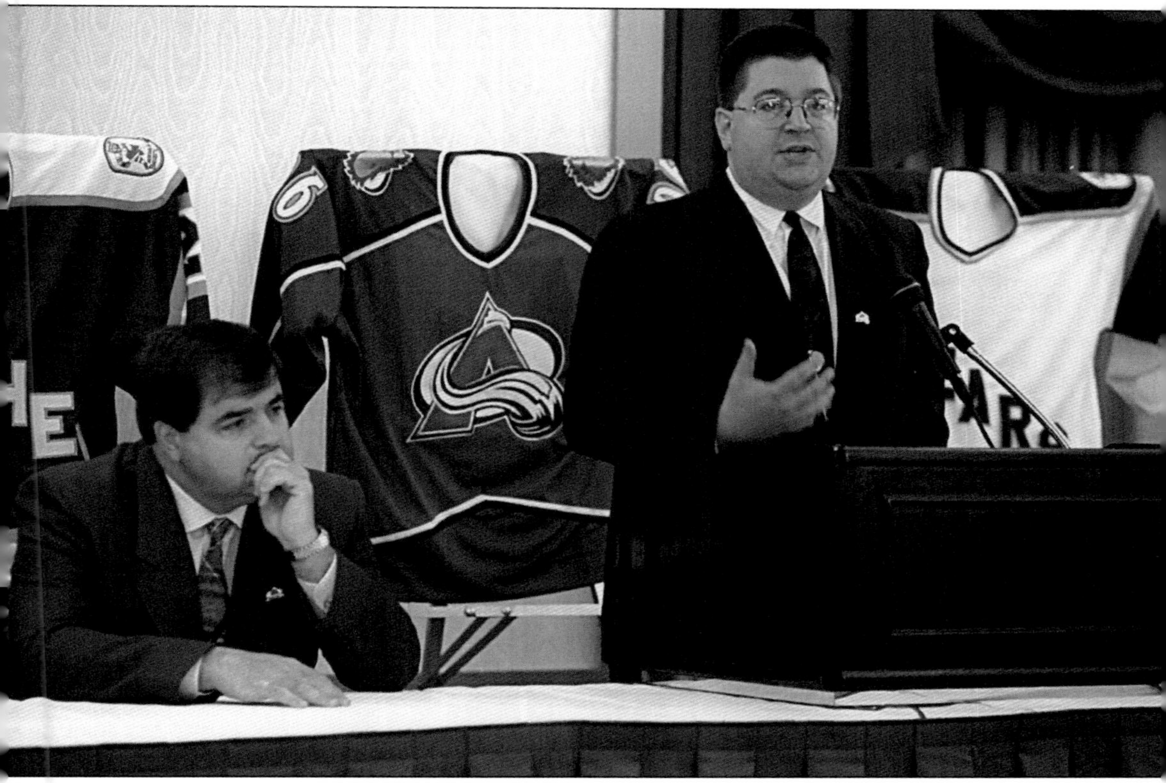

A New Era. Amid a sometimes-contentious breakup of a 12-year affiliation with Philadelphia, Bears president Jay Feaster (standing) announces a new five-year affiliation with the Colorado Avalanche at a Hotel Hershey press conference on March 21, 1996. Colorado general manager Pierre Lacroix (seated) would see the Avalanche, the relocated Quebec Nordiques, win the Stanley Cup in 1996 in their first season in Denver. The affiliation change meant that many of the former Cornwall Aces, who became intense Hershey rivals by eliminating the Bears from the playoffs in 1994 and 1995, now became Bears, and many former Bears became heated rivals when the Flyers debuted their own AHL club, the Philadelphia Phantoms, at the Spectrum for the 1996–1997 season. Bob Hartley, who fans disliked while he was in Cornwall, became beloved as Hershey's new head coach, while former coach Bill Barber became a Hershey boo bird target. (Peter R. Rekus/*Patriot-News*.)

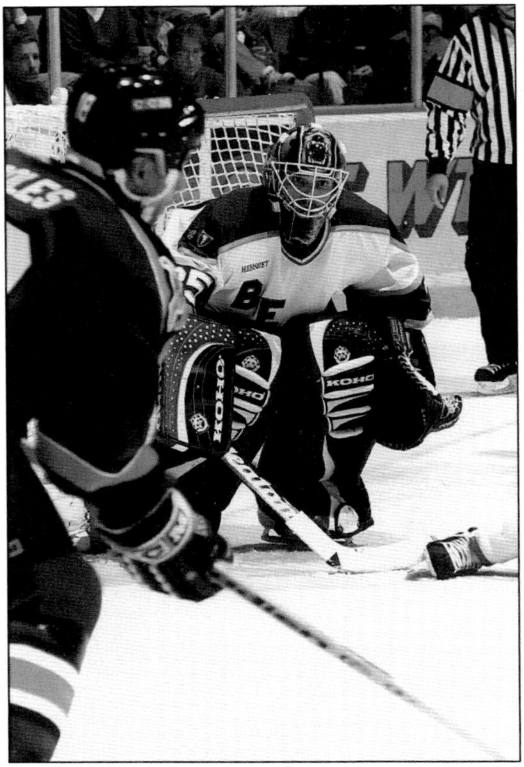

A Net Advantage. J.F. Labbe (eyeing a Bruce Coles chance) had arguably the greatest single season for a goalie in Hershey history. He went 34-22-9 and led the AHL with a 2.52 GAA. Labbe was named the AHL's MVP and its top goalie. In the playoffs, he made 102 saves in the final two games of a classic second-round series against Philadelphia. He also won the Calder Cup in 2000 with Hartford and ranks No. 9 in all-time AHL wins (202). (Bill Duh and Bruce Tyson/Just Sports.)

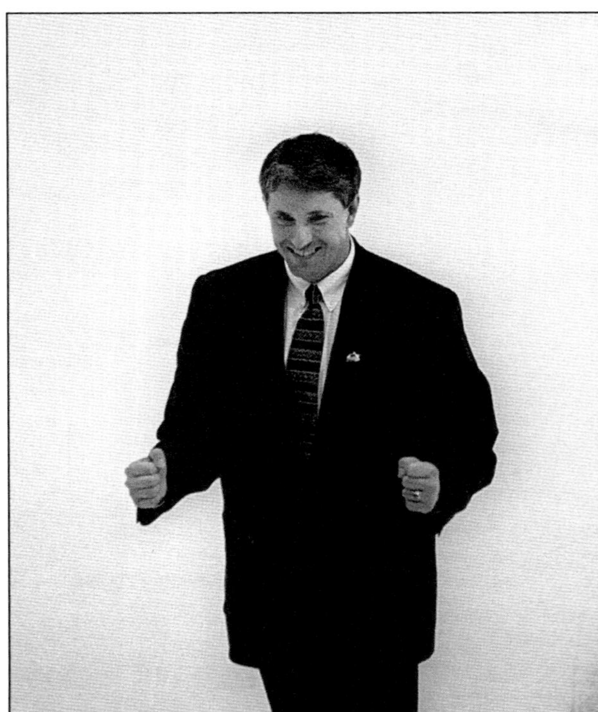

Uncle Bob. Bob Hartley, seen celebrating the Game 7 conference finals win over Springfield on May 31, 1997, led Hershey to a 43-22-5-10, 101 points, record. The Bears finished second to Philadelphia (111 points) in the Mid-Atlantic Division. It was the first 100-point season since 1988 and just the third in club history. Hartley directed a 23-game playoff marathon (the longest title march in AHL history) as the Bears faced elimination five times. (Gary Dwight Miller/*Patriot-News*.)

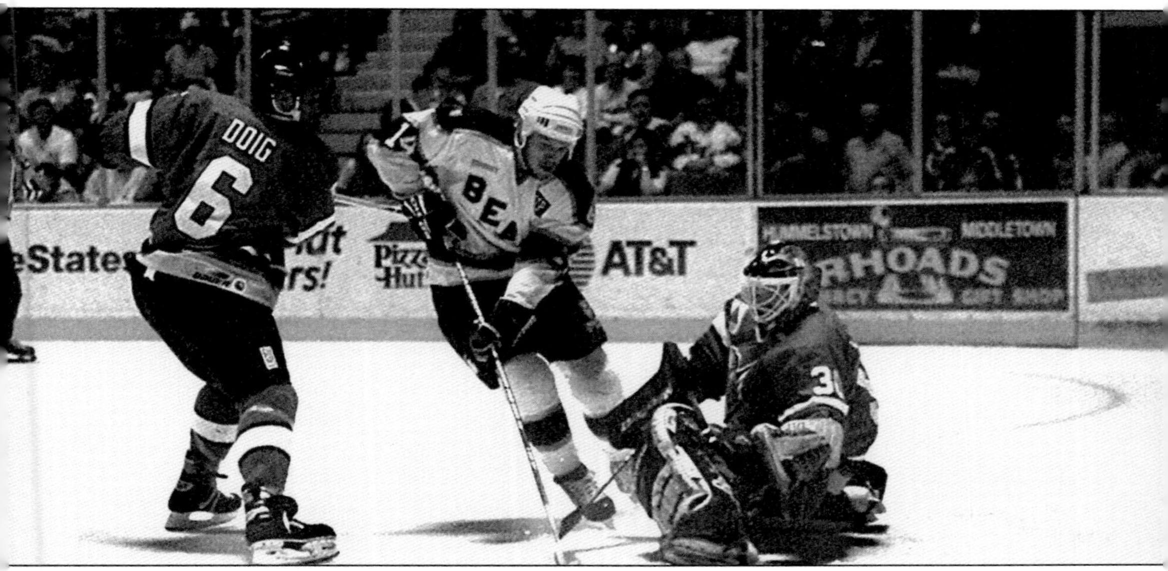

STRANGER THAN FICTION. Hershey, drained by the Philadelphia series, lost the first two games of the Southern Conference finals at home to Springfield. The Bears, perilously close to a 0-3 series deficit, trailed 3-1 in the third period of Game 3 in Springfield before tying it 3-3 on goals by Cory Banika and Steffon Walby. Walby's goal, with 40 seconds left in the third period, stood, even though Hershey's Eric Veilleux illegally cross-checked defenseman Brent Thompson into goalie Manny Legace. Springfield's Kevin Brown scored the apparent game-winner with 12 seconds left, but that goal was waved off when referee Denis Larue ruled that Reggie Savage's skate was illegally in Hershey's crease. When Mike McHugh won it 4-3 for Hershey at 2:53 into overtime, Legace (seen on the right in Game 2) snapped and slashed Larue, earning a 10-game suspension that set the stage for a Hershey series revival. Thompson became Hershey's captain in the 2002–2003 season. (Peter R. Rekus/*Patriot-News*.)

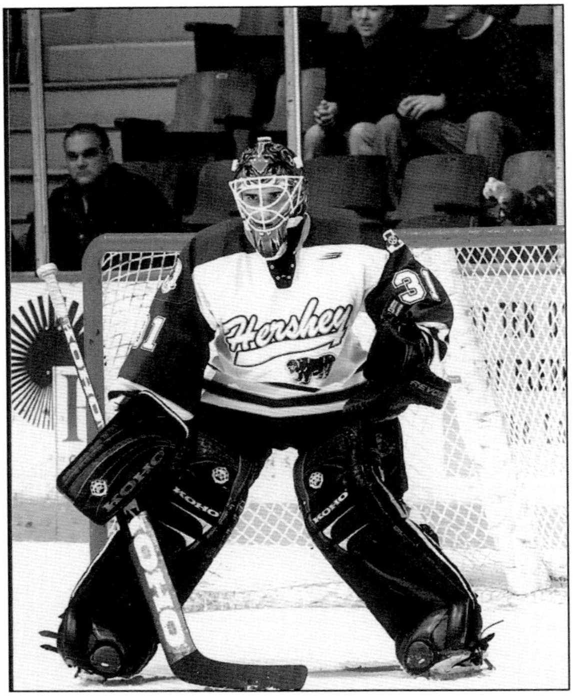

JUNIOR ACHIEVEMENT. J.F. Labbe, overcome by the flu, had to leave Game 7 against Springfield at 8:44 of the first period. Newly arrived junior eligible Marc Denis, age 19, a first-round pick with just 16 seconds of professional experience, stepped in and stopped 21 of 22 shots in a 3-1 win that advanced Hershey to the finals against Hamilton. Denis (left) set the NHL single-season record for minutes played in the 2002–2003 season (4,511 for Columbus). (Bill Duh and Bruce Tyson/Just Sports.)

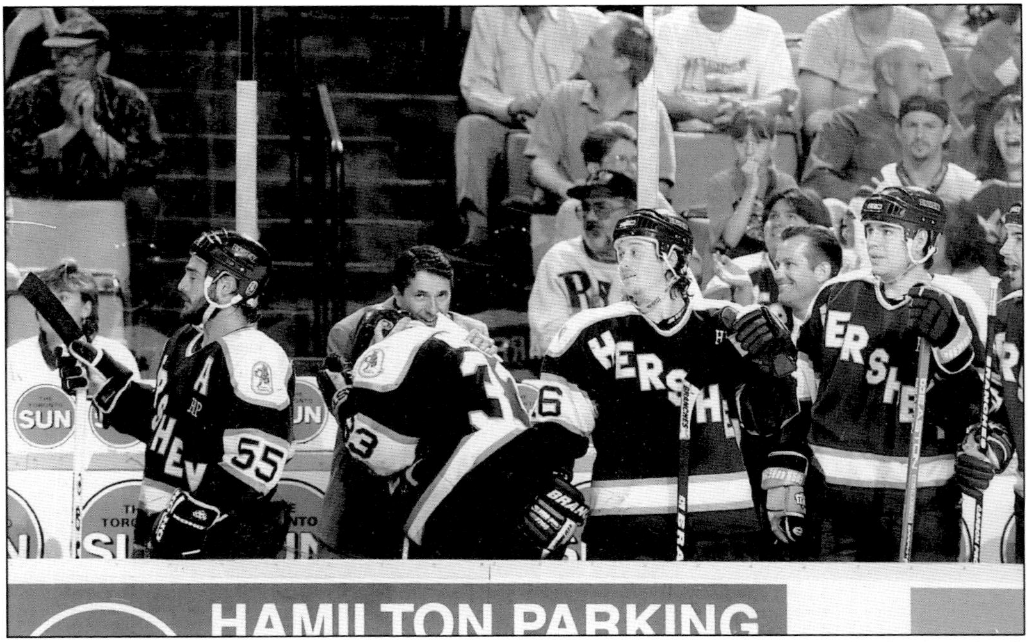

BULLDOG EFFORT. The Calder Cup finals against Hamilton could not match the back-to-back seven-game epics against Philadelphia and Springfield for drama. Hershey won the first two games at home and clinched the championship in five. Bob Hartley congratulates Mike McHugh during Game 5 (above). Christian Matte's goal at 4:40 of the second period broke a 1-1 tie and stood as the game-winner at Copps Coliseum. Josef Marha (22 points) led the AHL in playoff scoring. (Bill Duh and Bruce Tyson/Just Sports.)

Pure Joy. Captain Mike McHugh lifts the Calder Cup. McHugh, a veteran of just 20 NHL games with Minnesota and San Jose, had two overtime playoff winners and won the Jack Butterfield Award as playoff MVP. Winger McHugh and defenseman Paul Jerrard were the only two holdovers from the days of the Philadelphia affiliation. "We worked harder than any other team in the league," McHugh said. "For me, this is my Stanley Cup." (Michael Fernandez/*Patriot-News*.)

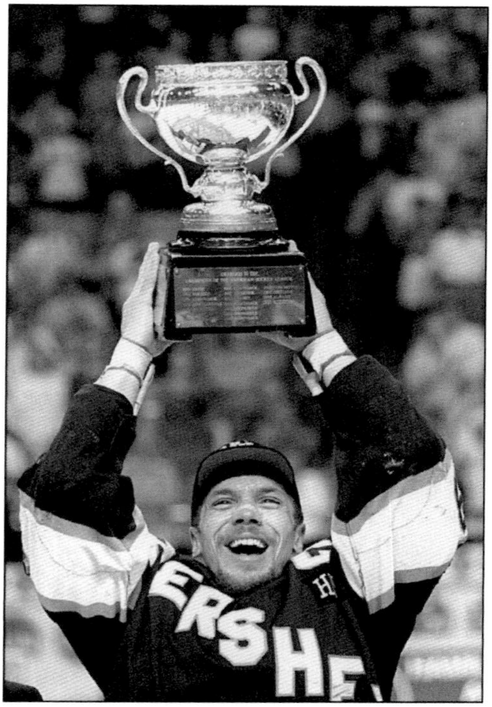

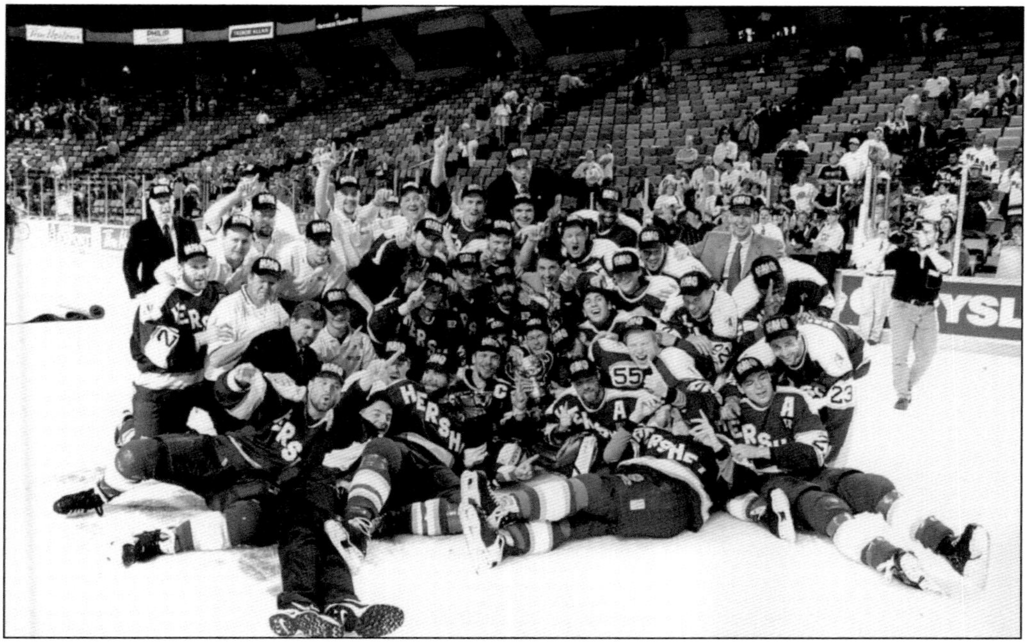

A Copped Cup. The Bears celebrate at Copps Coliseum on June 13, 1997. The date is the latest an AHL season has ever finished. The "HIP" emblem on the left front of the team jerseys was in honor of volunteer equipment manager Harry Hipple, who collapsed on the team bench at Hersheypark Arena and died of a heart attack at 74 before a morning skate on January 31, 1997. (Bill Duh and Bruce Tyson/Just Sports.)

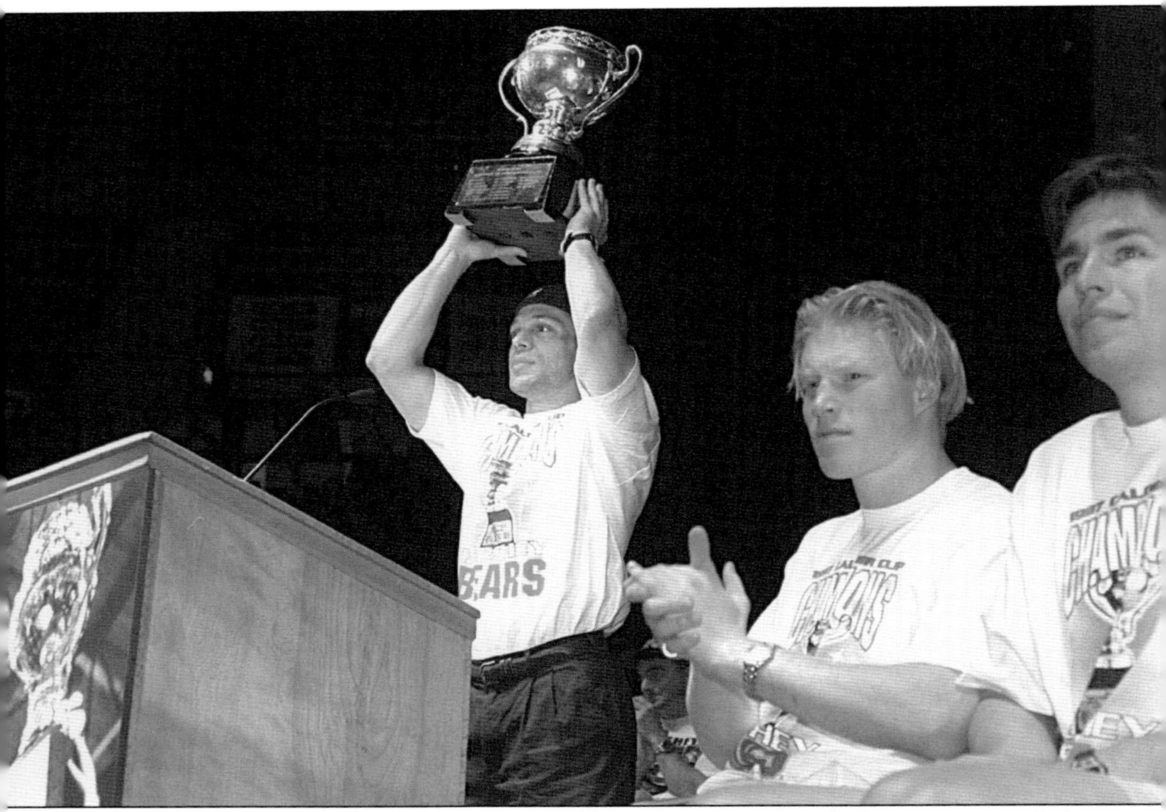

ATCH'S GAME. Mike McHugh raises the Calder Cup to the approval of a raucous crowd of more than 7,000 at a Hersheypark Arena victory rally on June 15, 1997, as Wade Belak (seated left) and Blair Atcheynum (seated right) watch. Atcheynum led Hershey with 42 regular-season goals, but his biggest score was the game-winner 42 seconds into triple overtime of Game 6 against Philadelphia. Hershey appeared finished after a 3-0 Game 5 loss in a feisty series in which the clubs set an AHL single-game playoff record with 340 combined penalty minutes in Game 2. Atcheynum's goal won Game 6 3-2 and forced Game 7, which Hershey won 3-2 at the Spectrum. Atcheynum suffered a broken ankle in Game 7 and did not return until Game 4 of the finals against Hamilton. When the Bears hung their Calder Cup banner on October 4, 1997, J.F. Labbe and Doug Friedman played for visiting Hamilton, which won 2-0 on a Labbe shutout. (Peter R. Rekus/*Patriot-News*.)

Four

Individual Recognition

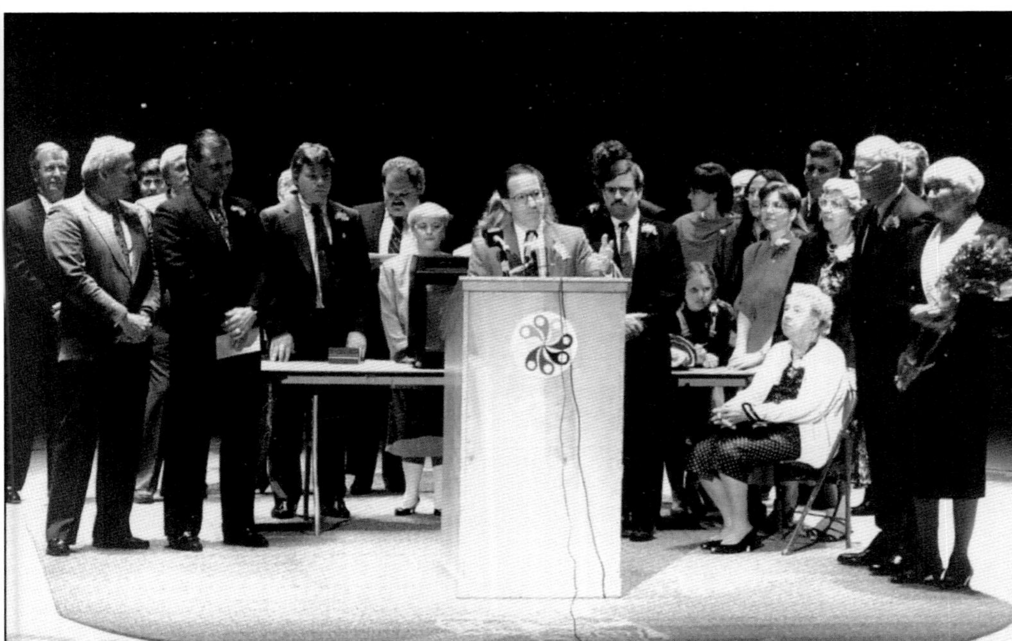

A Clutch and Grab Session. Virtuoso NHL broadcaster Mike Emrick (at the podium), an aficionado of Frank Mathers and Hershey hockey, served as master of ceremonies at Frank Mathers Night on March 9, 1991. No. 3 was retired in ceremonies highlighted by the presence of family, friends, and former players. Mathers's mother, May (seated), was in her 90s. Mathers, born March 29, 1924, in Winnipeg, Manitoba, originally wanted to be a dentist. (Hershey Bears.)

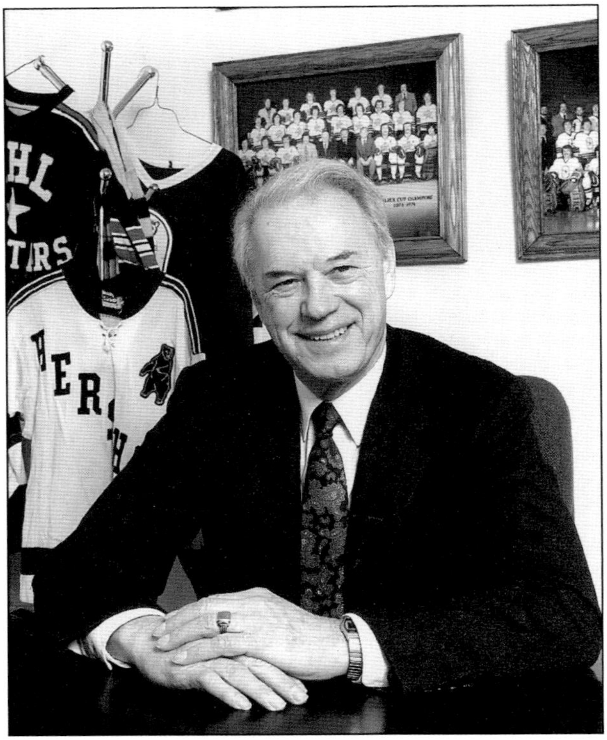

Greatness and Class. In an association that spanned from 1956 to 1991, Frank S. Mathers became the most towering figure in Bears history. He was part of six of the club's eight Calder Cups as either a player-coach, coach, or executive. In 1987, Mathers was awarded the prestigious Lester Patrick Trophy for outstanding service to hockey in the United States. In 1992, his legend was capped by induction into the Hockey Hall of Fame in the builder's category. (Hershey Bears.)

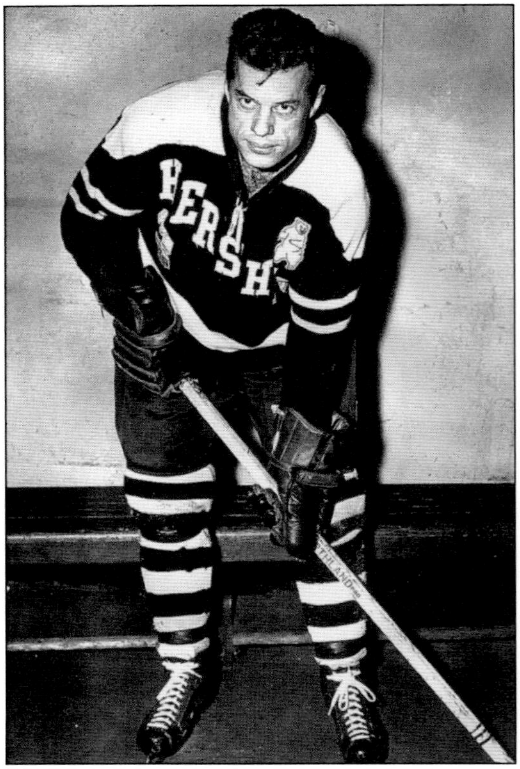

Mathers Moments. Frank Mathers played 23 career games with the Toronto Maple Leafs and also won two Calder Cups with Pittsburgh. He also played fullback in the Canadian Football League with Ottawa, Winnipeg (appearing in a Gray Cup title game), and Regina (while serving as a pilot with the Royal Canadian Air Force). In the 1961–1962 season, Mathers, twice named AHL Executive of the Year, added business manager to his titles when Baz Bastien returned to the revived Pittsburgh Hornets. (Hershey Bears.)

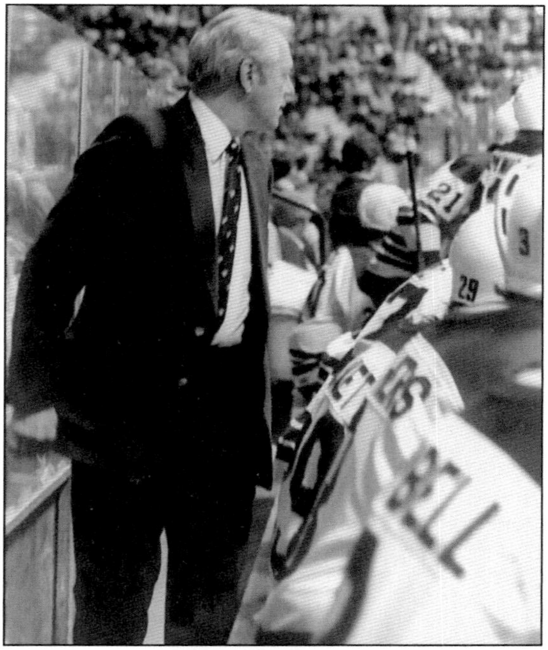

A BENCH ENCORE. Frank Mathers, who retired as a player after the 1961–1962 season, coached the Bears from 1956 to 1973. In the 1984–1985 season, he went back behind the bench (right) to coach 37 games on an interim basis after Gary Inness was fired. That brought his career coaching record in Hershey to 610-513-134. Mathers's club records for wins (610) and games coached (1,257) are considered unbreakable. Mathers finished below .500 just once (1959–1960) in 17 seasons. (Hershey Bears.)

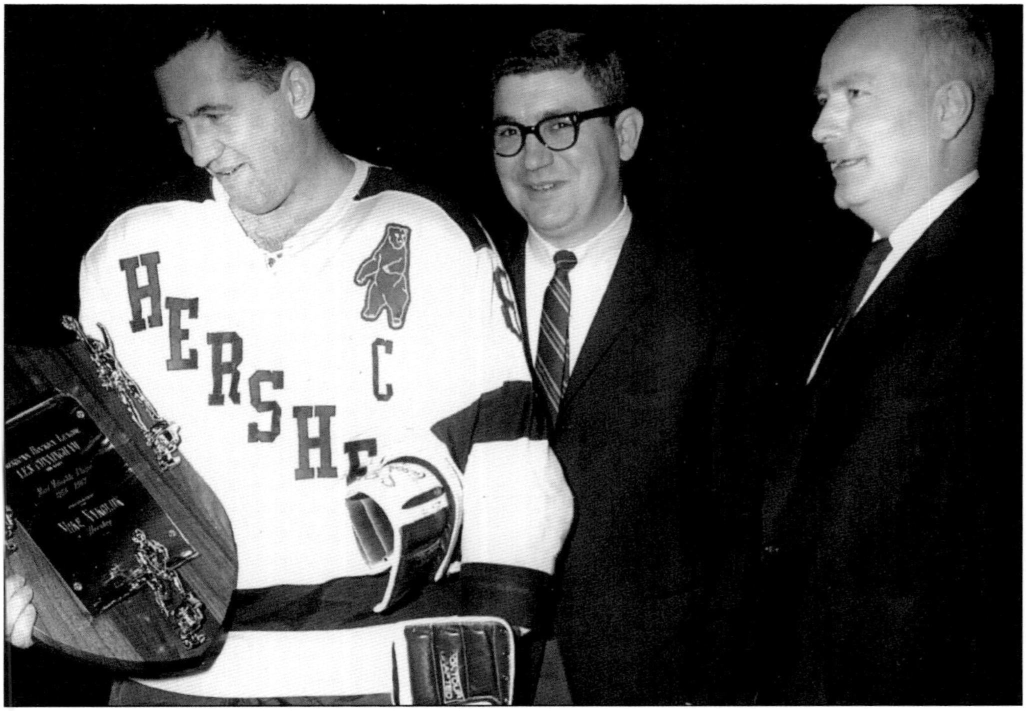

THE BIG BEAR. Center Mike Nykoluk (1958–1972), being presented with the Les Cunningham Award as 1966–1967 AHL MVP by Jack Button (middle) and Jack Butterfield (right), owns the club records for career points (808), assists (636), and games played (972). He is also near the top of the AHL record books for games played (No. 4 with 1,069), points (No. 6 with 881), playoff games (No. 3 with 112), and playoff assists (No. 2 with 62). (Hershey Bears.)

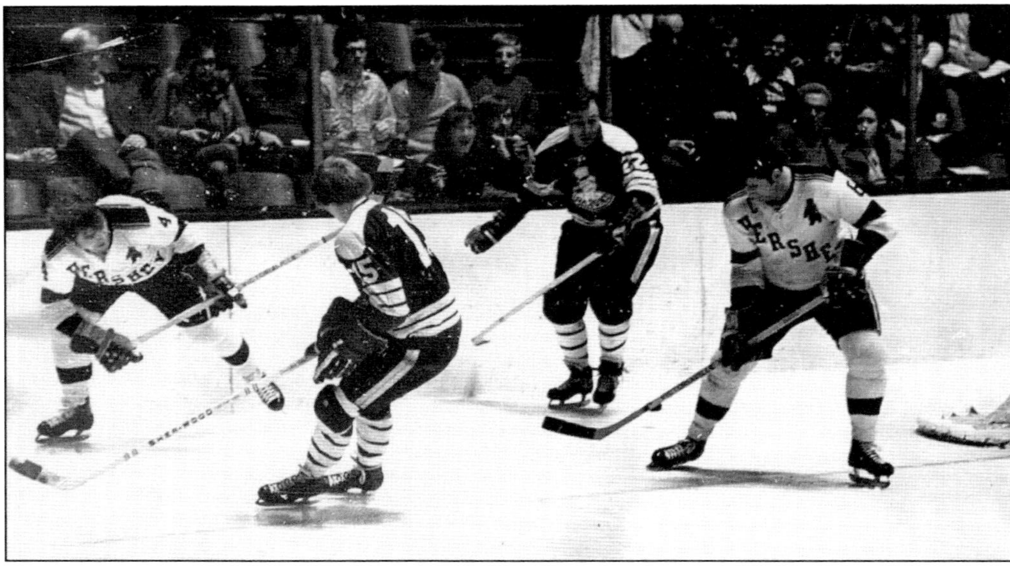

A POWERFUL PRESENCE. Mike Nykoluk (far right) scored 172 career regular-season goals and 13 playoff goals for Hershey. He ranks No. 1 in club history in playoff games (103), playoff points (73), and playoff assists (60). The two-time AHL All-Star, a veteran of 32 games with Toronto, retired after the 1971–1972 season. Nykoluk served as an assistant coach with the Philadelphia Flyers (1972–1978) and New York Rangers (1978–1980) and as Toronto's head coach (1981–1984). (Hershey Bears.)

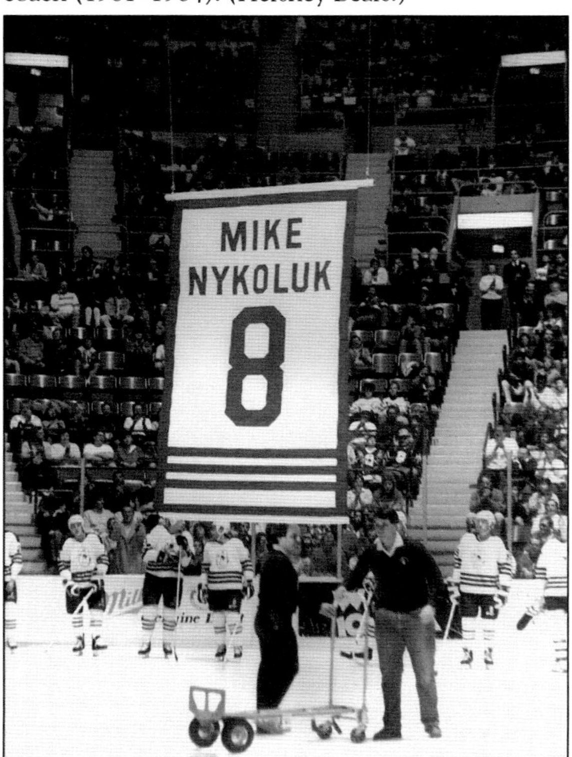

A DANGLING DIGIT. Mike Nykoluk's No. 8 was the first number retired in Hershey history. It was retired on March 29, 1972, before a game against Rochester that was the penultimate home game of Nykoluk's career. The club also staged a Mike Nykoluk Night on February 9, 1991, as an added honor. (Hershey Bears.)

ARNIE KULLMAN (1948–1960). Nobody wore hallowed hockey digit No. 9 longer in Hershey than Arnie Kullman. The center played 753 regular-season games for the Bears, second only to Mike Nykoluk. Kullman is No. 3 in career points (619), No. 2 in goals (253), and No. 4 in assists (376). Kullman, who played 13 career NHL games with Boston, led Hershey in scoring in the 1951–1952 and 1954–1955 seasons and holds the record for most career AHL All-Star Game assists (6). (Hershey Bears.)

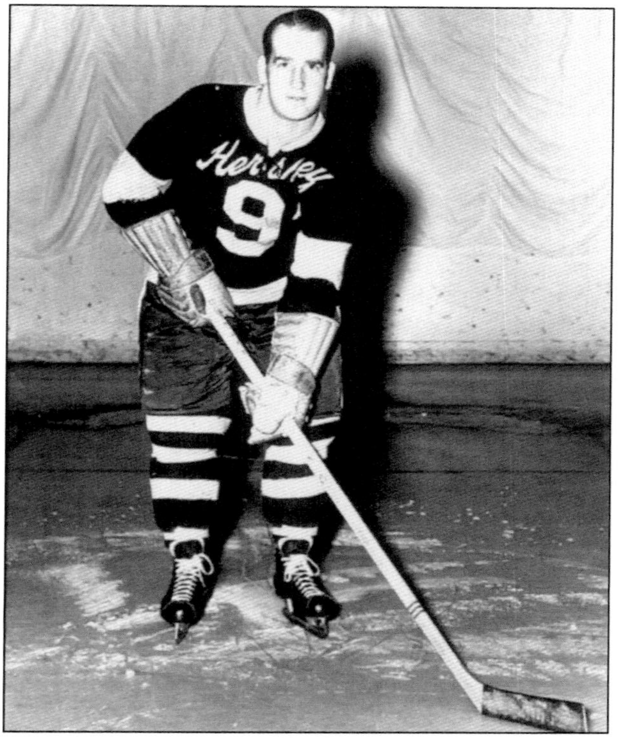

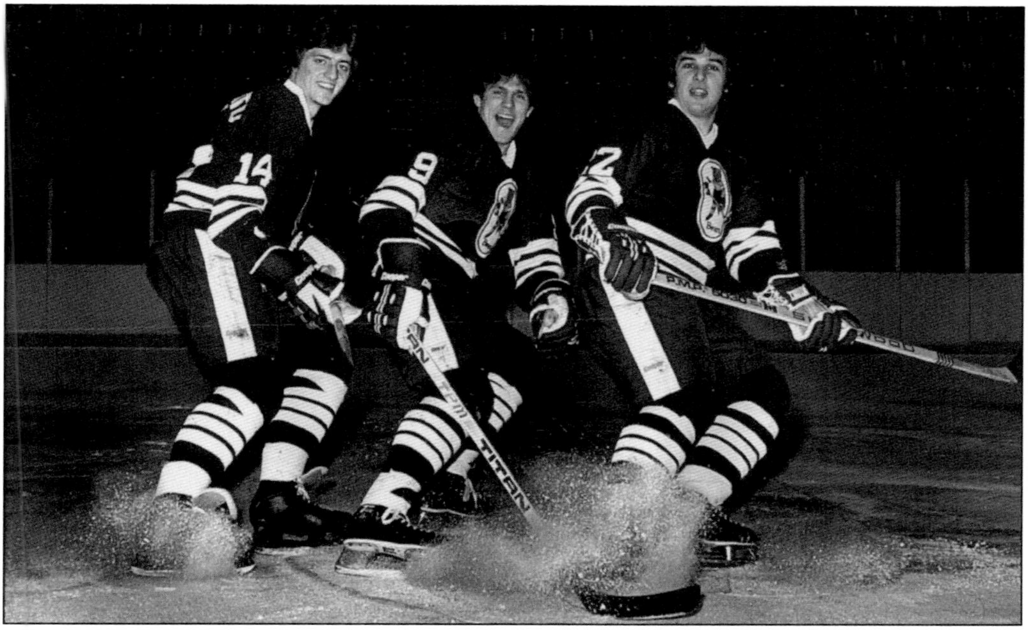

TIM TOOKEY (1980–1982, 1985–1987, 1989–1994). Tim Tookey (center), with Tony Cassolato (left) and Errol Rausse (right), generated the familiar shout of "Tooh-Key!" from fans with his scoring feats. In 529 career Hershey games, the center scored 693 points (No. 2 all-time), 251 goals (No. 3), and 442 assists (No. 2). Tookey's also third in all-time Hershey playoff scoring (52 points) and ranks fourth in AHL history in points (974). (Peter R. Rekus/Hershey Bears.)

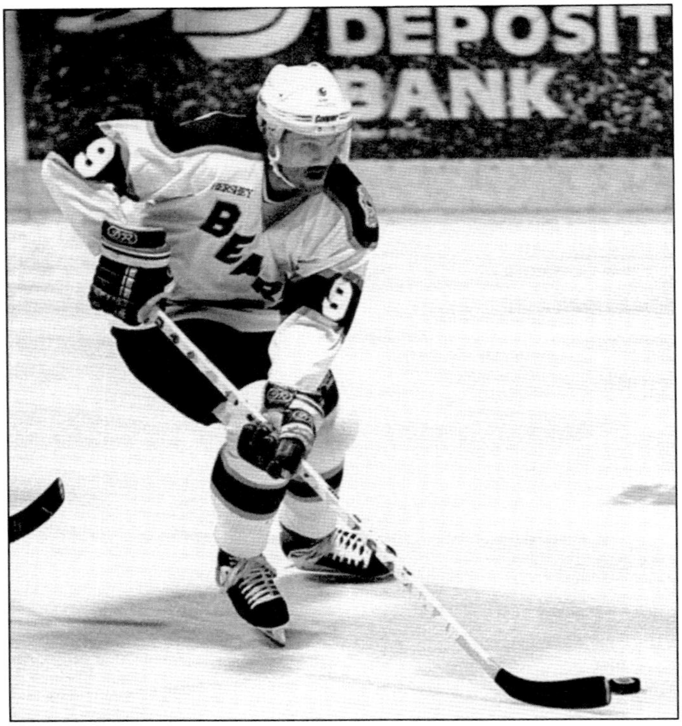

Triple Figures. Tim Tookey (left), Bill Sweeney, Bruce Boudreau, and Peter White are the only players in AHL history to score 100 points or more three times. Tookey holds the Hershey record for most points in a season (124 in 1986–1987). The three-time All-Star was AHL playoff MVP in the 1985–1986 season and AHL regular-season MVP and scoring champ in the 1986–1987 season. He won the Fred T. Hunt Memorial Award in the 1992–1993 season for sportsmanship and dedication. (Laura Mathews/*Patriot-News*.)

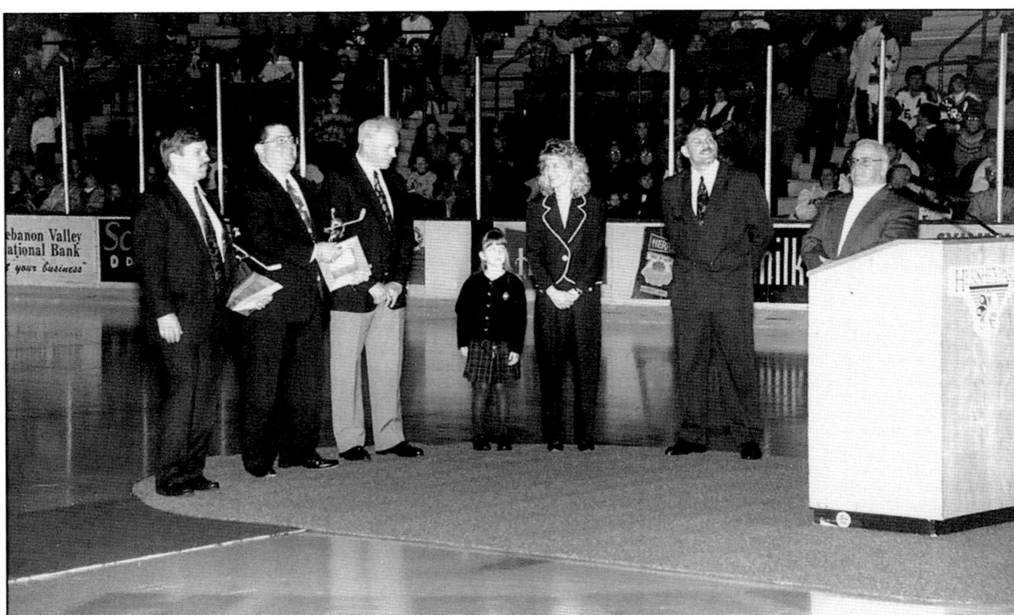

The Immortal No. 9. Arnie Kullman (far right) retired in 1960, the same year Tim Tookey (second from the right) was born. On December 6, 1997, they watched their No. 9 be retired at Hersheypark Arena. Tookey played 106 career NHL games for Washington, Quebec, Pittsburgh, Philadelphia, and Los Angeles. He also played for Fredericton, Baltimore, New Haven, and Providence in the AHL. (Hershey Bears.)

A Hat Trick. Willie Marshall, who played for Hershey from 1956 to 1963 during an AHL career that spanned from 1952 to 1972, celebrates a hat trick in November 1962. The center is the AHL's all-time leader in games played (1,205), points (1,375), goals (523), assists (852), playoff points (119), and playoff assists (71). In Hershey history, Marshall ranks No. 5 in points (570 in 439 games), No. 4 in goals (226), and No. 5 in assists (344). (Hershey Bears.)

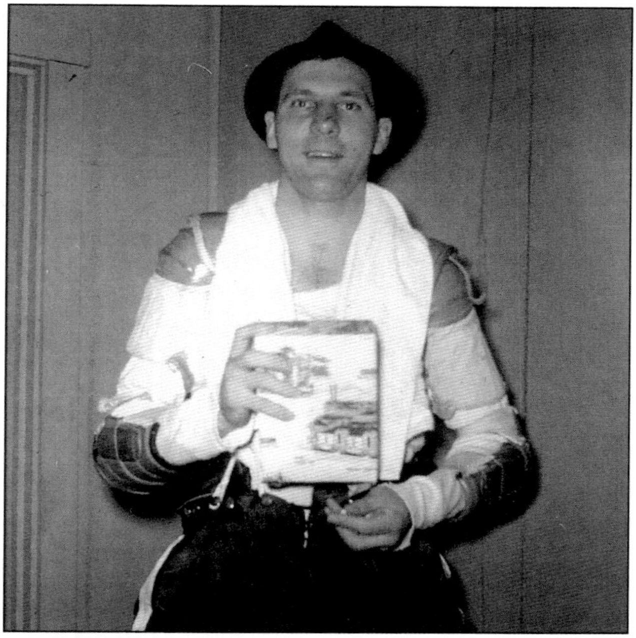

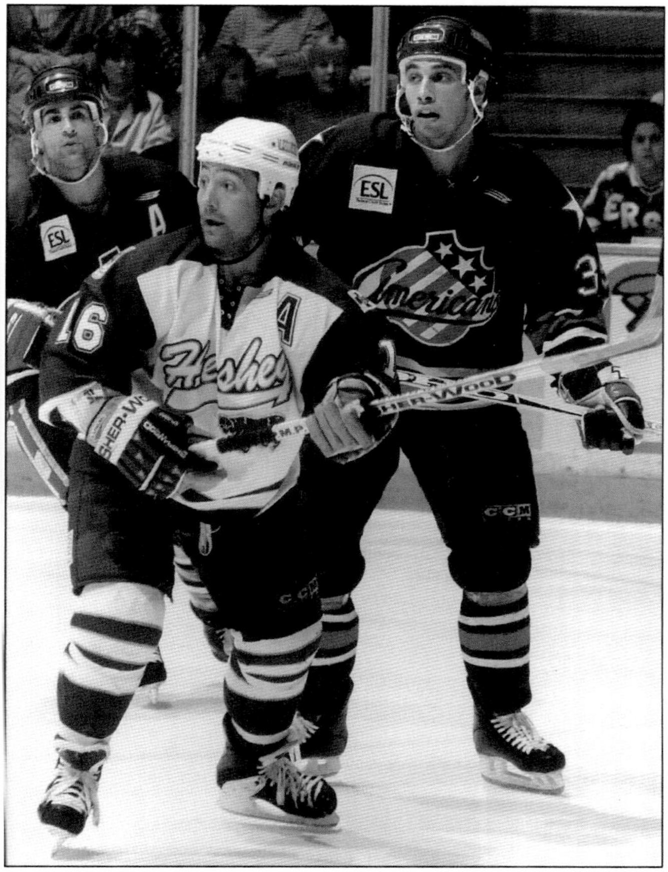

Mitch Lamoureux (1986–1989, 1993–1995, 1997–1999). Lamoureux, whose AHL career spanned from 1982 to 1999, ranks No. 8 in all-time Hershey scoring (448 points in 413 games). The center is in the top 25 in AHL history in points (816) and goals (364). In the 1993–1994 season, Lamoureux set the AHL record for most power-play goals in a season (27), which is now shared with two others. He won the Fred T. Hunt Memorial Award in the 1998–1999 season for sportsmanship and dedication. (Bill Duh and Bruce Tyson/Just Sports.)

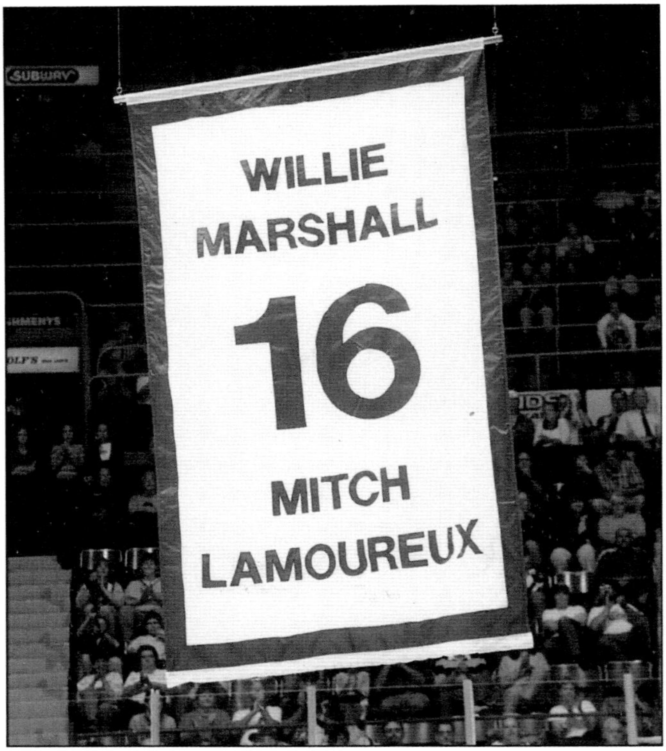

SWEET SIXTEEN. On October 2, 1999, the No. 16 worn by Mitch Lamoureux and Willie Marshall was retired. Both were small players who left large legacies. "Wee Willie" was five feet nine inches tall and weighed 160 pounds, and Lamoureux was five feet six inches tall and weighed 190 pounds. Lamoureux also played for Baltimore, Providence, and Maine in the AHL and in 73 NHL games, 70 with Pittsburgh. Marshall played 33 career NHL games for Toronto and also played for Pittsburgh, Rochester, Providence, and Baltimore in the AHL. (Bill Duh and Bruce Tyson/Just Sports.)

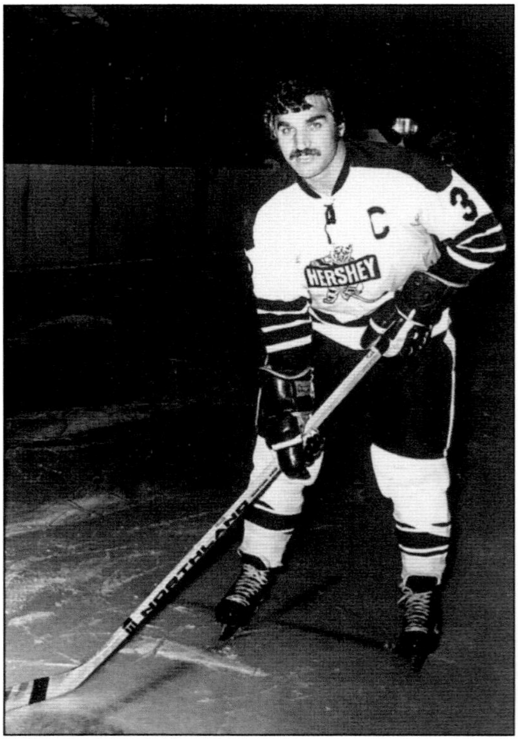

RALPH KELLER (1963–1974). Ralph Keller played more games (737) and produced more points (408) than any defenseman in Hershey history. The two-time AHL All-Star also played more playoff games (73) and scored more playoff points (73) than any Hershey defenseman. Only Mike Nykoluk and Arnie Kullman played more games for Hershey. Keller went on to serve as head coach of the IHL's Fort Wayne Komets from 1974 to 1978. (Hershey Bears.)

Stellar Keller. Frank Mathers (right) congratulates Ralph Keller as his name is added to the already retired No. 3. The ceremony took place on December 1, 2002, at the Giant Center. (Bill Duh and Bruce Tyson/Just Sports.)

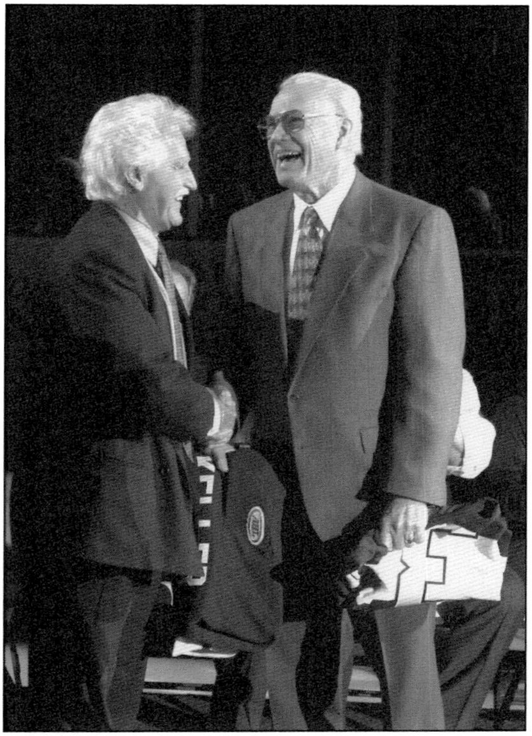

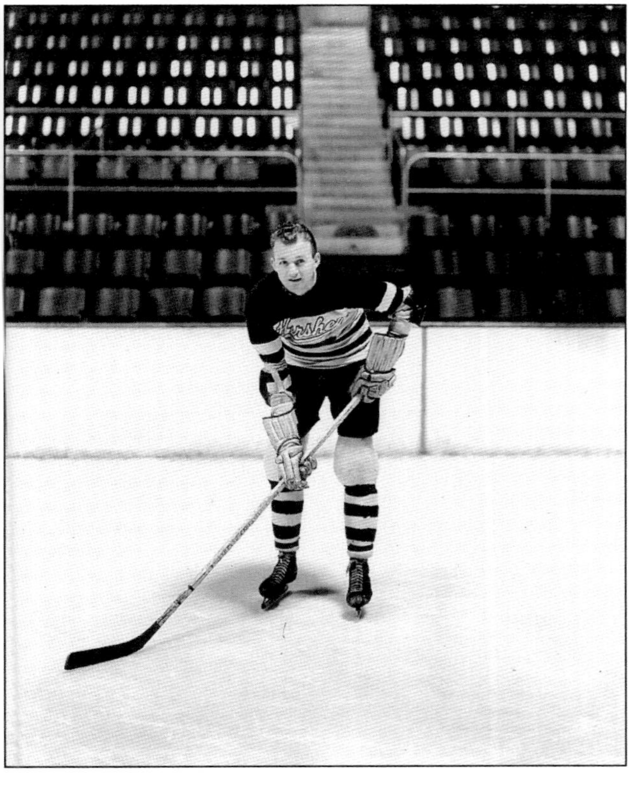

Harry Frost (1938–1943, 1945–1946). Right winger Harry Frost was a three-time AHL All-Star. He played nearly 300 games and scored more than 200 points for the Bears. (Hershey Bears.)

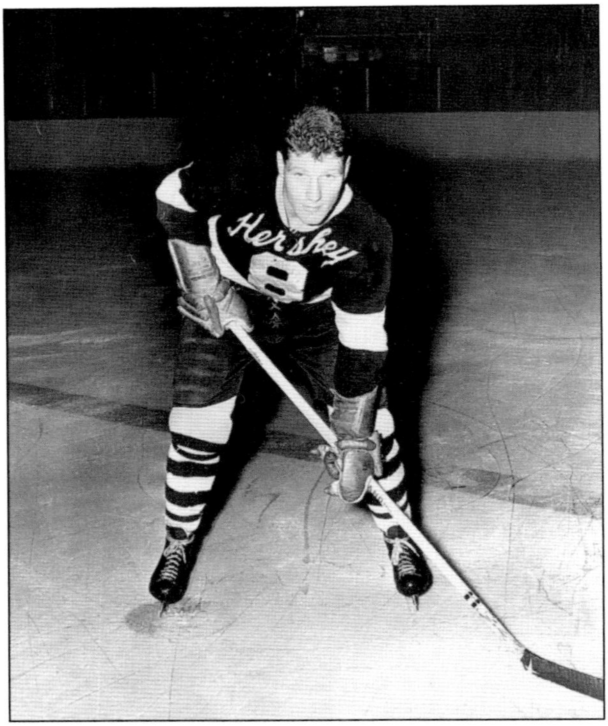

GEORGE "RED" SULLIVAN (1949–1954). Center George "Red" Sullivan scored 119 points in the 1953–1954 season, becoming the first Bear to score more than 100 points in a season and the first to be named AHL MVP. It stood as a club record until Tim Tookey broke it in the 1986–1987 season with 124 points. Sullivan's 89 assists in the 1953–1954 season still stand as the AHL single-season record. He went on to coach the New York Rangers (1962–1966), Pittsburgh Penguins (1967–1969), and Washington Capitals (1974–1975). (Hershey Bears.)

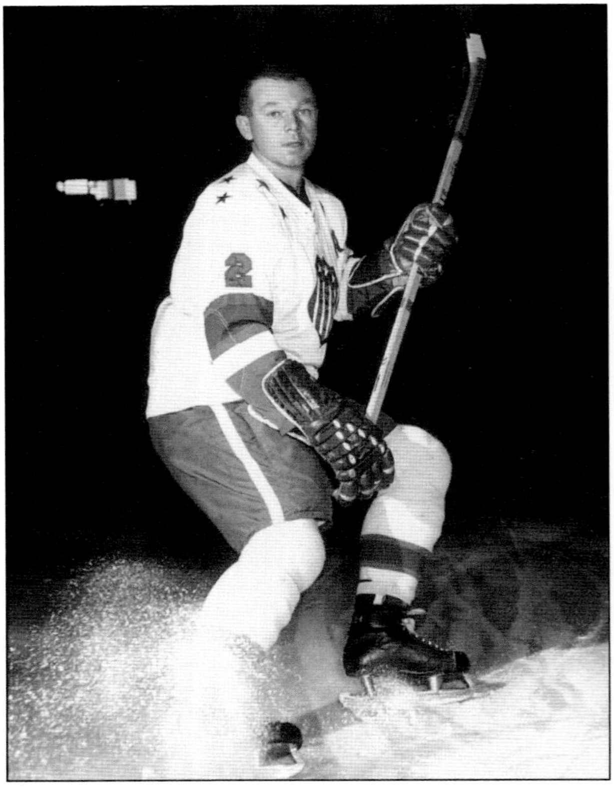

DON CHERRY (1954–1957). Defenseman Don Cherry has blazed a trail of entertainment and controversy for more than 50 years. It started in Hershey, where Cherry made his professional debut for the Bears in the 1954–1955 season, scoring 7 goals and earning 125 penalty minutes in 63 games. Cherry met his late wife, Rose, while playing in Hershey. "Grapes" went on to greater fame as a coach for Rochester, the Boston Bruins, and Colorado Rockies and as a broadcaster. (Hershey Bears.)

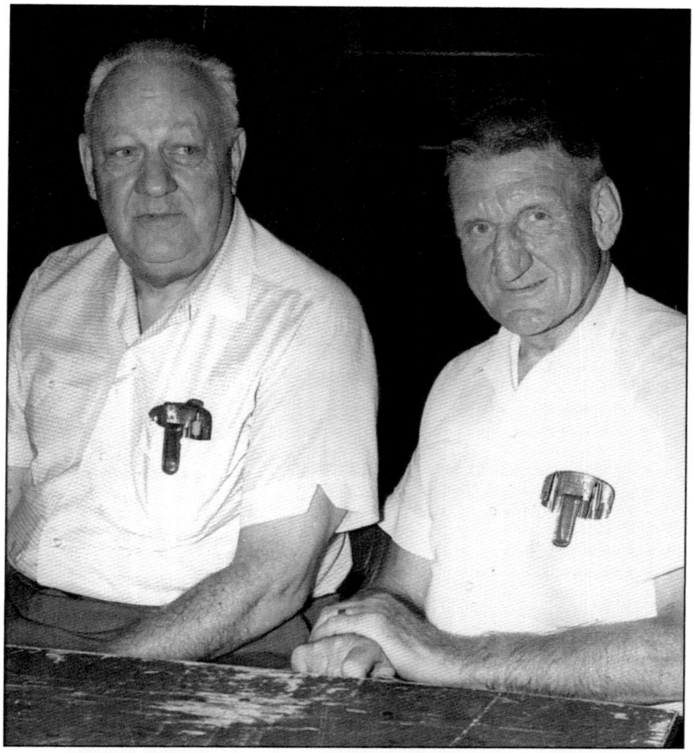

Call Him J.B. John B. Sollenberger (left), shown with Lloyd Blinco in 1964, was posthumously honored with the James C. Hendy Memorial Award as top executive in 1968 and the Lester Patrick Trophy in 1971. The John B. Sollenberger Trophy is awarded annually to the AHL's leading scorer. The longtime Hershey general manager retired as club president in 1962. Sollenberger helped establish the Big 33 Game and twice tried to relocate NFL teams to Hershey. (Hershey Bears.)

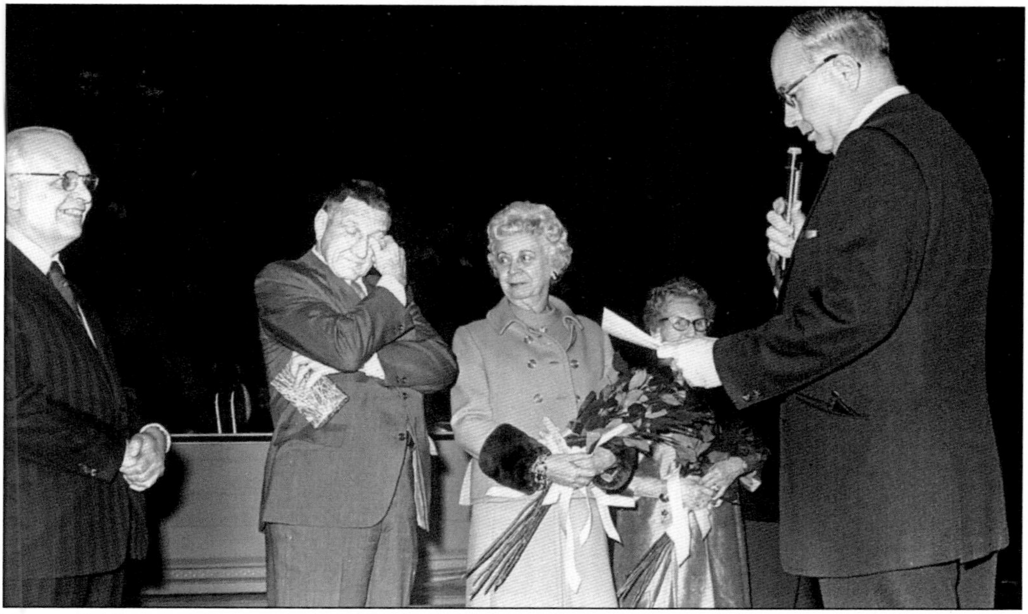

Lloyd S. Blinco. His career as a Hershey player or executive spanned from 1932 to 1973. Blinco (seen second from the left at his retirement night in 1973) was inducted into the Pennsylvania Sports Hall of Fame in 1970, the first hockey representative honored. He played in the days when a real bear mascot was kept in a cage at the Ice Palace. The animal once was paraded in New York's Madison Square Garden and left a mess on the ice. (Hershey Bears.)

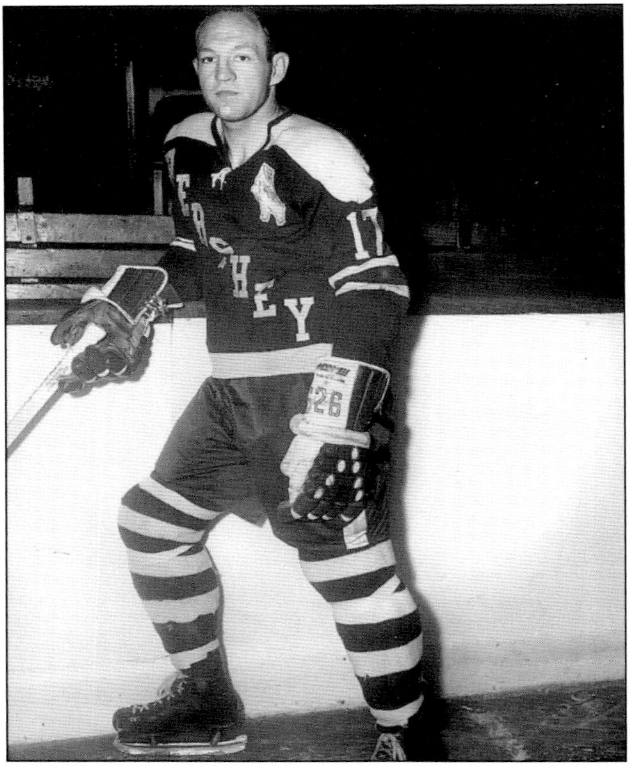

Bob Leiter (1963–1964, 1965–1966, 1967–1971). Center Bob Leiter ranks 19th in all-time Hershey scoring (304 points in 348 games) and was an AHL All-Star in the 1970–1971 season. (Hershey Bears.)

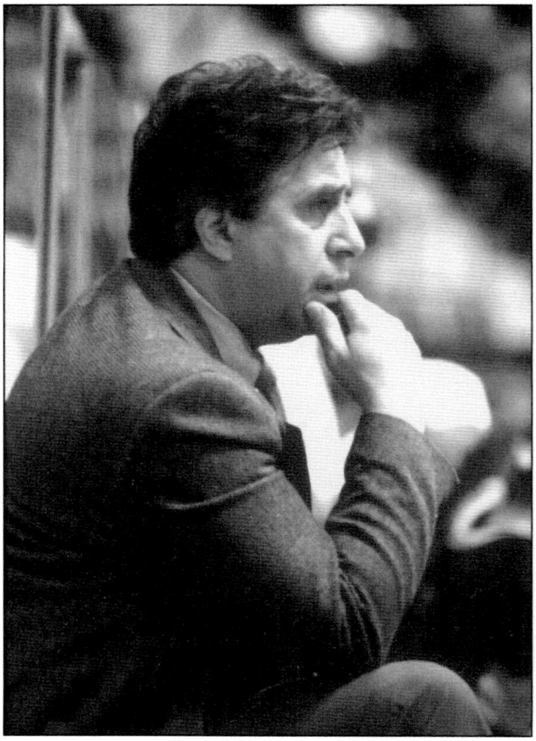

Gene Ubriaco (1963–1967). Gene Ubriaco, left wing, scored 42 goals for Hershey in the 1965–1966 season. Shown here with the Baltimore Skipjacks, he went on to a coaching career that included a stint leading the Pittsburgh Penguins (1988–1990) and Mario Lemieux. (Hershey Bears.)

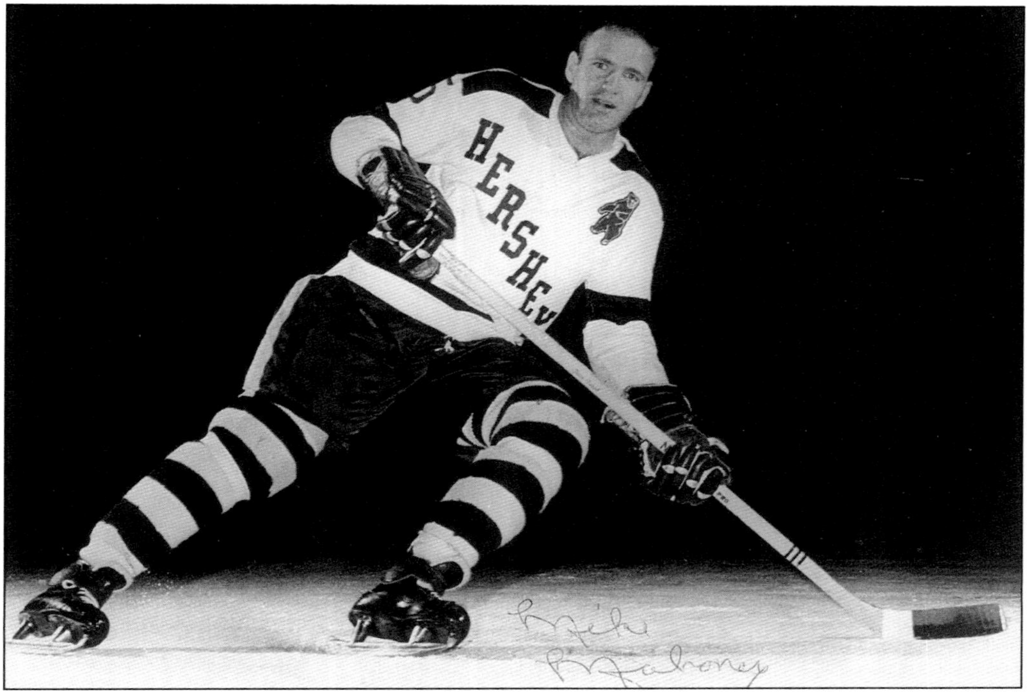

MIKE MAHONEY (1961–1971). Mike Mahoney ranks No. 3 in all-time games played by a Hershey defenseman (536) and No. 5 in blue-line scoring (195). (Hershey Bears.)

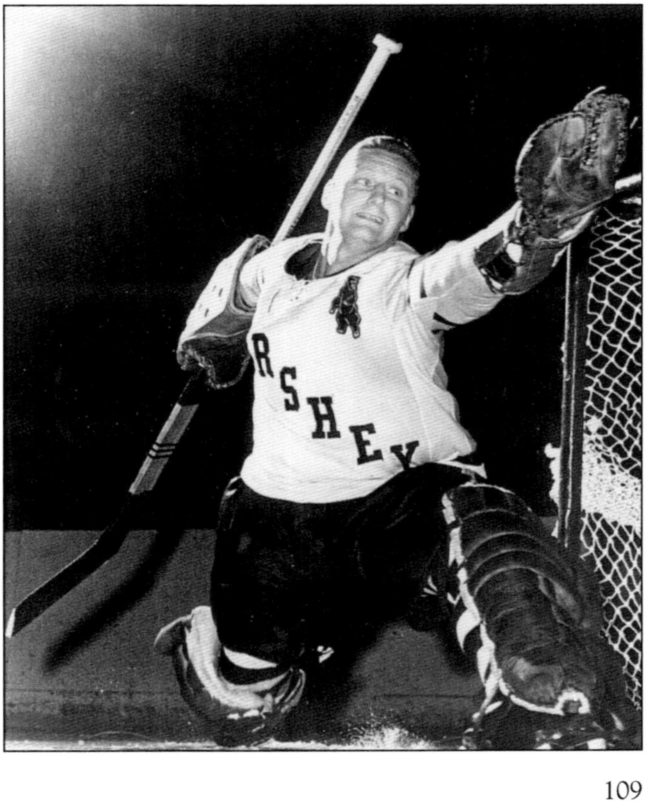

ED CHADWICK (1962–1964). Goalie Ed Chadwick ranks No. 8 in Hershey wins (65). Chadwick, whose career spanned from 1952 to 1968, is No. 10 in AHL history in wins (196). (Hershey Bears.)

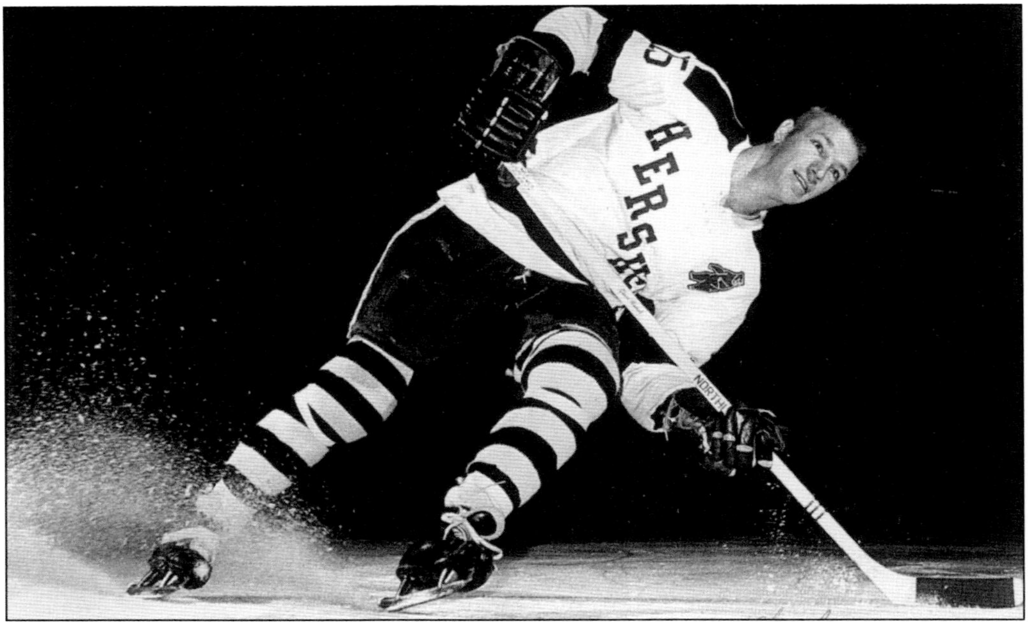

Myron Stankiewicz (1960–1968). Left winger Myron Stankiewicz ranks No. 12 in Hershey history in scoring (399 points in 522 games). (Hershey Bears.)

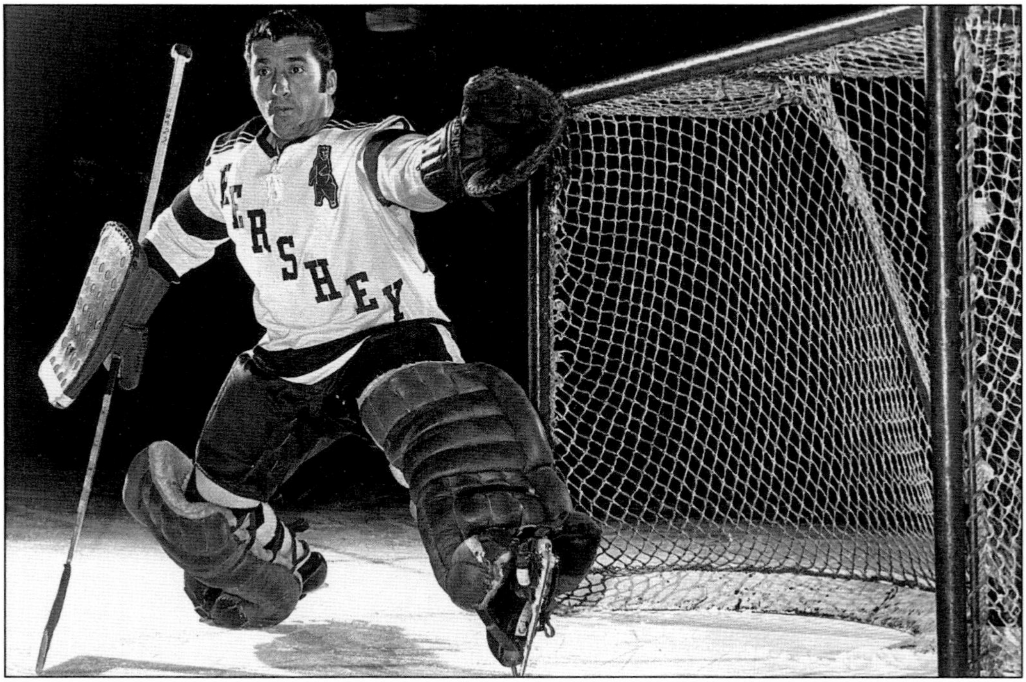

Andre Gill (1962–1972). Andre Gill ranks No. 3 in games played (309) and wins (139) on Hershey's all-time goalies list. He is No. 5 in shutouts (12). In the 1966–1967 season, Gill went 29-17-10 with four shutouts and won the AHL's Harry "Hap" Holmes Memorial Award for outstanding team goaltending. Gill, in the top 25 in all-time AHL wins, also played for the World Hockey Association's Chicago Cougars (1972–1974). (Hershey Bears.)

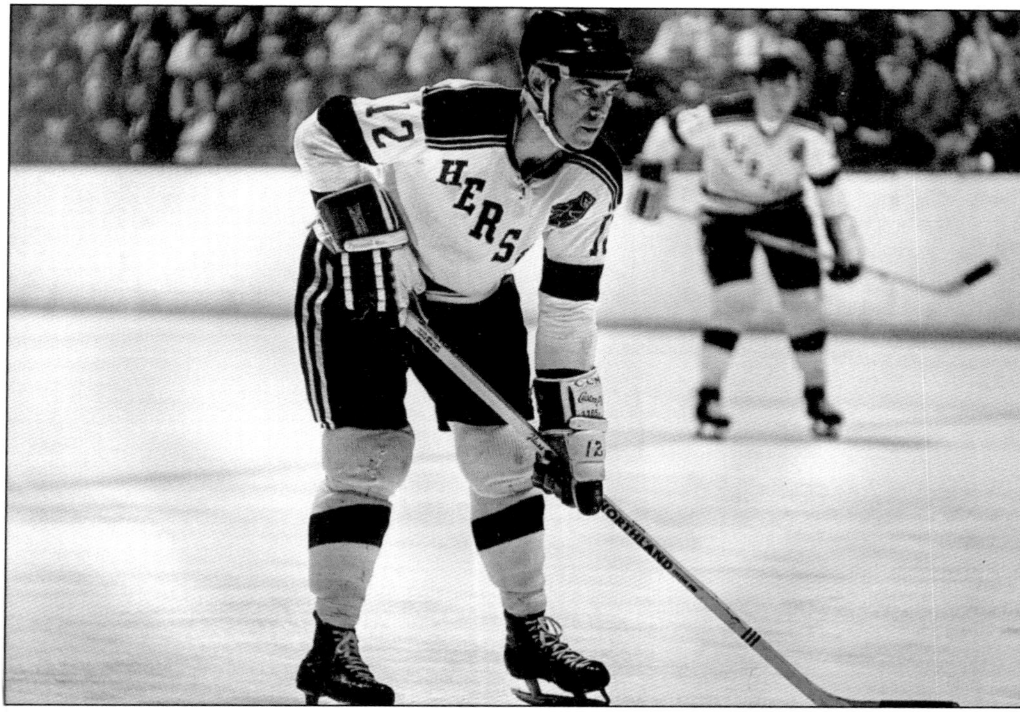

Roger DeJordy (1962–1970). Left winger Roger DeJordy ranks No. 7 on Hershey's all-time scoring list (448 points in 531 games). The two-time AHL All-Star is one of five players who have played in more than 60 playoff games (62) for the Bears. (Hershey Bears.)

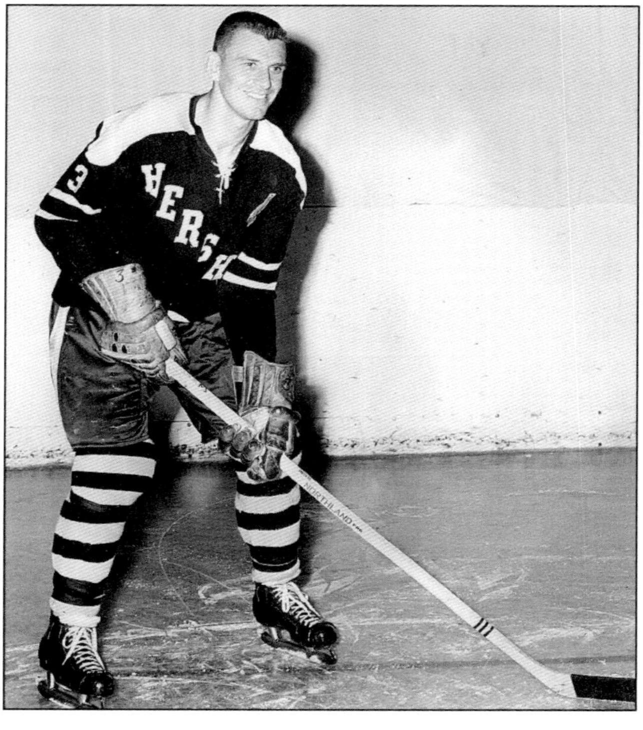

Marc Reaume (1960–1964). In the 1962–1963 season, Reaume became the first Bear to win the Eddie Shore Award, given to the AHL's outstanding defenseman. Reaume produced 86 points in 241 games for Hershey. He also played 344 NHL games for Toronto, Detroit, Montreal, and Vancouver. (Hershey Bears.)

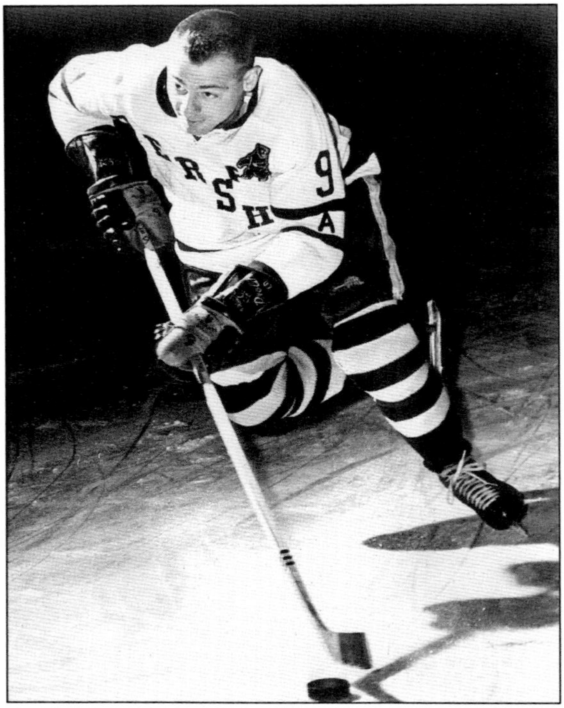

PETE CONACHER (1960–1966). Pete Conacher, left wing, scored 296 points in 404 Hershey games. Conacher also played in 229 NHL games for the New York Rangers, Toronto, and Chicago. (Hershey Bears.)

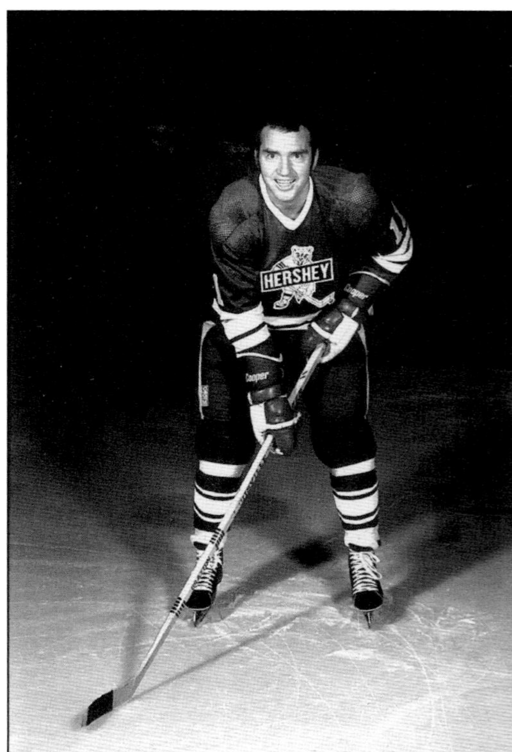

JEAN-GUY GRATTON (1969–1972, 1975–1976). Right winger Jean-Guy Gratton won the John B. Sollenberger Trophy for the 1975–1976 season as the AHL's leading scorer (93 points). Gratton had 221 points in 269 Hershey games. (Hershey Bears.)

Colin Campbell (1974–1975). Colin Campbell, defenseman, played 636 NHL games for Pittsburgh, Colorado, Edmonton, Vancouver, and Detroit and served as head coach of the New York Rangers from 1994 to 1997. Campbell went on to become executive vice president and director of hockey operations for the NHL. (Hershey Bears.)

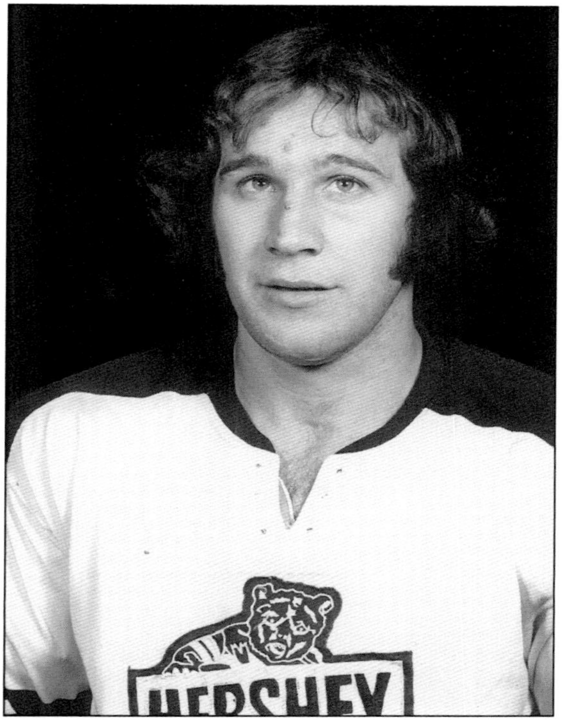

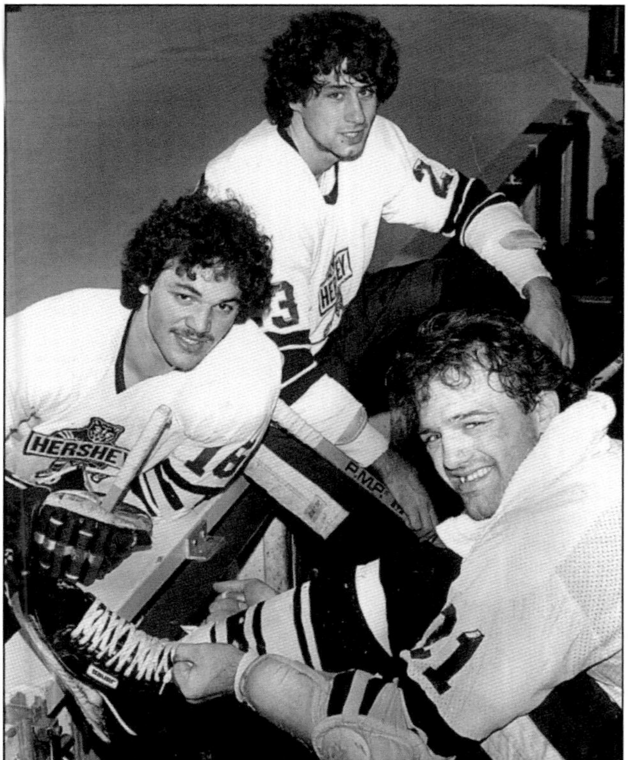

Lou Franceschetti (1979–1984) and Gary Rissling (1978–1981). Lou Franceschetti (left) and Gary Rissling (right) are shown here with Glen Currie. Right winger Franceschetti ranks No. 17 in all-time Hershey scoring (314 points in 347 games) and played 459 NHL games for Washington, Toronto, and Buffalo. Winger Rissling ranks No. 8 in all-time Hershey penalty minutes (690) and No. 10 in AHL history (1,743). (Norman Arnold/*Patriot-News*.)

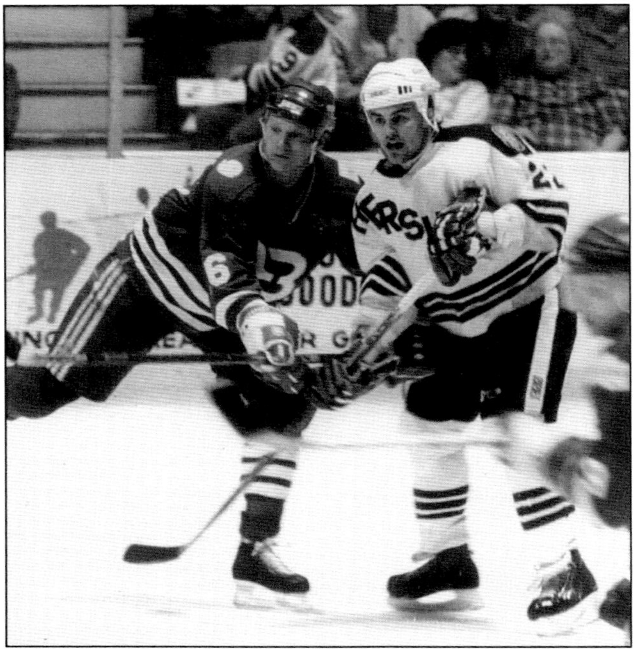

Don Biggs (1987–1990). Don Biggs (on the right) scored 274 points in 219 games for Hershey. The right winger won the AHL MVP award for Binghamton in the 1992–1993 season when he set the league record for most points in a season (138). (Hershey Bears.)

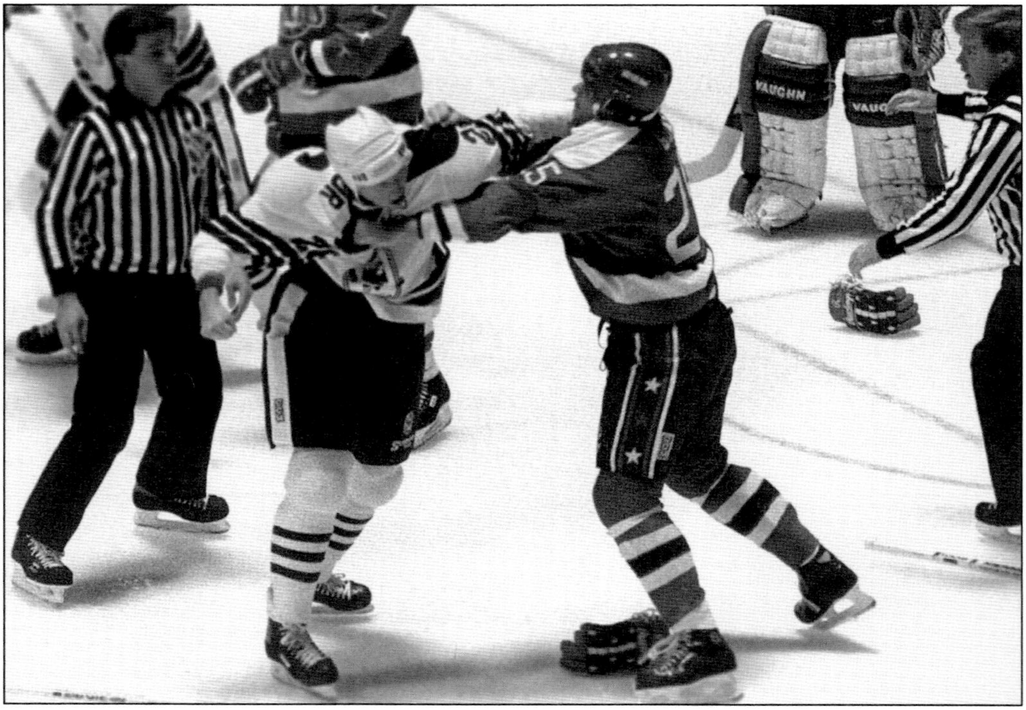

Don Nachbaur (1984–1990). Center Don Nachbaur (left), taking a swing at Baltimore Skipjack Alain Guay, ranks No. 5 in all-time Hershey penalty minutes (1,014). The team captain from 1985 to 1987 went on to serve as head coach for the WHL's Seattle Thunderbirds and Tri-City Americans and assistant coach for the AHL's Philadelphia Phantoms. He also played 223 NHL games for Hartford, Edmonton, and Philadelphia. (Hershey Bears.)

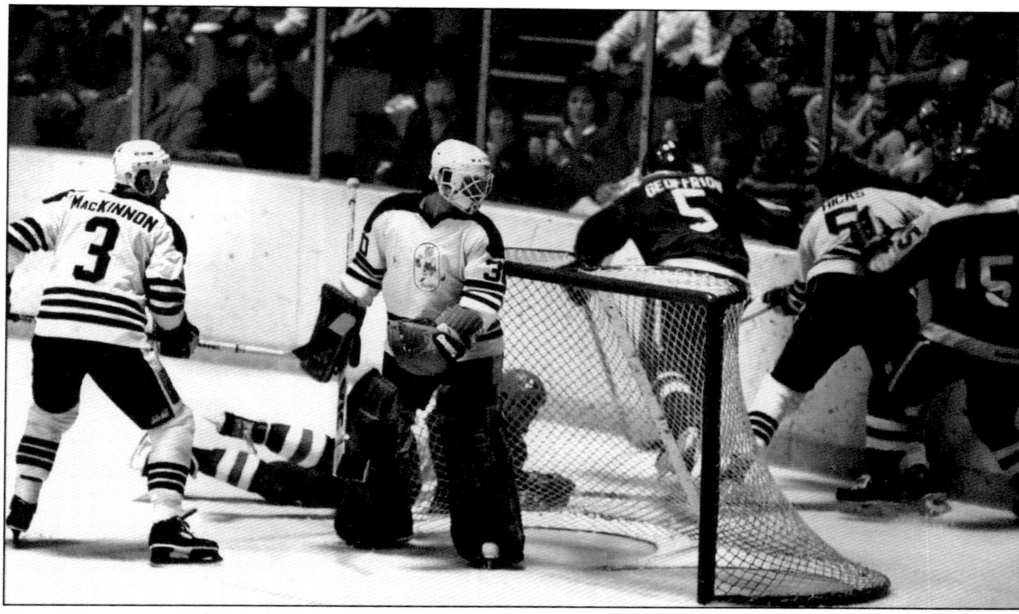

RON HEXTALL (1984–1986, 1989–1990). In the 1985–1986 season, goalie Ron Hextall backstopped Hershey to the Calder Cup finals and became the only Bear to ever win Rookie of the Year. In Game 2 of the Southern Conference finals against St. Catherine's, Hextall beat up three different Saints during a bench-clearing brawl. An NHL rookie in the 1986–1987 season, he led Philadelphia to the Stanley Cup finals and is one of five players from a losing team to win the Conn Smythe Trophy. (Hershey Bears.)

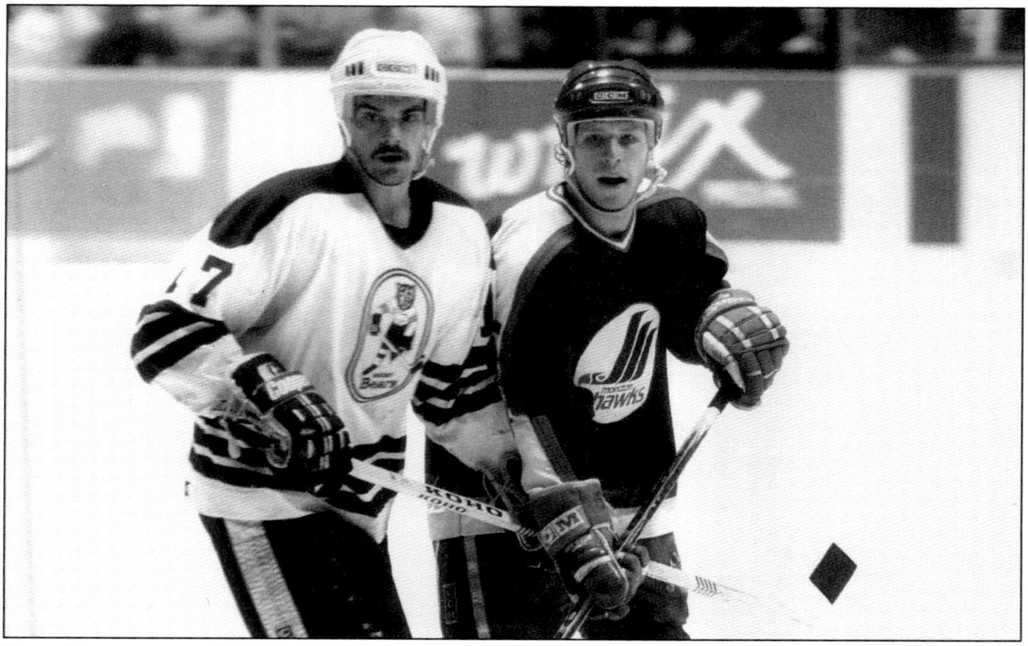

ROSS FITZPATRICK (1984–1990). Ross Fitzpatrick (left) was a two-time AHL All-Star who scored 372 points in 299 games for Hershey. The left winger also ranks No. 16 in AHL history with 308 goals. (Hershey Bears.)

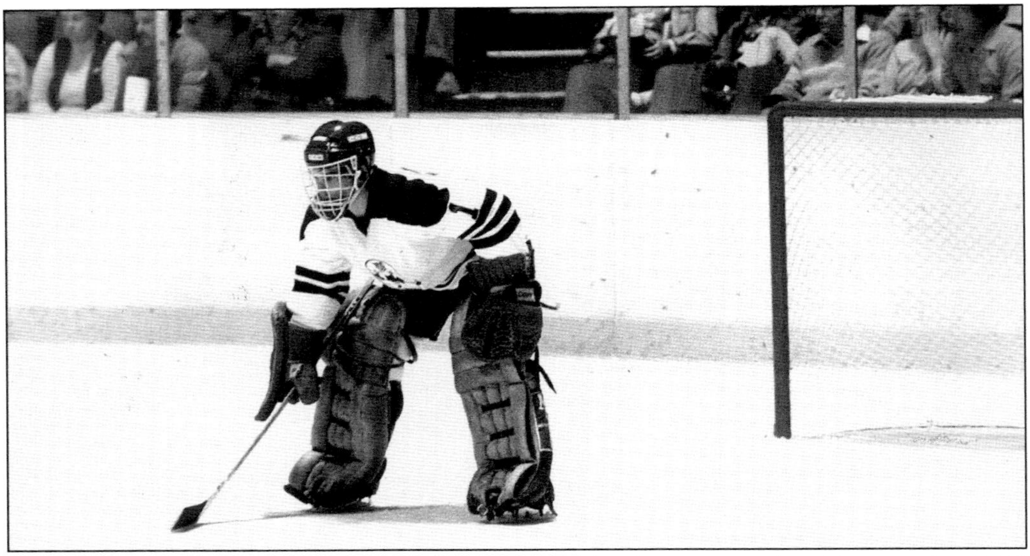

ROLLIE BOUTIN (1978–1982). Rollie Boutin ranks No. 5 in games played by a goalie (160) and wins (83) in Hershey history. Boutin was a second-team AHL All-Star in the 1980–1981 season, when he went 32-15-5. He holds the Hershey record for most saves in a regular-season game (52 against New Haven on January 27, 1981). (Hershey Bears.)

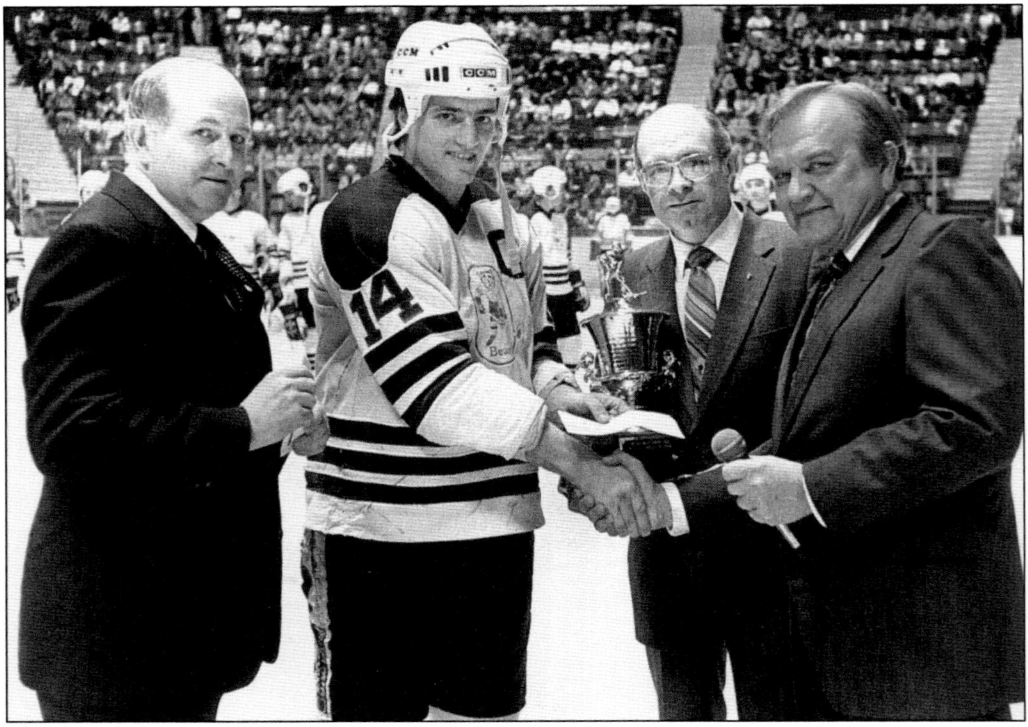

TONY CASSOLATO (1979–1983). Center Tony Cassolato won the Fred T. Hunt Memorial Award for sportsmanship and dedication in the 1980–1981 season. Cassolato scored 305 points in 276 Hershey games and set the club single-season record for goals (53) in the 1982–1983 season. (Hershey Bears.)

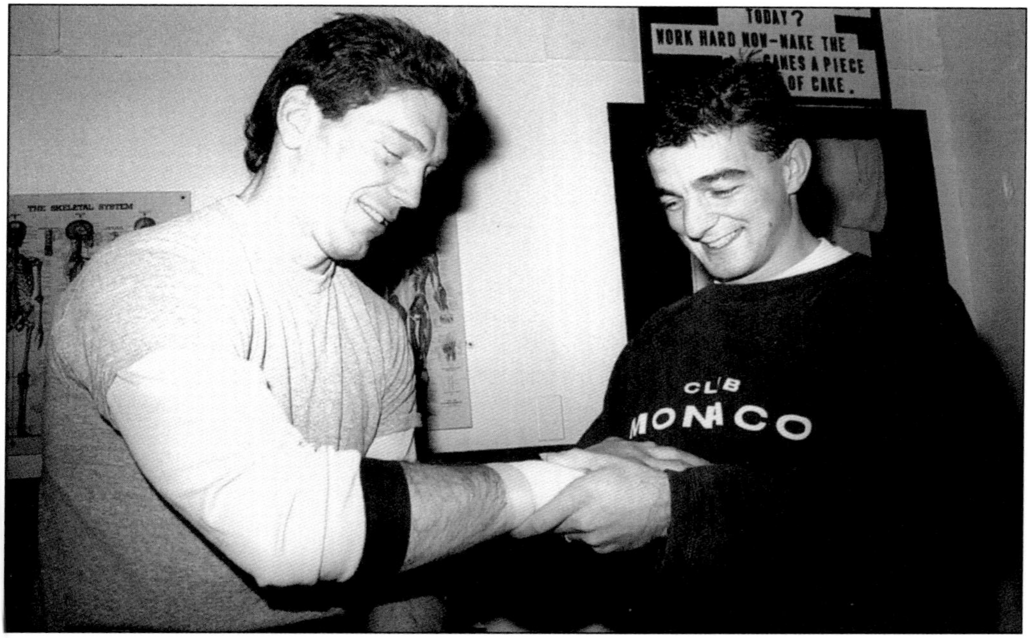

MIKE STOTHERS (1984–1992). Mike Stothers (left) gets taped by trainer Dan "Beaker" Stuck. The defenseman is Hershey's all-time penalty minutes leader (1,519) and ranks No. 7 in AHL history (1,840). Stothers went on to serve as assistant coach of the Bears, Philadelphia Phantoms, and Philadelphia Flyers before becoming head coach of Owen Sound in the OHL. (Hershey Bears.)

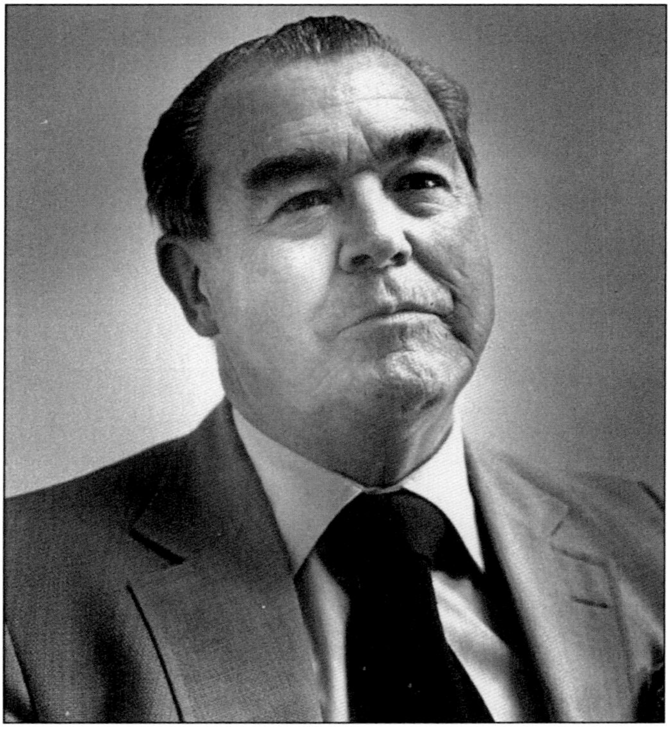

BRENT I. HANCOCK. The prime keeper of Bears history, Brent I. Hancock, served as the club's publicist from 1935 to 1982. Hancock, who served with the U.S. Marines in the South Pacific in World War II, won the AHL's Ken McKenzie Award for the outstanding public relations and marketing executive of the 1980–1981 season. (Hershey Bears.)

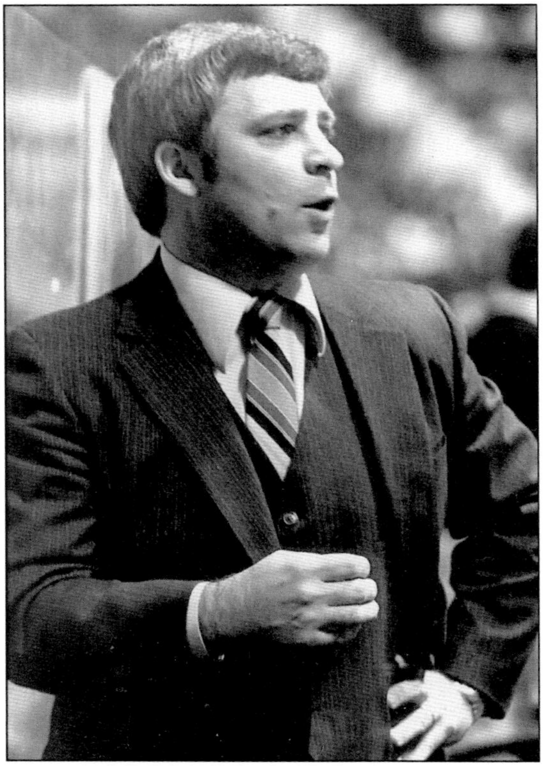

Bryan Murray. Murray coached Hershey to a 47-24-9 record in the 1980–1981 season before becoming an NHL head coach and/or general manager for Washington, Detroit, Florida, and Anaheim. As general manager in Anaheim, Murray put together a roster that reached the 2003 Stanley Cup finals against eventual champion New Jersey. (Hershey Bears.)

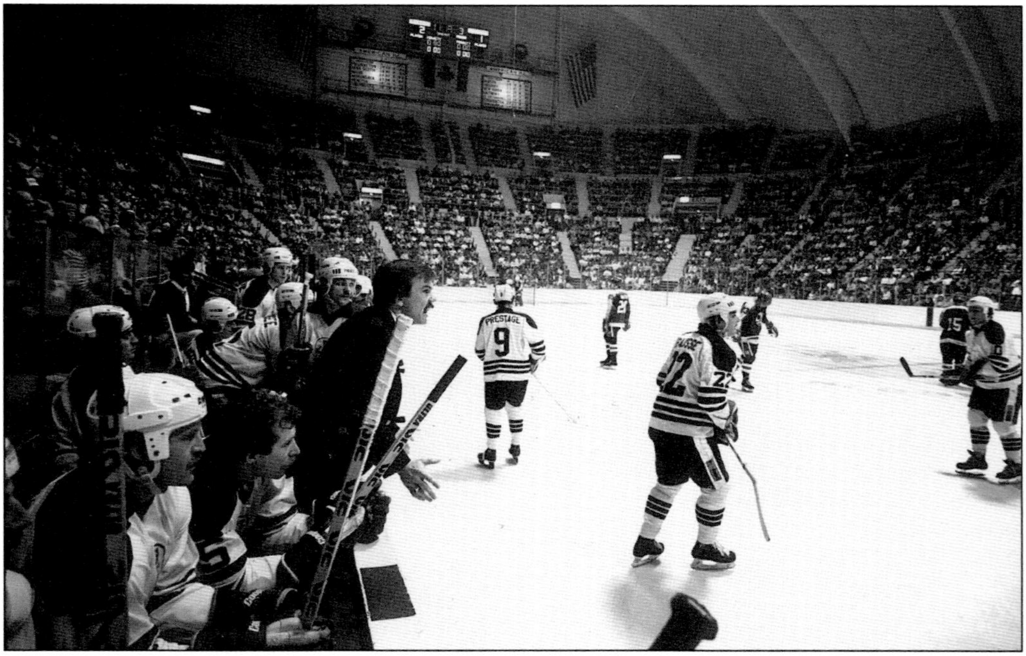

Gary Inness. As a goalie (1973–1974, 1978–1980) and head coach (1981–1985), Gary Inness participated in 297 Hershey regular-season games. He also played 162 NHL games for Pittsburgh, Philadelphia, and Washington and in the WHA with Indianapolis. (Hershey Bears.)

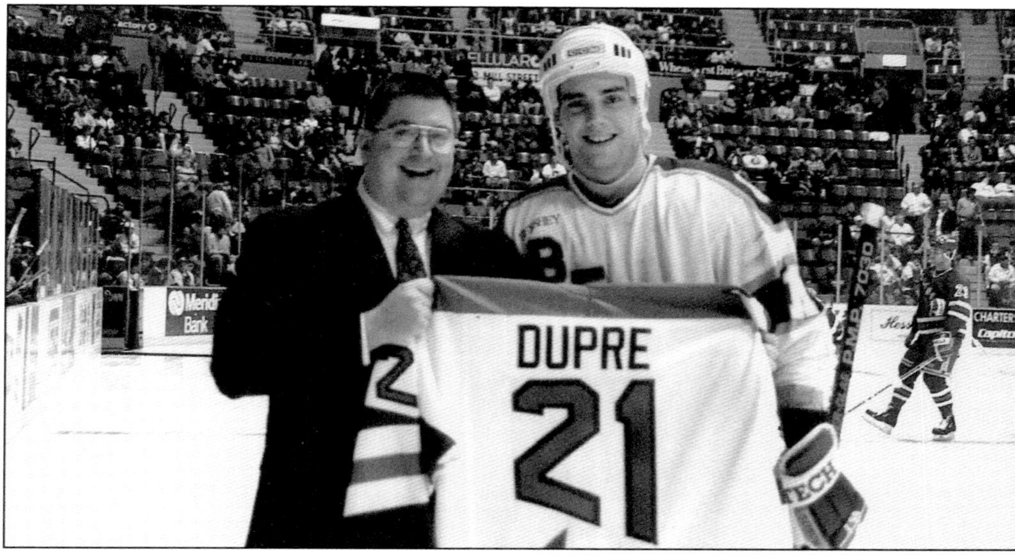

JAY FEASTER. Jay Feaster (left), who served as president and general manager of the Bears, presents Yanick Dupre with his 1995 AHL All-Star Game jersey. Feaster won the James C. Hendy Memorial Award for outstanding executive in the 1996–1997 season. He went on to become assistant general manager and general manager of the Tampa Bay Lightning. Under Feaster in the 2002–2003 season, the Lightning won the first division title and playoff series in their history. (Hershey Bears.)

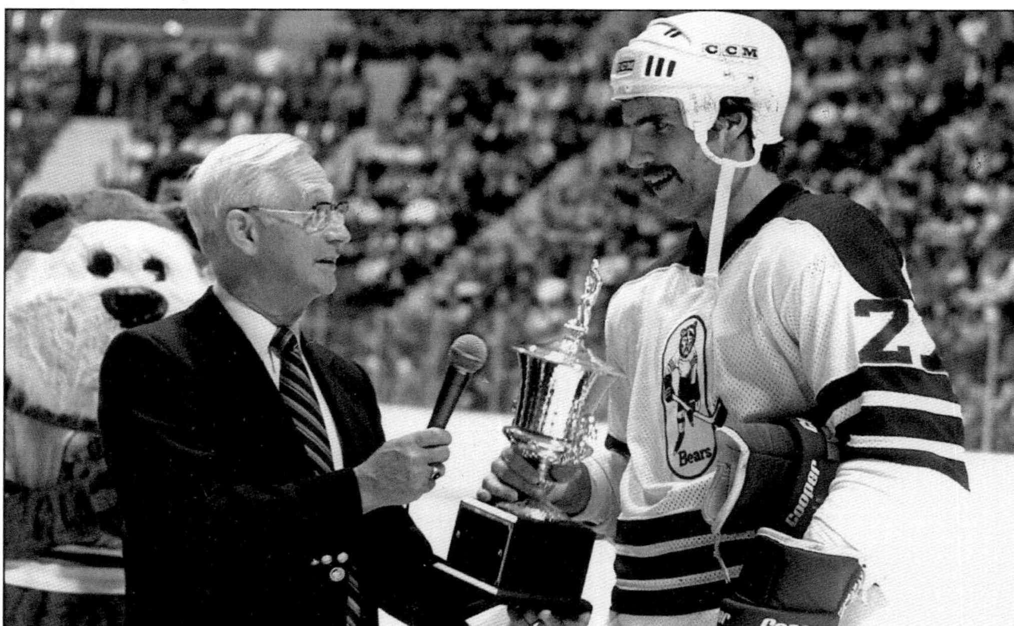

MARK LOFTHOUSE (1977–1981, 1987–1989). Right winger Mark Lofthouse (right) led the AHL in scoring in the 1980–1981 season (103 points). On January 7, 1981, he set Hershey's single-game scoring record with eight points (four goals, four assists) during an 11-2 victory over Rochester. Lofthouse produced 262 points in 259 Hershey games. He also played in 181 NHL games for Washington and Detroit. (Hershey Bears.)

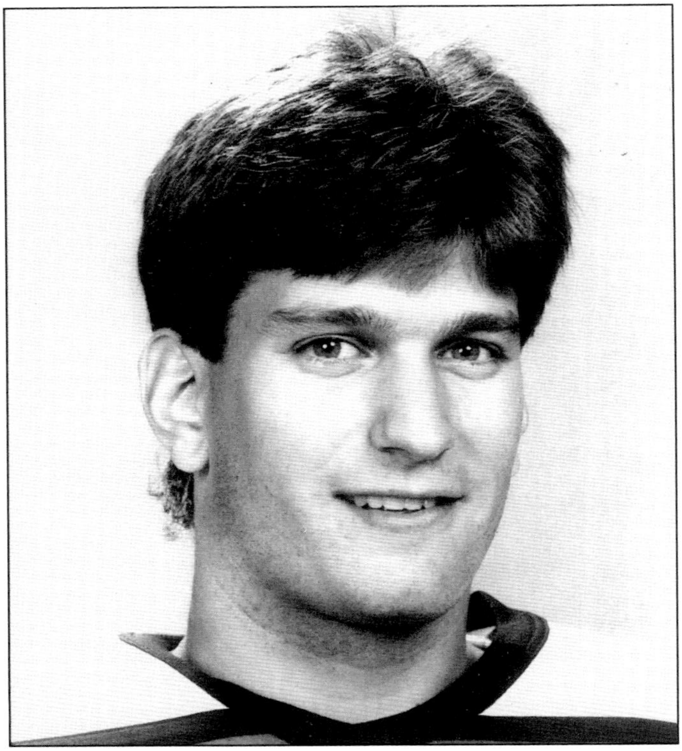

Darren Rumble (1989–1992, 1995–1996). Defenseman Darren Rumble ranks No. 6 in all-time scoring by Hershey blueliners (172 points in 267 games). Rumble won the Eddie Shore Award as the AHL's top defenseman in the 1996–1997 season with the Philadelphia Phantoms. (Hershey Bears.)

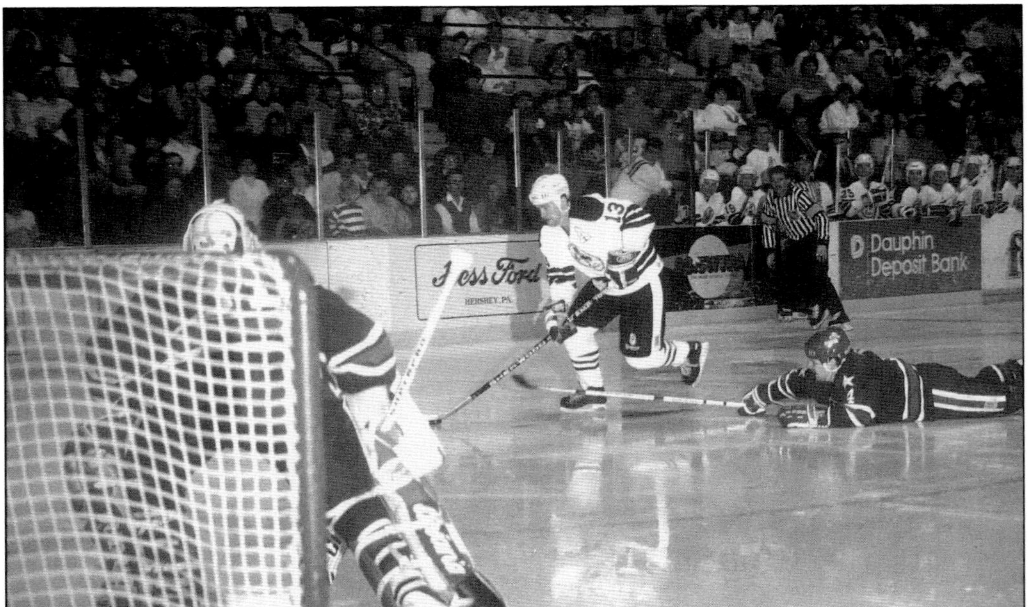

Brian Dobbin (1985–1991). Right winger Brian Dobbin ranks No. 4 in all-time Hershey playoff scoring (47 points in 53 games). In the regular season, Dobbin produced 399 points in 315 Hershey games. (Hershey Bears.)

Chris Jensen (1988–1993). Right winger Chris Jensen produced 297 points in 283 Hershey games. Jensen also played 74 career NHL games with the New York Rangers and Philadelphia Flyers. (Hershey Bears.)

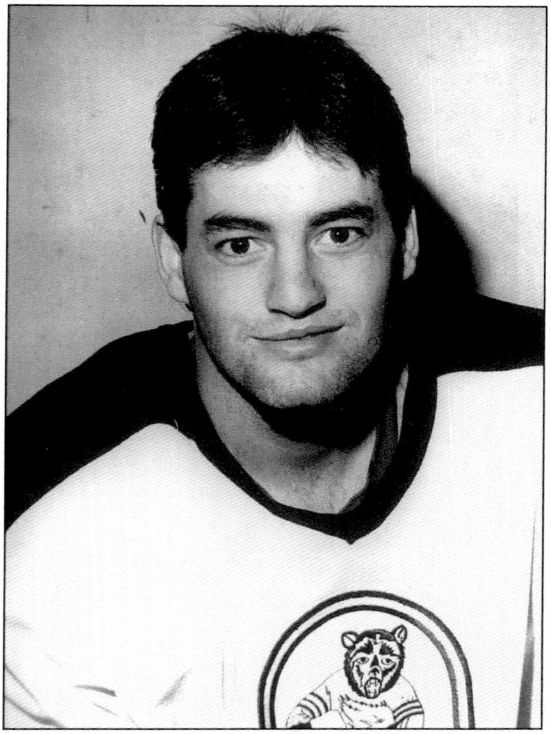

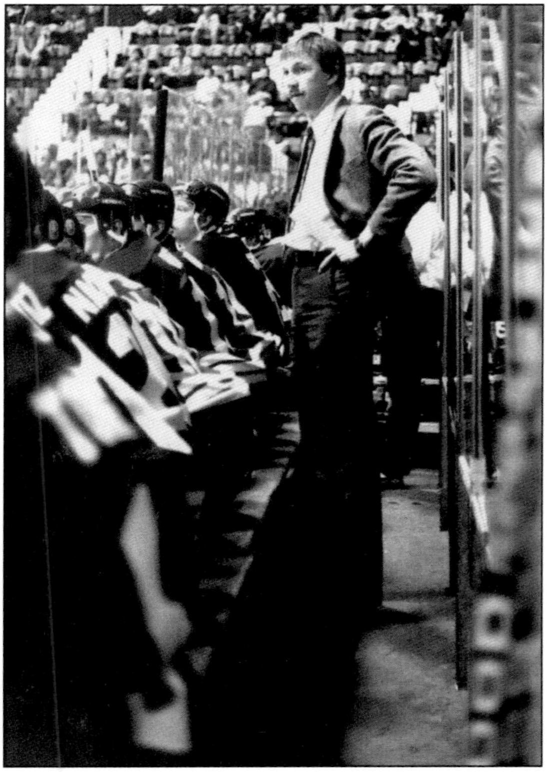

John Paddock (1985–1989). John Paddock has fashioned the greatest coaching record during the AHL's era as the NHL's primary developmental league. He is the only coach in history to lead three different franchises—Maine (1983–1984), Hershey (1987–1988), and Hartford (1999–2000)—to the Calder Cup. Paddock, who has also coached the AHL's Binghamton Rangers and Binghamton Senators, served as head coach of the NHL Winnipeg Jets from 1991 to 1995. (Hershey Bears.)

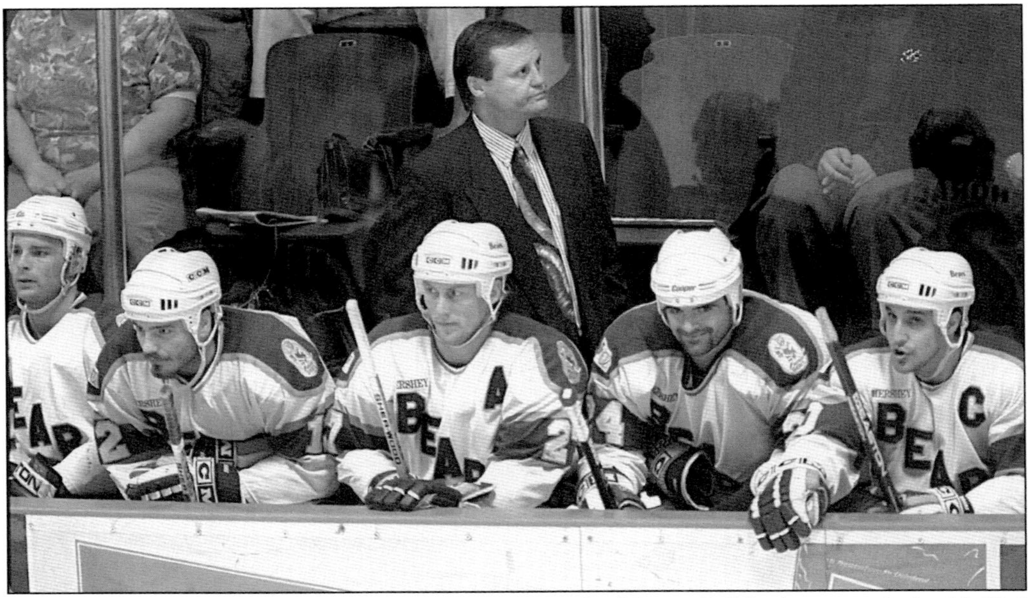

Bill Barber (1984–1985, 1995–1996). Hockey Hall of Famer Bill Barber compiled a 28-27-8 record in two partial seasons as Hershey's head coach. Barber replaced Gary Inness in the 1984–1985 season (after an interim stint by Frank Mathers) and Jay Leach in the 1995–1996 season. Barber led the Philadelphia Phantoms to the Calder Cup in the 1997–1998 season and then served as the Philadelphia Flyers head coach from 2000 to 2002. He was NHL Coach of the Year for the 2000–2001 season. (Charles Lewis/*Patriot-News*.)

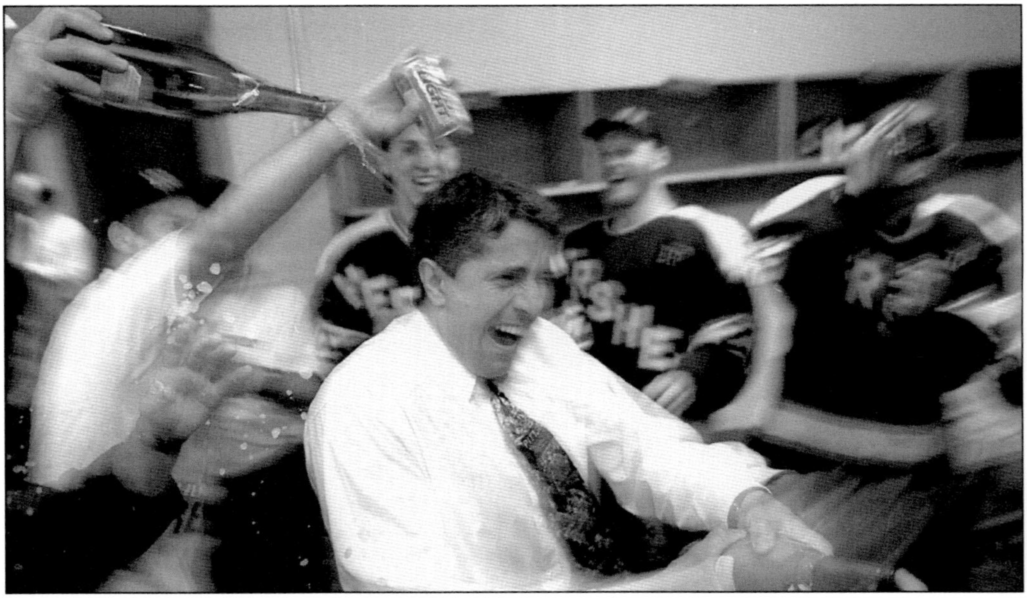

Bob Hartley (1996–1998). Bob Hartley, celebrating the 1997 Calder Cup win in the team's Copps Coliseum locker room, became head coach of the Colorado Avalanche in 1998. He led the Avalanche to the Stanley Cup in 2001, becoming the first former Hershey coach to lead a club to the NHL title. Hartley became coach of the Atlanta Thrashers in 2003 after being fired by Colorado in December 2002. (Michael Fernandez/*Patriot-News*.)

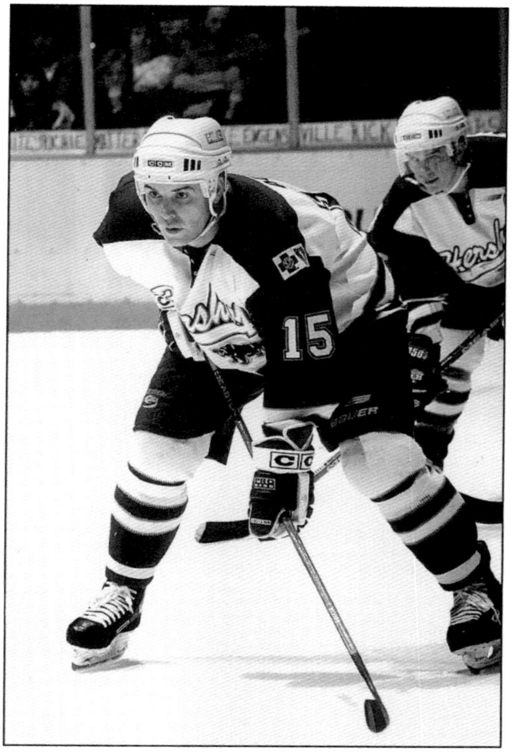

SERGE AUBIN (1997–2000) AND CHRISTIAN MATTE (1996–2000). Serge Aubin (left) scored 42 goals and earned first-team AHL All-Star honors in the 1999–2000 season before going on to an NHL career with Columbus and Colorado. Two-time team MVP Christian Matte (right) led the AHL in scoring in the 1999–2000 season (104 points) and also was a first-team All-Star. Matte produced 291 points in 253 Hershey games. (Bill Duh and Bruce Tyson/Just Sports.)

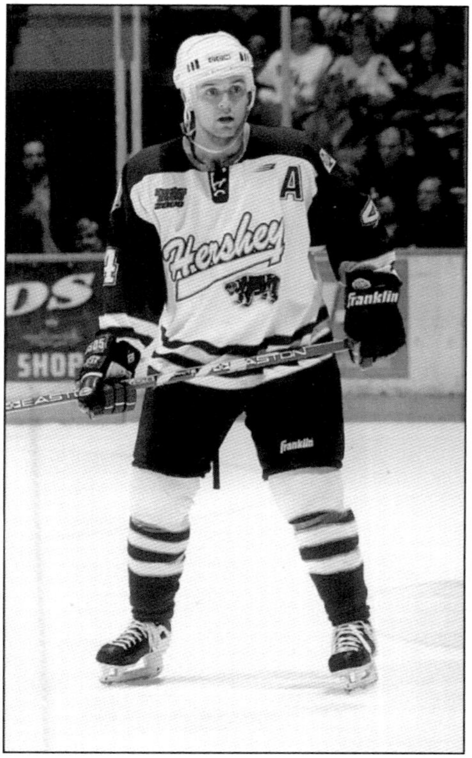

MIKE GAUL (1997–2000). Mike Gaul set the AHL record for most assists by a rookie defenseman (47) in the 1997–1998 season. He holds the club record for most points by a defenseman in a single season (69 in 1999–2000), when he was a second-team AHL All-Star. Gaul ranks No. 7 in all-time scoring by Hershey defensemen (168 points in 168 games). (Bill Duh and Bruce Tyson/Just Sports.)

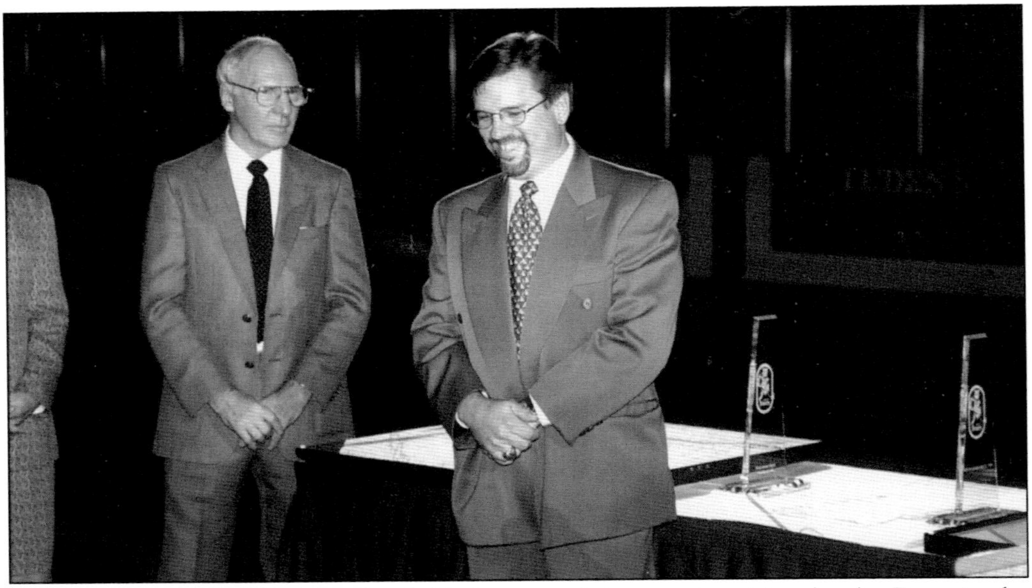

Doug Yingst. Doug Yingst, a Frank Mathers protégé, started working for the Bears in the 1982–1983 season and has risen to become the club's president and general manager. Yingst (above right with Willie Marshall), whose first season as general manager was the 1996–1997 Calder Cup campaign, won the Ken McKenzie Award for outstanding marketing and public relations executive for the 1987–1988 season and the James C. Hendy Memorial Award for outstanding executive in the 1999–2000 season. (Bill Duh and Bruce Tyson/Just Sports.)

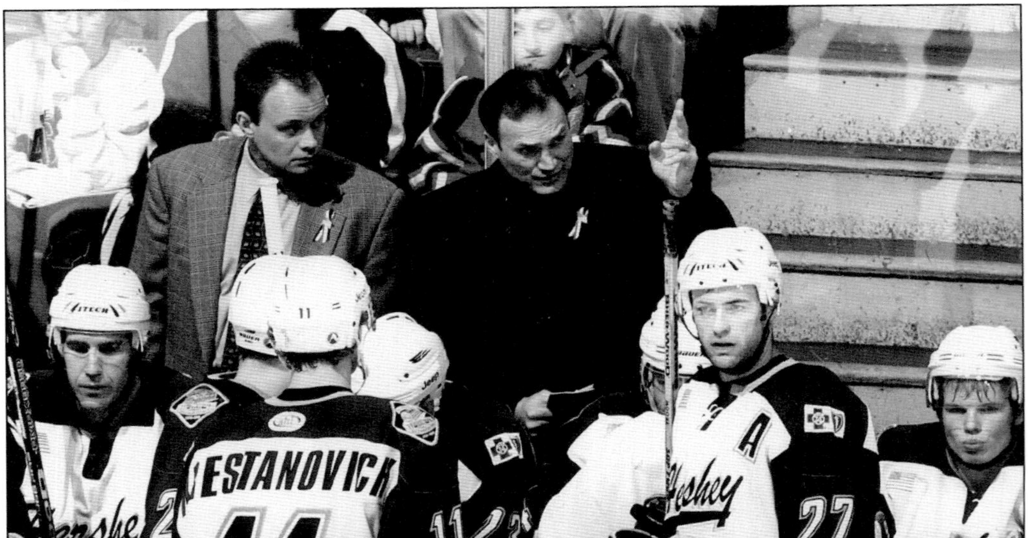

Mike Foligno (1998–2003). Mike Foligno, a 15-year NHL veteran, led the Bears to the conference finals twice during a five-season tenure. Foligno (standing on the right) left on June 14, 2003, to become the head coach-general manager of the Sudbury Wolves in the OHL. He ranks No. 3 in Hershey wins (186-154-44-16) and games coached (400). Assistant Paul Fixter (standing on the left) succeeded Foligno on July 1, 2003, becoming the 20th man to serve as AHL head coach in the club's history. (Bill Duh and Bruce Tyson/Just Sports.)

Five

GIANT CHANGE

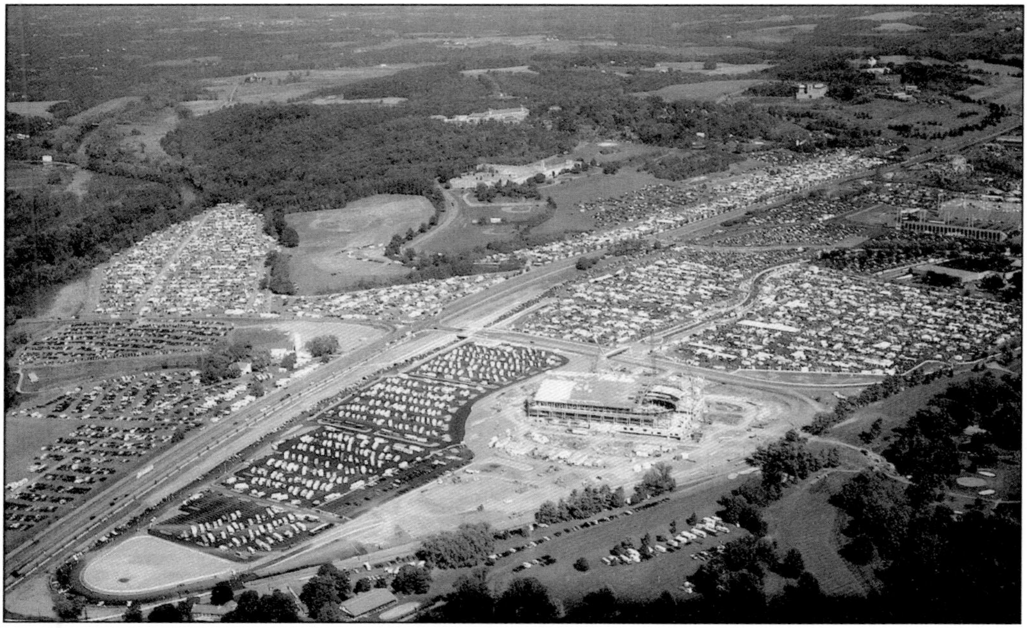

UNDER CONSTRUCTION. This is an aerial shot of Giant Center taken on October 2, 2001. On November 1, 2001, the final roof truss was placed at the south end and the building was topped off. By 1999, plans were underway in earnest to replace Hersheypark Arena, pressed by the forces of time and sports economics. A narrow main concourse, no luxury suites, and a relative lack of concession and restroom facilities meant it was not state of the art in building convenience. (*Patriot-News*.)

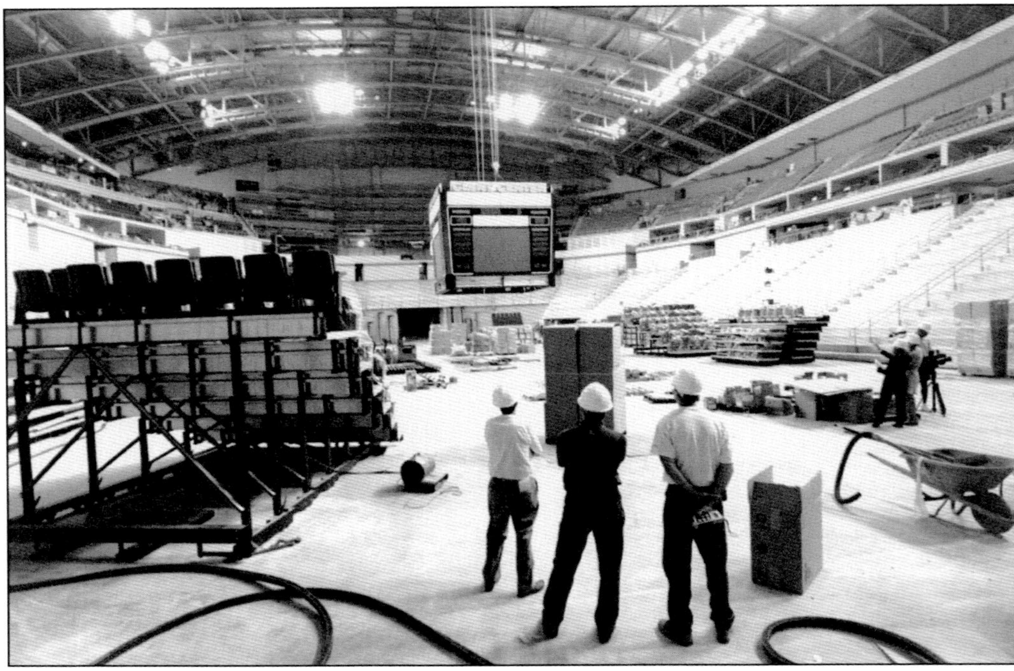

AN OVERHEAD ATTRACTION. Giant Center's $1.2 million scoreboard is raised on August 12, 2002. On December 2, 1999, Hershey Entertainment revealed that the celebrated architecture firm HOK Sport, which also designed Baltimore's Camden Yards, would design Hershey's new arena. In a Hersheypark Arena ceremony on December 6, 1999, Gov. Tom Ridge announced that the state would contribute $25 million to the new arena's $75 million cost. (Sean Simmers/*Patriot-News*.)

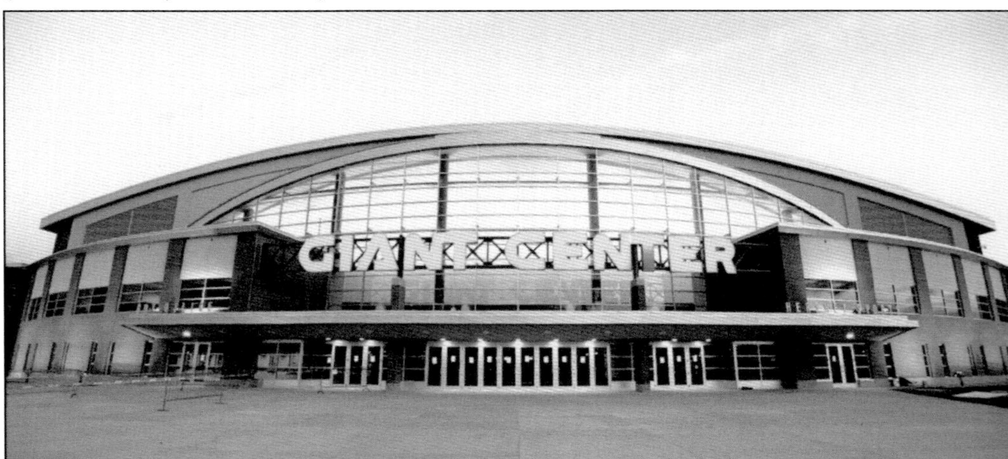

ARENA ECHOES. HOK Sport architects sought to echo Hersheypark Arena, particularly its arched roof, in Giant Center. The ceremonial groundbreaking was held on November 8, 2000. Giant Foods paid $4.5 million for 10-year naming rights. On June 12, 2002, the 10-hour ice-floor foundation pour took place. The two-foot foundation had to be level to within the thickness of a nickel from end to end. The Giant Center sign was mounted outside the arena on June 18, 2002. (John C. Whitehead/*Patriot-News*.)

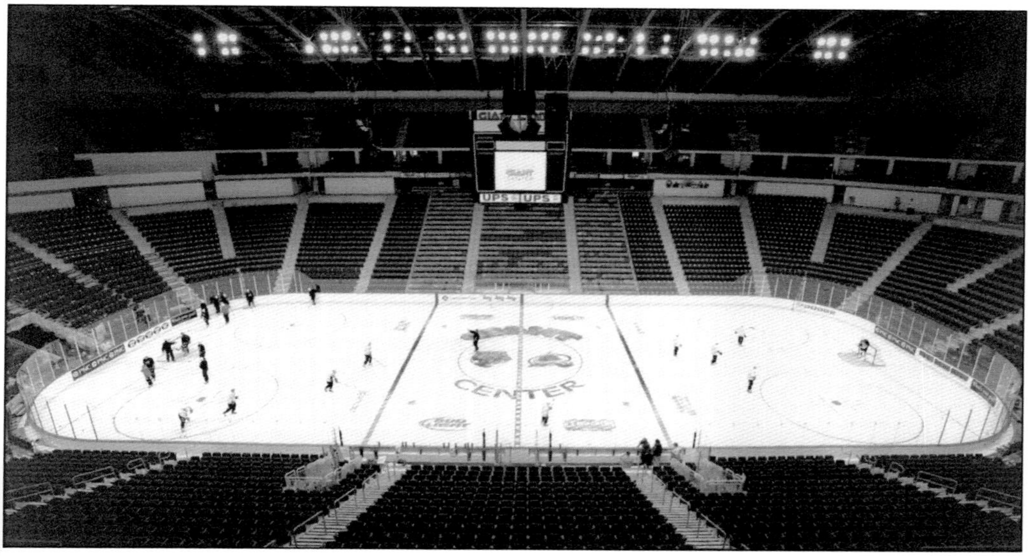

First Strides. The Bears held their first-ever practice at Giant Center on October 8, 2002. They raved about the NHL caliber of the 295,000-square-foot building that seats 10,500 for hockey (maximum capacity is 12,500), including 40 luxury suites and 688 club seats. Giant Center's grand opening happened on October 15, 2002, with a Cher concert. Team facilities include a main home dressing room, auxiliary dressing room, weight room, and rehabilitation pool. (Michael Fernandez/*Patriot-News*.)

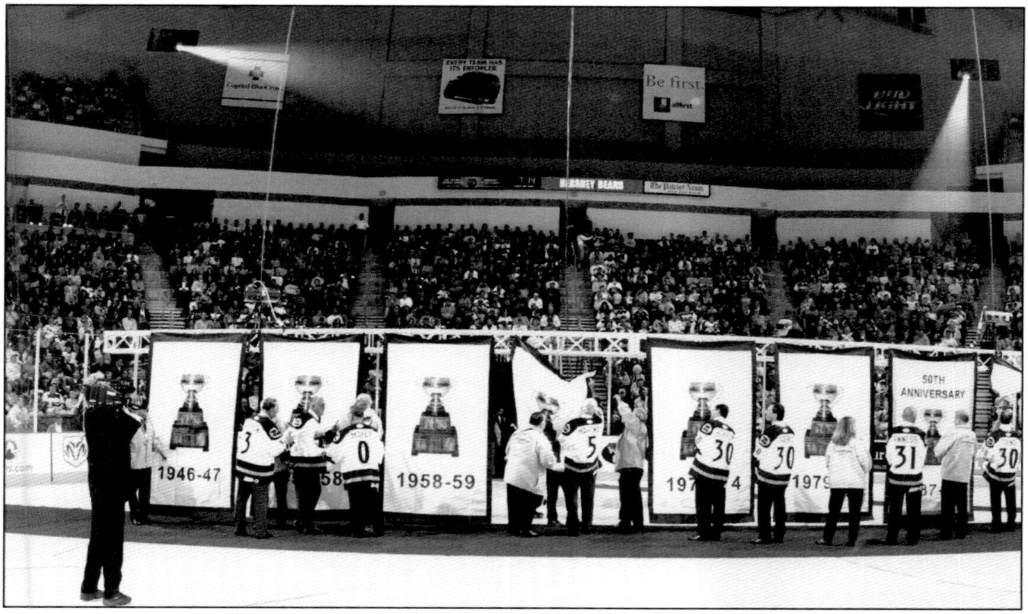

A Banner Event. Fans and former players raise banners representing all eight Calder Cup championships in ceremonies before the Bears played their first Giant Center game on October 19, 2002. ESPN commentator Barry Melrose served as master of ceremonies. A club-record crowd of 10,789, including Gov. Mark Schweiker, attended the game. Frank Mathers garnered the loudest and longest ovation. Hershey beat Rochester 4-1. (Bill Duh and Bruce Tyson/Just Sports.)

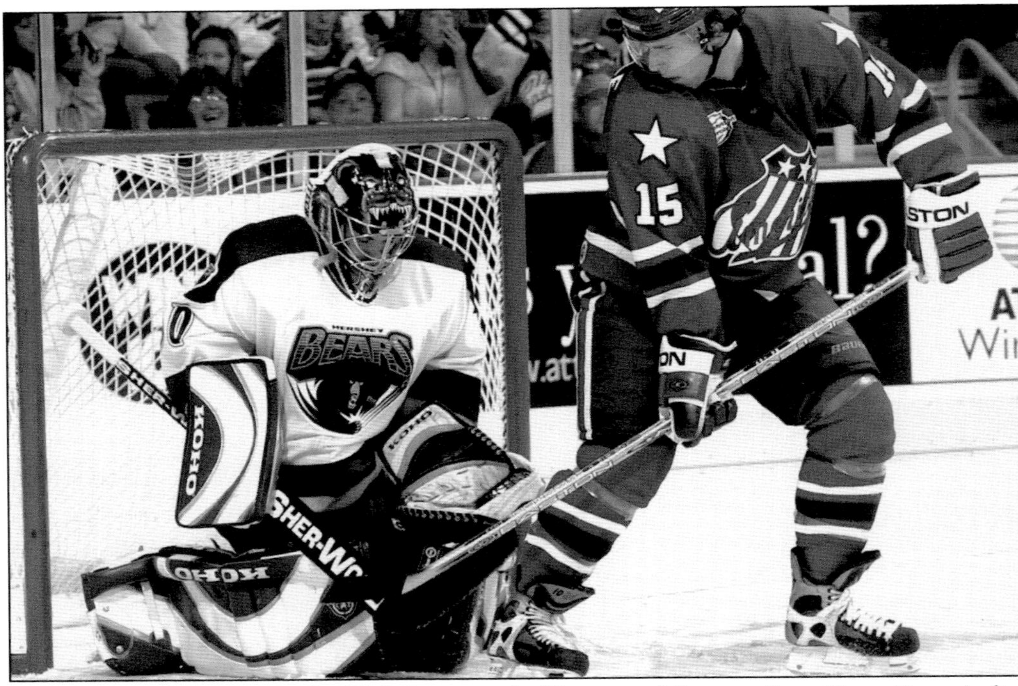

The Grand Opening. Goalie Phil Sauve made 32 saves while recording Giant Center's first win. Riku Hahl (Hershey) and Paul Gaustad (Rochester) took the first face-off. Rochester's Jason Botterill took the first shot at 1:30 of the first period, and Sauve made the first save on it. Hershey's Cail MacLean scored the first goal at 6:54 of the second on a power play. Hershey's Rob Voltera and Rochester's Doug Janik engaged in the first fight. (John C. Whitehead/*Patriot-News*.)

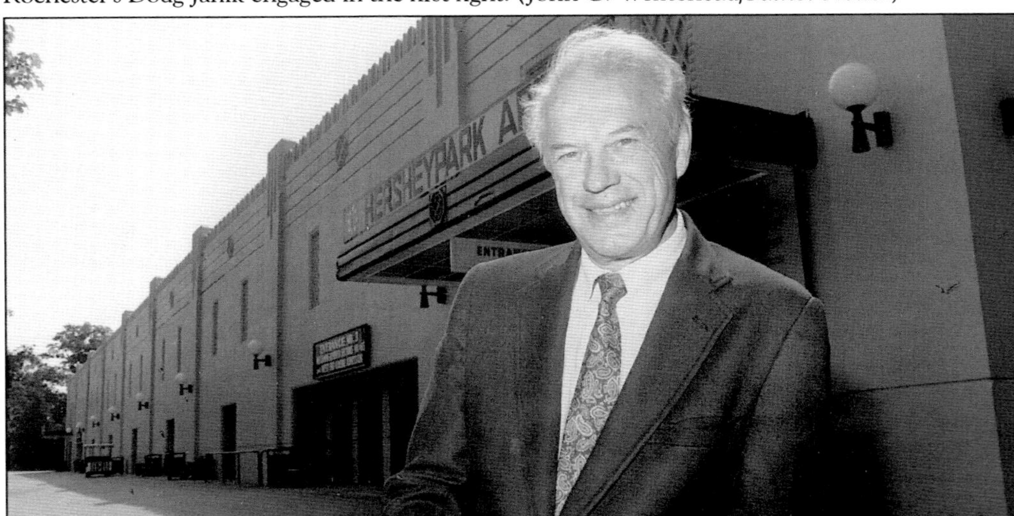

Historic Monuments. Giant Center will have to fill with more than a half century of memories before it can compare to Hersheypark Arena, where Frank Mathers and the Bears built an abiding hockey tradition. Listen close inside Hersheypark Arena and you still can hear the echoes of goal cries and stars of the game roll calls. Mathers and Hersheypark Arena are eternally tethered. As the old hockey adage goes, champions walk together forever. (Hershey Bears.)